The Scandinavian Theatre

A Short History

Drama and Theatre Studies

GENERAL EDITOR: KENNETH RICHARDS
ADVISORY EDITOR: HUGH HUNT

FREDERICK J. MARKER
AND LISE-LONE MARKER

The Scandinavian Theatre

A Short History

Basil Blackwell · Oxford

0 631 14840 4

Set in Monophoto Apollo
Filmset and printed in Great Britain by
BAS Printers Limited, Wallop, Hampshire
and bound by The Kemp Hall Bindery, Oxford

Contents

List of Plates   vi

Introduction   ix

ONE   The Middle Ages   1
TWO   The Humanist Stage   21
THREE   Renaissance Festivities   32
FOUR   Royal Troupes and Strolling Players   44
FIVE   Holberg and the Danish Comedy   55
SIX   Rococo Playhouses: from Kongens Nytorv
to Drottningholm   69
SEVEN   The Gustavian Age   82
EIGHT   Denmark's Golden Age   102
NINE   Ibsen Takes the Stage   132
TEN   August Strindberg   176
ELEVEN   The Modern Theatre   204
TWELVE   Since 1945   243

Chapter References   274

Bibliography   281

Index   291

Plates

1. Medieval devil motifs. Fresco in Maria Magdalene Church, Randers.
   Courtesy of Nationalmuseet, Copenhagen   8
2. Fresco in Sæby Church, Jutland.
   Courtesy of Nationalmuseet, Copenhagen   9
3. Medieval Hell-mouths. Fresco in Tybjerg Church, near Præstø, *c.* 1450.
   Courtesy of Nationalmuseet, Copenhagen   10
4. Fresco in Vallensbæk Church, near Copenhagen, 1450–75.
   Courtesy of Nationalmuseet, Copenhagen   11
5. Medieval elevated Paradise. Fresco in Tybjerg Church, *c.* 1450.
   Courtesy of Nationalmuseet, Copenhagen   12
6. Medieval Fool leads the procession to Golgotha. Fresco in Bellinge Church, Odense, 1496.
   Courtesy of Nationalmuseet, Copenhagen   13
7. Simultaneous staging in *The Tragedy of the Virtues and the Vices*, Copenhagen, 1634   18
8. Detail from royal procession of Christian IV, 1596   34
9. Painting by Heimbach of Queen Sophie Amalie in *Unterschiedliche Oracula*, 1655   40
10–12. Three Bérain-d'Olivet stage designs for Charles XII's French troupe in Stockholm, 1699   50, 51

13. Painting by Pehr Hilleström of a scene from *Orpheus and Eurydice*, Swedish Royal Opera, 1773.
Courtesy of Kungliga Teatern, Stockholm   85

14. Photograph of Carlo Bibiena setting for a Gustavian opera, *c.* 1774.
Courtesy of Drottningholms Teatermuseum   87

15–17. Three paintings by Pehr Hilleström of scenes from Gustavian opera, 1778–81.
Courtesy of Drottningholms Teatermuseum   88, 89

18. Painting by Hilleström of *The Conquest of the Galtar Rock*, Drottningholm, 1779.
Courtesy of Drottningholms Teatermuseum   90

19. Painting by Hilleström of a scene from Gustav III's *Helmfelt*.
Courtesy of Drottningholms Teatermuseum   93

20–21. Design by Desprez and photographed set for *Queen Christina*, 1785.
Courtesy of Nationalmuseum, Stockholm   96, 97

22. Design by Louis Jean Desprez for *Gustav Wasa*, 1786.
Courtesy of Nationalmuseum, Stockholm   98

23. Design by Thomas Bruun for *Dyveke*, 1796.
Courtesy of Teatermuseet, Copenhagen   105

24. Gothic impressions by Troels Lund.
Courtesy of Royal Theatre Library, Copenhagen   114

25. Design by C. F. Christensen for a tropical rain forest.
Courtesy of Royal Theatre Library, Copenhagen   116

26. Design by Christensen for *The Festival in Albano*, 1839.
Courtesy of Royal Theatre Library, Copenhagen   117

27–28. Johanne Luise Heiberg in two of her most famous roles.
Courtesy of Teatermuseet, Copenhagen   123

29. Costume sketches by Henrik Ibsen for *Olaf Liljekrans*, 1857   148

30–31. Designs by P. F. Wergmann for Ibsen's *The Pretenders*, 1864 and Munch's *Duke Skule*, 1865.
Courtesy of Royal Theatre Library, Copenhagen   152, 153

32. Scene photograph from the world première of *A Doll's House*, 1879.
Courtesy of Teatermuseet, Copenhagen   160

33. Rehearsal photograph from the world première of
   To Damascus I, 1900.
   Courtesy of Drottningholms Teatermuseum   192

34–36. Three designs by Carl Grabow for the world première
   of *A Dream Play*, 1907.
   Courtesy of Drottningholms Teatermuseum   194, 195

37. Design by Svend Gade for *A Dream Play* at the
   Lorensberg Theatre, 1916.
   Courtesy of Drottningholms Teatermuseum   210

38–39. Designs by Knut Ström for *The Saga of the Folkungs*,
   1920, and *Romeo amd Juliet*, 1922, at the Lorensberg
   Theatre.
   Courtesy of Drottningholms Teatermuseum   214, 215

40. Sketch by Ström for *To Damascus* III, Lorensberg
   Theatre, 1922.
   Courtesy of Drottningholms Teatermuseum   216

41–43. Three designs by Isaac Grünewald for *Samson and
   Delilah*, Royal Opera, 1921.
   Courtesy of Drottningholms Teatermuseum   220, 221

44. Design by John Jon-And for *Phèdre*, Dramaten, 1927.
   Courtesy of Drottningholms Teatermuseum   229

45. Projection design (Fairhaven) by Grünewald for *A
   Dream Play*, Dramaten, 1935.
   Courtesy of Drottningholms Teatermuseum   234

46. Design by Helge Refn for *Days on a Cloud*, Danish
   Royal Theatre, 1947.
   Courtesy of Teatermuseet, Copenhagen   256

47. Design by Helge Refn for *Vetsera Does Not Bloom for
   Everyone*, Frederiksberg Theatre, 1950.
   Courtesy of Teatermuseet, Copenhagen   257

48. Design by Erik Nordgreen for *The Blue Pekinese*,
   Danish Royal Theatre, 1954.
   Courtesy of Bodil Kjer and the designer   258

49. Design by Sven Erixson for *Richard III*, Dramaten,
   1947.
   Courtesy of Drottningholms Teatermuseum   262

50. Scene photographs from Ingmar Bergman's version of
   A Dream Play, Dramaten, 1970.
   Courtesy of Beata Bergström and Drottningholms
   Teatermuseum   271

The publication of these plates has been generously aided by a grant from Nordisk Kulturfond

Introduction

Rich in its history and traditions and strikingly cosmopolitan in its outlook, the Scandinavian theatre has nevertheless remained relatively unexplored territory to the reader unfamiliar with the Scandinavian languages. Remarkably enough, no general history of the Scandinavian stage has previously been available in English. Those capsule surveys or introductions to the subject that do exist have all too often been content to perpetuate time-honoured stereotypes and misconceptions—a favourite chestnut being what we can call the 'geographical-climatological fallacy', on the basis of which, viewing Scandinavia as a freezing and forbidding 'snowy mountain land slenderly attached to the rest of Europe', the writer of such introductions proceeds to draw some sweeping and rather dubious critical or cultural conclusions. In spite of the vigorous international interest in the more recognizable giants of Scandinavian drama—Holberg, Ibsen, Bjørnson, Strindberg—the theatrical context which fostered these figures has suffered undue neglect. In particular, modernism in Scandinavian drama has persistently been viewed as a phenomenon of sudden change, severing all connections with older traditions at a single blow. In fact, however, even so rebellious an artist as Ibsen was profoundly influenced in his art by the theatre of his own time.

Organization and selection, the Scylla and Charybdis facing any writer of a one-volume history of the theatre of a particular country or era, present an even more severe navigational challenge to the historian of the Scandinavian theatre. For one thing, the question of definition immediately poses itself. As fascinating and inviting as the lively theatre cultures of Finland and Iceland may be, a book whose aim is to provide a short history of the 'Scandinavian' stage which would place the major, internationally familiar dramatists of the North in context must necessarily limit itself to a discussion of theatre in Denmark, Sweden, and, somewhat later in the course of developments, Norway. The theatrical cultures of these three countries, like their languages, are intimately interrelated. As the following pages will often prove, few theatrical developments have taken place in one of these Scandinavian countries which have not had their parallels or repercussions in another. Without losing sight of these underlying bonds of cultural affinity, then, one must nevertheless preserve the outlook of comparative drama and literature. Nor is one's task made easier by the rather astonishing fact that no trans-national history of the Scandinavian theatre has yet appeared in a Scandinavian language. This is not to suggest that there is any paucity of books about Danish, Swedish, or Norwegian theatre history. For example, the classic work of Danish stage history, Thomas Overskou's *Den danske Skueplads i dens Historie* (1854–76), takes seven volumes totalling no less than 4,858 pages to chronicle the years from the founding of Grønnegadeteatret, Scandinavia's first national theatre, in 1722 to the rebuilding of the Royal Theatre in Copenhagen in 1874. Robert Neiiendam's continuation of Overskou's saga, bringing the story from 1874 up to 1892, occupies six volumes. In our own time, outstanding theatre historians like Agne Beijer, Gösta M. Bergman, Neiiendam, Torben Krogh, and Øyvind Anker have produced a veritable library of special studies treating individual figures and periods. Without this rich and enviable wealth of theatre scholarship in Scandinavia, the present volume could quite literally not have been attempted. Nevertheless, the very nature of these sources poses a difficult problem of selection and emphasis: which events, developments, plays, and performances should be included in order to characterize the theatrical style of a given era; which must be passed over in the interests of readability and synthesis? The question demands an answer, and the answer depends in the last analysis upon individual judgement. No solution can ever be the perfect one.

The objects of theatre research are, in our opinion, stage productions, and these are best characterized in a terminology which is reconstructive, because the work of the theatre historian is recreative and focuses upon the stylistic forces and artistic intentions operative at a given time. In a brief history that ranges from the Middle Ages to the present day, all-inclusiveness is obviously inconceivable, and certain great performances and theatre artists must be selected as points of emphasis, illustrating the development of theatrical styles and trends. In this process, designed to serve the interests of the general reader and to spare him a daunting superabundance of detail, the specialist may inevitably regret the omission of a favourite name or a parallel development. Let it be said at once, however, that the authors themselves have also had to bypass some inviting stopping places—Bournonville and the Danish ballet, for instance, or Tivoli's Pantomime Theatre and its remarkable traditions— in the interests of clarity and brevity. Considerable space has been devoted to the theatre since Ibsen, and the critic or student of modern drama, while he will find no new literary inter- pretations of the plays of Ibsen or Strindberg or Lagerkvist advanced here, may discover that by viewing these dramatists in their original theatrical contexts one comes to understand better why they fashioned their plays as they did.

Their theatrical heritage is an imposing one. Above all, this book has endeavoured to take the Scandinavian theatre out of its vacuum and consider it in relationship to developments in Europe as a whole, with the realization that, from the fifteenth century to the twentieth, cultural interaction with the rest of European theatre has played a major rôle in shaping Scandinavian stage forms and tastes. If it has been cosmopolitan in its outlook, the Scandinavian theatre has also been a lively and vigorous phenomenon for far longer than most outside observers seem to realize: the earliest liturgical drama, an Easter sequence from Linköping, dates from the thirteenth century; Sweden's oldest surviving play is from the latter part of the fifteenth century; the 250th anniversary of Scandinavia's first 'national' theatre was celebrated in 1972. The medieval theatre, the Humanist stage, the festivals of the Renaissance, and the activities of itinerant troupes in Scandinavia all have direct parallels elsewhere on the

Continent. Holberg's first play in 1722 established a lasting and continuous tradition of native playwriting that has remained an integral part of Scandinavia's flourishing theatre culture. At the centre of that culture stand its three national theatres, the 225-year-old Royal Theatre in Copenhagen, Dramaten in Stockholm (founded 1788), and Nationaltheatret in Oslo, which was seventy-five years old last year. To anyone unacquainted with the phenomenon of a great national repertory theatre, a glance at the statistics from a randomly selected season elicits both astonishment and a sense of envy and frustration when faced with a purely commercial theatrical system. To take such a random example: during the 1967–8 season, highlighted by the 800th birthday of the city of Copenhagen, the Danish Royal Theatre presented *sixty-five* productions, including sixteen plays (nine of them new), twenty-one operas (six new), and twenty-eight ballets (nine new), for a total of 518 performances, in a continually changing repertory pattern, on its two stages. As was realized in Scandinavia over two centuries ago, an active theatre culture is not free: running costs for the 1967–8 season totalled just under $6,000,000—of which gate receipts, from an average attendance of 76.5 per cent, made up only about one-sixth. Even these few bald statistics tend to throw the term 'national theatre' into bolder and sharper relief.

This history has been written primarily for the reader who has no Danish, Swedish, or Norwegian. All titles are referred to throughout in English translation, with the original title normally provided when a work is first mentioned. Both the scope of the study and the fact that a majority of its readers will be unfamiliar with the Scandinavian languages have made the compilation of an exhaustive footnote apparatus seem an unnecessarily cumbersome impediment. Instead, it has appeared more reasonable to limit footnotes largely to direct quotations and to supplement them with a summarized guide (pp. 274–80) to the principal published references relevant to each chapter. In the notes, full bibliographical citations are given only for those items *not* listed in the Bibliography at the back. Often, however, facts about the important productions discussed—for example, the world première of *A Doll's House* or William Bloch's direction of *An Enemy of the People* or Craig's staging of *The Pretenders*— have been drawn directly from unpublished primary sources (promptbooks, ground plans, sketches, rehearsal logs, and so on) and from newspaper and periodical archives.

Our work on this project has been made both easier and pleasanter by the willing assistance of a large number of individuals and institutions. In particular, it is a pleasure to acknowledge the valuable help and cooperation of the following: Drottningholms Teatermuseum and its *intendant* Barbro Stribolt; Teatermuseet, Copenhagen, and its curator Klaus Neiiendam; Universitetsbibliotek, Oslo, and its theatre librarian Øyvind Anker; Nationalmuseum, Stockholm, and Børge Magnusson of its Graphics Collection; De danske Kongers kronologiske Samling, Rosenborg Castle, and *museumsinspektør* Niels Jessen; and the staffs of the Danish Royal Library, the Danish Royal Theatre Library, Roskilde Kommunebibliotek, Nationalmuseet and Universitetsbiblioteket (Copenhagen).

We are deeply grateful to Professor emeritus Agne Beijer for his advice and for giving us a memorable day with him in the Drottningholm collection. Among those from whose interest and encouragement our work has benefited, we are especially indebted to Professor Evert Sprinchorn of Vassar College, to ambassador Emil Blytgen-Petersen, and to such notable men of the theatre as Thorvald Larsen, Erik Nordgreen, and Helge Refn. On the editorial side, the patience and help of Dr. Kenneth Richards and Mr. J. K. D. Feather of Basil Blackwell and Mott have saved the study from numerous pitfalls.

Finally, we owe a very substantial debt of gratitude to Nordisk Kulturfond for a grant to permit publication of the illustrations, and to the Canada Council for two research grants which enabled us to carry this project to completion.

'To reconstruct a past world, doubtless with a view to the highest purposes of truth—what a work to be in any way present at, to assist in, though only as a lamp-holder!' George Eliot once wrote. As lamp-holders to the conspicuous splendour of the Scandinavian stage, then, we can only hope that some of its lustre is reflected in these pages.

Toronto   *Frederick J. Marker*
January, 1975   *Lise-Lone Marker*

CHAPTER ONE

The Middle Ages

The theatre in Scandinavia, like that of other European countries, has its roots in the liturgical ceremonies of the Middle Ages. Although the great mystery cycles which flourished elsewhere on the Continent seem not to have taken hold here, the development of other types of medieval religious and secular drama followed a familiar pattern. Bishop Ethelwold's tenth-century *Concordia Regularis,* which specified the ritual of *Quem quaeritis,* the announcement of the Resurrection by the angel on Easter morning, has a close parallel in a thirteenth-century Easter sequence which survives from Linköping in Sweden. This brief Swedish liturgic play, performed by priests and acolytes during the service on Easter morning with Christ's tomb as the central focus, contains the seeds for the gradual growth of a more dramatically elaborate Easter performance.

In these later Resurrection plays, as popular in Scandinavia as they were in France and Germany, a variety of episodes drawn from the Gospels were enacted as vividly as possible by the priests for the pleasure and edification of their congregations. In 1475, a so-called Marian Chapel was erected in the Church of Our Lady in Flensborg, and the four priests of the church, known as Marians, 'acted . . . during Lent the tragedy of Our Lord Jesus Christ, and laid Him in a walled-up grave.'[1]

[1] Quoted in Torben Krogh, *Ældre dansk Teater,* p. 14.

1

The practice persisted until 1527, while the holy sepulchre itself, covered by a large stone, could be seen in the Marian Chapel as late as 1864. In a letter from 1506, the Swedish priest Hans Jacobi in Söderköping mentions having secured a *ludus resurrectionis* which may have been acted by the teachers and students of Söderköping's Latin School. As late as 1635, the accounts of a Danish town refer to a mummer who had 'for two days acted at the town hall the story of Christ's Resurrection.'[2]

The sepulchre-crypts which designated Christ's tomb in these Easter dramas, several of which may still be seen in Scandinavian churches and museums, formed the midpoint of other related rituals as well. A Swedish description runs as follows:

They used to come to church early on Easter morning so that the women could anoint Jesus, whose image of stone or wood was laid out in a crypt, which was formed like a sepulchre and placed by the altar, and upon which a guardian angel was seated. This I have seen in two churches in Uppland such as Vada and Skarplöfstad [Vester-Löfsta]. They oiled the image with fragrant balsam, traces of which are still to be found on the above-mentioned crypt. They also crawled on their knees around these sepulchres to do penance for their sins.[3]

Similarly, forgiveness of sins could be obtained by walking around the sepulchre which stood in the Danish Church of Saint Peter in Næstved: seventy days indulgence was allowed anyone who 'walked about the grave of the Lord, praying for peace, for good weather, for the welfare of the Danish kingdom, and for those buried here.'[4]

Rituals such as the burial of Christ's cross were not tolerated by the Reformation, and zealous Lutheran prelates strove to banish sepulchres from the churches. A Swedish church edict of 1591 strictly prohibited the ritual of the symbolic burial of the Cross and the Resurrection at Easter. During the visit of the Polish King Sigismond to Sweden in 1594, immense popular anger was provoked when Roman Catholic priests buried a picture of Christ which was subsequently taken up from its grave on Easter morning.

[2] *Ibid.*, p. 15.
[3] H. Hillebrand, *Sveriges Medeltid,* III, p. 647.
[4] Krogh, p. 4.

Christmas, the second great feast of the Church, was another occasion for dramatic representation in Scandinavia, and the resultant Epiphany plays enjoyed a longer life than any other medieval form. Their action was universally familiar. In solemn procession the priests who impersonated the Magi moved up the centre aisle. One pointed with his sceptre at a star, which was carried forward on a pole or moved through the church by means of a wire. At the altar the procession halted before the crib. The Magi sacrificed to the new-born babe and, after they had fallen on their knees in prayer, an angel appeared to them in the shape of a boy clad in white. As the drama developed, the tyrannical Herod put in an appearance, and the three kings paused at his throne on their way to the manger.

With the coming of the Reformation to Denmark in 1536, Epiphany plays were unconditionally banished from the churches. Their popular appeal continued unabated, however, and it gradually became customary at Epiphany time for students of the Latin schools to march in procession from house to house in the guise of the Magi. Donations were gratefully accepted. In these later remnants of the ancient Church rituals, the three scholars impersonating the Magi were always clad in white, and high paper caps lavishly decorated with gilt emphasized their regal splendour. The blackened face of one of the students alluded to the tradition that one of the Wise Men was black. The three kings were often joined by a crowd of other Biblical figures. In Bergen in Norway, where these processions have survived almost to our own day, the Magi were accompanied by 'Mary with the child in a little cradle, Joseph with an axe in his hand' and 'some secondary figures.'[5] One might also meet such characters as Herod or old Simeon, and a Judas was usually entrusted with the duty of collecting donations in a purse which he continually displayed. In Sweden, folk figures were added. Occasionally a fool would join the motley troupe. Always at the head of the procession, carried on a pole, moved the crucial symbol of the shining star.

The ancient Epiphany rituals seem to have had deep roots in Halland in Sweden, where the strictures of the Reformation failed to banish these star processions from the churches. Three short Epiphany dramas from this district are extant, two

[5] Sagen and Foss, *Bergens Beskrivelse* (Bergen, 1824), p. 590.

3

from Falkenberg and a third from Laholm. All three plays, which appear to stem from a common source, combine dialogue with incidental songs, fragments of ancient Epiphany melodies sung both by the actors and the audience. In one of the two Falkenberg texts appear Herod, his servant, the Magi, three soldiers, and Judas with his purse. After the usual preliminaries, the drama begins in the following manner:

Herod
Come forth, my servant!

Servant
What wishes my lord and master?

Herod
I command you to bring forth a chair for me, for I am so bitter in my heart that I know not on which foot or toe to stand. My servant, bring forth a chair.

Servant
It shall be done.

Song
>   Herod he asked
>   All those whom he saw,
>   If Christ would be born
>   In Bethlehem town.

Herod
Come forth, my servant!

Servant
What wishes my lord and master?

Herod
I command you to find the three Wise Men. I will speak a word or two with them.

Servant
It shall be done.

Song
>   And we nod and we bow
>   Both for great and for small,
>   That's why we have come now
>   To great Herod's hall.

The Magi then appear before Herod, who orders them to go and seek the new-born King of the Jews. In his ferocity this favourite tyrant of the Middle Ages warns that if they are not back within three nights and three days, they will be put to death. The Wise Men set off, but Herod, sensing treachery, decides to saddle up and ride to Bethlehem himself. A song then relates the slaughter of the Innocents, after which the servant returns to assure his master in conclusion that he 'took the new-born babes, pierced their hearts and crushed their bones.'

The staging of this little playlet was obviously simple in the extreme. Even the slaughter of the Innocents, an attractive opportunity for medieval realism, remained off-stage. The sole prop mentioned in these Swedish dramas is the chair, perhaps a reminiscence of Herod's regal throne in the older ceremonies within the church. The second Falkenberg play is very similar to the first, but the Laholm text introduces another important processional figure, the Virgin Mary. When the Magi ask her about the new-born King, she replies with a fragment of a Christmas song which is her only speech in the drama. In other Epiphany plays from Bergen, probably based on scholastic traditions of German derivation, Joseph is added as the mid-point of some rather irrelevant comic scenes. Significantly, the plays acted by the Bergen students were described as 'farces,' and a diary entry from 1665 mentions 'the customary *ludos comicos* which presented the three kings and the star.'[6]

When such plays concluded, the moment came to address a tactful reminder to the audience that art requires its reward, usually collected by Judas in his purse. In one instance the villainous Herod himself rises from his chair and appeals directly to the spectators:

> Your pardon that I am so bold
> To step before you here;
> My question to you now is this:
> Will there be some cheer?

When the players had finished passing the hat, they sang a

[6] Cf. Krogh, p. 300, and H. Wiers-Jensen, 'De liturgiske Skuespil og deres sidste Udløbere i Norden i Stjernespillet,' *Norvegia sacra*, I (Christiania, 1921), p. 62f.

song of thanks, sometimes shrewdly contrived to become less complimentary if the take did not meet expectations.

Miracle plays dramatizing the lives and legends of the saints constituted a genre universally popular throughout Europe in the Middle Ages and undoubtedly represented in Scandinavia as well, although little is known about specific performances here. In the preface to *Tobie Comedia,* a play published in 1550 and usually attributed to Olaus Petri, the biblical translator and counselor to Gustav Vasa who inspired Strindberg's *Master Olof,* the author argues that wise men have long used the performance of moral comedies and tragedies to instruct the common people about right and wrong in the world. 'Our forefathers,' he adds, 'had done the same in this country as in other countries since the coming of Christianity, with songs, rhymes, and comedies about holy men.' In Sweden a religious play of this type is found as early as the latter half of the fifteenth century. Entitled *De uno peccatore qui promeruit gratiam* and listed in G. E. Klemming's bibliography of Swedish drama as the oldest surviving play in the language, this work has its origin in the Maria cult which so profoundly shaped medieval drama and depicts a sinner's forgiveness through the (initially reluctant) intercession of the Virgin Mary. The fact that this very brief text was actually intended for performance is indicated by the stage directions and by a prologue in which the speaker greets the audience and calls for silence.

A remarkable series of medieval Danish frescoes and other religious works of art, clearly sharing the visual imagery of dramatic performances, offers additional vivid evidence of a tradition of miracle productions (see p. 8ff). The fool and the Devil, two of the most predominant and treasured characters on the medieval stage, make frequent appearances in these church frescoes. A painting from 1503 in Skiveholme Church depicts a fool playing two instruments at once, a medieval trait which re-appears in the Elizabethan theatre. An unusual fresco in Bellinge Church on Fyn, dating from 1496, shows another fool leading the procession to Golgotha (Plate 6). One of the most colourful of all Scandinavian devils dominates a fresco in Maria Magdalene Church in his traditional mask and guise of a hairy, fantastic animal (Plate 1). Many of the localities appearing in these paintings are clearly related to the mansions which stood on the medieval stage. The familiar Hell-mouth, designed as a dragon's head combined with a castle-like prison, is pictured in Selsø Church on Zealand. Vivid frescoes of souls being literally thrust or dragged into the mouth of Hell adorn a variety of Danish churches, while one, offering a contrast to these horrors, shows the whiter and more fortunate souls being led with folded hands into the city of eternal bliss, in this case an elevated Paradise reached by a flight of stairs (Plate 5).

By far the best example of medieval religious drama in Scandinavia is the *Ludus de Sancto Canute duce,* a Danish miracle play about the Holy Duke Knud. On January 7, 1131, Knud Lavard was murdered in a forest near Haraldsted by Magnus, and his legend relates that a well sprang from the spot of the slaying and miracles took place at his grave. The martyr quickly became a national folk hero, and to the great joy of the people his son, King Valdemar the Great, succeeded in having him canonized in 1169. No doubt it soon became customary to perform a play based on these dramatic incidents in Ringsted, where he was buried. The existing version of this old play, a close adaptation in verse dialogue of the Latin legend read each year in the Church of Saint Bendt in Ringsted on the anniversary of the murder, stems from the early sixteenth century.

No fewer than thirty speaking parts appear in the *Ludus de Sancto Canute duce,* in addition to which a large number of non-speaking extras, representing privy counselors, courtiers, and crowds of citizens, were needed to swell the festive processions and silent tableaux of this colourful medieval pageant. At the centre of the picture are the figures of Knud, depicted as the *rex pacificus,* the ideal and pious ruler, and Magnus, boldly drawn as the envious embodiment of evil and godlessness, driven on by demonic malice. The framework for this quintessential clash of good and evil was an elaborate one. The action spans nearly thirty years, and the scene shifts to a variety of locations. At the heart of the production was the simultaneous or polyscenic principle of mansion staging. In the prologue the Herald asks the spectators to 'hold their peace and make room,' indicating that the acting area was probably not clearly demarcated and that the lavish spectacle which followed made use of a simultaneous open performance area rather than

7

a raised stage. Presumably the numerous mansions or localities were erected around the largest square in Ringsted, close to the church where the martyr was held in special veneration—a technique which parallels both the Vissingen passion play and the Lucerne Easter play.

Chief among the mansions required was the royal court of Roskilde, which occupied a central position. In addition, the audience saw a locality for the Danish Privy-council, various castles and manors, a gallows, and the ill-fated grove where Knud is slain. Assuming some topographical arrangement of the

1. Medieval devil motifs. One of Scandinavia's most formidable representations of the Evil One: fresco in Maria Magdalene Church, Randers

2. A medieval devil and an angel battle for a soul: fresco in
Sæby Church, Jutland

mansions akin to Renwart Cysat's plan for the Lucerne passion,
the localities on Zealand were probably grouped together while
another section of the acting area was reserved for Knud's
castles in Jutland and Slesvig. In general, both individuals and
elaborate processions moved freely and frequently from mansion to mansion, occasionally even on horseback. Messengers
journeyed busily from castle to castle. When the Privy-council
meets in its mansion and reaches a decision which it wishes to
present to King Harald, a stage direction notes that the counselors 'journey to Harald's castle' and one of them simply shouts
to the king: 'Harald, look out and go here forth, the Privy-
council has arrived.' At his castle in Ribe Knud is named Duke
of Slesvig, after which he immediately 'rides to Slesvig, takes
up residence in the castle' and delivers an address to the inhabitants there.

As might be expected, the taste for scenes of gory realism
which gradually became more pronounced in the medieval
theatre is strongly in evidence in the *Ludus de Sancto Canute
duce*. The audiences of the period relished such scenes of
torture and execution, familiar from a daily life in which hang-

9

ing, drawing, and quartering were regarded as public entertainment. In this category belongs a rather drastic presentation in the play of the punishment of a thief. After Knud was sent to Slesvig by King Niels, the legend relates that he demonstrated his righteous spirit through his strict treatment of the numerous criminals who ravaged and plundered the country during this restless age. In the drama, 'the thieves are chased, one of them is caught and is brought before the Duke.' That Knud's men manage to capture only one robber after what is surely an animated chase sequence relates to the simple fact that it was difficult to stage more than one good execution at a time.

3. Medieval Hell-mouths. Souls being driven into the mouth of Hell: fresco in Tybjerg Church near Præstø, c. 1450

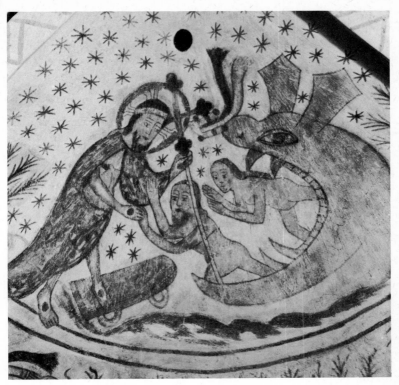

4. Christ's descent into Hell: fresco in Vallensbæk Church
near Copenhagen, 1450–75

Knud's men are, however, explicit concerning the fate of the
other thieves: 'We have both impaled them and buried them
alive.' The hanging of the captured robber is handled ex-
peditiously. The criminal himself is not given a single line; one
of the Duke's men tells his master what the offender has to say
in his own defence. Direct speech by the thief was avoided because a dummy was probably used for the actual execution,
thereby allowing greater freedom in the range of tortures inflicted. The entire action came to a standstill during this grim
episode, and dialogue was not to resume until 'after the thief
has been hanged'.

This relatively simple hanging sequence is, however, a mild
example of medieval sensationalism compared with the scenes

11

of torture and mayhem which animate the *Dorotheæ Komedie, Comoedia de Sancta virgine Dorothea,* the only other extant example of a Scandinavian miracle play. This text is a Danish verse translation and partial adaptation of a Latin prose drama by Knight Chilian, published in 1507. The Danish version, dated 1531 and attributed to the Odense school-master Christiern Hansen, is a perfect instance of the miracle play form. The basic material offered everything that the audiences of the period could reasonably demand, including several conversions, a variety of miracles and a whole series of satisfying scenes of corporeal punishment. Saint Dorothea suffered martyrdom in Asia Minor during the reign of Diocletian at the beginning of the fourth century. In the legend, the pagan ruler Fabritius lusts for the beautiful Dorothea but is spurned because she prefers to 'live in poverty until she may gain heaven

5. Whiter, pious souls are admitted to an elevated Paradise reached by stairs: fresco in Tybjerg Church, *c.* 1450

after her death.' Enraged, Fabritius has her whipped, flogged and brought to the stake, but by a miracle she remains unharmed. She converts her two sisters to Christianity, with the result that the villainous Fabritius has them burnt at the stake. Dorothea herself is thrown into prison for her faith and must ultimately yield her young life to the executioner's axe. Before she dies, she delivers such an inviting description of the joys of Paradise that a young pagan, Theophilus, promises to embrace the true faith if she will send him a sign from heaven. The miracle takes place—an angel presents Theophilus with a basket of fragrant flowers and herbs gathered from the meadows of Paradise—and he immediately keeps his promise.

In a prologue, or *argumentum*, preceding the play, a short survey of the action is provided for an audience hardly expected to be as familiar with this legend as with the nationalistic tale of Knud Lavard. The 'argumentor' then leads the players

6. A medieval Fool leads the procession to Golgotha: fresco in Bellinge Church, Odense, 1496

into the acting area and introduces the principal characters one by one. Although influenced in some respects by the emerging interest in classical drama at this time (it is, for example, divided into five acts), the *Dorothea* rests squarely upon medieval conventions and principles of staging. It requires a mansion stage accommodating Fabritius's 'house,' Dorothea's 'house,' a prison, a temple with pagan idols, and the crucial localities where the hapless victims are tortured and put to death. That such structures could be relatively elaborate can be deduced from the fact that Dorothea's 'house' was equipped with a practical door. When Fabritius's henchmen come to the chaste woman's home, 'they knock upon the door.' When they are denied entrance, the door is broken down with a stone and the mother is forced to conceal her frightened daughter.

For the play's gruesome torture scenes, the technical artistry of the medieval theatre's *maître de secrets* was of utmost importance. When Dorothea refuses categorically to renounce her faith, Fabritius commands the executioner and his helper:

> With stake and iron bind her fast,
> Then let her body feel the whip,
> Next tar and oil on her cast,
> For our gods she will not worship.

After 'she is whipped,' the executioner orders his assistant to fetch some fire. In what is apparently a humorous interlude, the helper tries long and hard to find sparks in the ashes but must at last resort to flint and steel. The stake is finally prepared, and the unfortunate victim is stripped of most of her clothing. The flames dance up about her, but by a miracle her body remains untouched. Fabritius then casts Dorothea into prison, but she is soon dragged before him again. After a vain attempt to force the saint to worship pagan idols, he hands her back to the executioners and orders them to torture her with glowing tongs 'set upon her hands and feet.' The executioner helpfully explains to the poor girl in detail what she may expect:

> I shall now hang you by your feet,
> And with the strongest rope you tie,
> To twist your arms and legs a-wry,

And stifle your mouth from all breath,
And finally torture you to death.

Jean Fouquet's famous miniature of the martyrdom of Saint Apolline is the best medieval illustration of how near to reality such a torture scene could come.

The highpoint of the entire production remained, however, the beheading of Dorothea, a *secret* which undoubtedly followed all the rules of the art. A saint of this importance could naturally not be executed without the presence of a considerable audience. Even Fabritius himself, who until then had apparently not left his mansion, is seized by the desire to attend the bloody spectacle. He orders his horse to be saddled and commands the executioner to bring the girl to the scaffold, declaring: 'I will be there at once with some a-riding, and some on foot for those who like walking.' Surrounded by a crowd of spectators, the heroine is led to the block. Tension builds as the executioner draws his sword and bluntly bids his victim to 'Stretch forth thy neck with greatest haste/And I shall chop as I've been taught.' Dorothea recites a last prayer and once again affirms her faith. Still another exciting effect remained in store for the audience: an angel appears with 'apples and roses which grow in the fields of Paradise.' The heroine requests him to hand the flowers to Theophilus, after which she is decapitated.

The medieval farce, a popular secular genre in Scandinavia, belonged chiefly to Carnival time or Shrovetide. It was a venerable custom that this season was devoted to merry-making and masquerades, and the *Fastnachtsspiel* or Carnival play emerged in Scandinavia at an early date. In 1447, the prior of the Monastery of Saint John in Odense, wishing to establish a school at the monastery, had to promise not to permit 'cum scolaribus (suis) ... choreas et ludos carnispriviales ... celebrari.'[7] In this respect the Scandinavian theatre was more or less exclusively under German influence, stemming primarily from nearby Lübeck. Here, the Carnival farce was cultivated energetically by an upper-class association called the *Zirkelgesellshaft,* and performances are recorded as early as 1430. German merchants in Bergen carried their native Carnival

[7]. S. Birket Smith, *De tre ældste danske Skuespil* (Copenhagen, 1874), p. 12.

customs to Norway, and a play about the Judgement of Paris performed by Lübeck's *Zirkelgesellshaft* in 1455 had a direct counterpart in a related Danish farce.

Despite their popularity, very few of these medieval farces have survived in Scandinavia. *Paris' Dom/The Judgement of Paris,* one of two extant Danish farces, is a popularized and rather coarse exploitation of the humanist cultivation of classical subjects. Bellona, goddess of strife, presents Paris with the apple which he must award to the contestant whom he finds most beautiful. Juno, Pallas Athene and Venus all court his favour, but enchanted by the physical charms of Venus, which he takes the opportunity to describe in very tangible terms, Paris accords her the prize. Pallas responds by castigating the lechery of man and its utter disregard of justice. *Den utro Hustru/The Unfaithful Wife,* which like its companion piece is a short one-act Danish farce found in the same manuscript which contains the Dorothea miracle play, exhibits the characteristic traits of the German Carnival play. Three ardent suitors seek the favours of a wife whose husband is away on a pilgrimage. Two of them, a peasant and a monk, are quickly shunned by the virtuous woman, and even a nobleman's elegant courting fails to move her. Not satisfied with a refusal, the third suitor seeks out a witch whom he promises a reward if she can bring the beautiful woman into his power. The witch conjures up a devil, an inept specimen of infernal power who fails miserably and is given a thrashing by the old crone. The latter now decides to take matters into her own hands, and appears before the wife with a dog, pleading tearfully for alms. When asked why she is so unhappy, the old crone instantly replies that her dog is actually her own daughter, once a beautiful girl who, when she spurned the love of a young man, was thus transformed. The sad tale makes such an impression on the virtuous wife that she resolves at once to yield to the nobleman's demands, since, as she puts it, 'ere I became a dog like this, I'll say yes to all he might wish.' A Swedish example of this genre is *Een Lustigh Comedia om Doctor Simon/A Merry Comedy about Doctor Simon,* a sixteenth-century farce in which the prologue and epilogue clearly stamp it as an itinerant piece performed by travelling players. The play deals with a peasant and his wife who quarrel over a pair of trousers, the symbol of domestic power and authority. The wife, who bears the unusual nick-name Doctor Simon, wins out in the end; the beaten husband must resign the rule of the house and tolerate the fact that she 'now has gotten to wear the pants.'

The scenic requirements for the performance of these itiner-ant farces were extremely modest. There would be no question of an actual platform stage or of elaborately constructed man-sions. The acting area was the floor or ground itself, on which the necessary localities were designated in the simplest possible way, by means of a chair or a bench. Just as on the mansion stage, which was the grander model for this technique, the actors remained visible throughout the performance and moved freely from one locality to another.

We may imagine that the troupe of itinerants arriving at a house to perform *The Unfaithful Wife* was preceded by a musician. When the players had entered the room and a space had been cleared for them, they arranged themselves 'in order' at the rear of the stage. The 'crier'—normally the leader of the troupe—then stepped forward to deliver his introductory speech *ad populum*. Called Preco in both Danish farces, the crier presented a summary of the action and, with the aid of a pointer or staff, introduced the characters to the audience. *The Unfaithful Wife* required at least three localities, or *standorte*, which may be called 'the wife's room,' 'the witch's room,' and a public bath in which the amorous peasant is washed and shaved. In addition, there would be at least one neutral locality where characters not bound to these *standorte* could re-main when not participating in the action. There are a number of indications in the text that the principal localities were suggested by a chair, on which the actors occasionally sat. Directions in the text illustrate the continual movement of the characters from one locality to another: 'the peasant returns to his wife', 'the nobleman goes to the witch and says', 'the witch goes with her dog to the wife', and so on. At the conclusion of the play, the actors arranged themselves in the same order as at the beginning, and Preco came forward to deliver his final speech. His closing lines—'Thus will I go out the door,/Give me something to drink before'—allude to the fact that the players were customarily treated to beer or wine before continuing on their way to the next engagement.

7. Simultaneous staging in the 1634 performance of *The Tragedy of the Virtues and the Vices* in Copenhagen

Probably the most illuminating single piece of evidence concerning the medieval theatre in Scandinavia is an unusual picture which illustrates the survival of the principles of simultaneous staging in a production given in Copenhagen in 1634. This unique piece of iconography (Plate 7) depicts the performance of the German morality play *Tragoedia von den Tugenden und Lastern/The Tragedy of the Virtues and the Vices* which, although produced as part of a typical Renaissance festivity, nonetheless exemplifies perfectly the older medieval principles and conventions. It was acted during the spectacular thirteen-day celebration held by King Christian IV in 1634 to mark the wedding of the crown prince to Princess Magdalene Sibylle of Saxony.

The action of this German prose morality begins in the customary medieval manner with Prologus, who requests silence and summarizes the plot. The story is allegorical: King Fastus (Pride), the Prince of the Vices who lives in the Castle of the Dragon, attacks the Virtues—Faith, Hope, Charity, Truth, Patience, and Courage—who reside in the Castle of Hope. Driven back through the intervention of the archangel Raphael, Fastus consults his advisers about the best way to conquer the Virtues, whom he cannot subdue in battle. The Vices decide to feign friendship in order to lure the Virtues into their power. Three 'simple and honest' Virtues actually let themselves be duped and accept the Vices' invitation. They are overpowered and made prisoners, but Raphael again comes to the rescue with his flaming sword. He liberates the Virtues and sets fire to the Castle of the Dragon, as devils drive the godless Vices into Hell-mouth. The comic relief in this 'tragedy' is supplied by the fool Hans Bratwurst, a servant in the Castle of the Dragon who functions as the ironic *raisonneur*.

The Tragedy of the Virtues and the Vices was staged on a section of the castle square in Copenhagen. A round, lavishly decorated tent served as the mansion of the Virtues, the Castle of Hope, while an open, quadrangular structure with entrances at opposite ends was constructed to house the Vices in the Castle of the Dragon. As the picture shows, this latter mansion was covered by an ornate gothic roof supported by pillars. At the close of the drama, this Vicious abode was bombed with fireworks, exploded, and burned. The table ignited and the chairs exploded as the guests saved themselves at the last moment. The pyrotechnic climax was reached when the pillars at the four corners of the building, each with a sphere at the top and six spheres on its pedestal, spouted fire simultaneously, devils fired rockets from several high poles, numerous ground pieces exploded, and the Hell-mouth into which the Vices were driven belched forth its infernal flames.

True to venerable tradition, the Hell-mouth and the Castle of Hope stood farthest from each other, at opposite ends of the stage. The Virtues' mansion, in the form of a canopy or tent, was so designed that its inhabitants could appear by entering before it, as seen in the picture, but it did not provide for any interior action. In contrast, the play's central and principal mansion, the Castle of the Dragon, was a completely open structure clearly designed to allow the audience to see the action taking place inside it. In this way, everyone could watch the excesses of the Vices, obviously of greater interest than the pious behaviour of the Virtues. Finally, the open quality of this mansion was of considerable practical importance because the production took place at night, in the dim glow of artificial illumination. Only in the play's spectacular closing apotheosis was the entire stage setting bathed in the flood of light which we see depicted in this unusually vivid medieval scene picture.

Long before the 1634 production of *The Tragedy of the Virtues and the Vices* took place, however, the Scandinavian theatre had moved in new directions. The religious character of medieval drama altered in the face of the new forces of cultural change accompanying the Reformation. The Renaissance made new currents felt both at court and in the schools. Nevertheless, the theatrical techniques of the Middle Ages continued to sustain a remarkable continuity long after the spirit and the age of medieval drama had faded.

CHAPTER TWO

The Humanist Stage

The twin forces of the Reformation and Renaissance Humanism profoundly affected the Scandinavian theatre. Performances of medieval religious plays disappeared and were replaced in popular favour by the school drama, a genre which stood at the zenith of its appeal from the mid-sixteenth to the mid-seventeenth century. A repertoire of Latin plays both ancient and new, translations of these, and original dramas in the vernacular was acted by university and Latin school students in the larger Scandinavian towns. These productions were supervised by local teachers, often themselves either the author or the adapter of the piece. The burgeoning Humanist concern with classical civilization and literature shaped the selection of plays and brought the classical genre patterns of tragedy and comedy to bear on native drama. Throughout this entire period, however, medieval staging conventions continued to retain their supremacy.

Throughout northern Europe, dramatic performances at schools and universities enjoyed strong encouragement during the Reformation, exemplified by the enthusiastic espousal by Luther and Melanchton of theatrical activity as an excellent pedagogical tool for educating youth to high morals and good manners. Next to the Bible, Melanchton could think of no more useful books than tragedies. Reflecting this attitude is a Swedish church ordinance from 1572 which heartily recommends the acting of comedies and tragedies 'so that both those who play and those who watch may be instructed and improved'.[1] When King Gustav II Adolf consulted his bishops in 1620 to find means of advancing learning and knowledge in Sweden, one piece of advice given him was to follow the example set by other European countries, which encouraged their professors of rhetoric to teach their students to present plays. In Norway, a comparable Bergen ordinance dated 1617 decreed that the local school-masters should 'let their pupils enact short Christian comedies as academic exercises . . . according to ancient custom, so that youths can become accustomed to polite behaviour and good manners.' This ordinance specifically mentioned 'the good people' of the town as a potential audience for these performances, which were clearly not envisioned solely as intermural exhibitions. 'The master himself,' we are told, 'accompanies his pupils, directing their action and playing in a proper manner.'[2] This mention of a performance leader present throughout the production brings to mind the figure of the medieval *régisseur* as he is depicted in Jean Fouquet's miniature of the *Mystère de Sainte Apolline*.

Numerous recorded performances of Plautus and Terence in Scandinavia testify to the importance attached to these dramatists. Their plays, read in the original both at the Latin schools and at the universities, were performed from the early decades of the sixteenth century as exercises in rhetoric. An official decree from 1574 urged the students of the University of Copenhagen to present public performances of Terence, universally the more preferred of the two playwrights because of his supposedly more elevated tone and the edifying moral *sententiæ* prevalent in his comedies.

Of greater interest, however, are the native dramas nurtured by the scholastic theatre tradition. These plays, usually based on biblical (particularly Old Testament) subjects, were at first no more than free adaptations of foreign models. From Sweden, such titles as *Holofernis och Judiths Commoedia, Rebecka,* and *Tobie Comedia* are strikingly typical. School performances in Danish embraced such characteristic subject matter as *Abel and Cain, David and Goliath, Kong Salomons Hyldning/Allegiance to*

---

[1] Nils Personne, *Svenska teatern*, I, p. 17.
[2] Øyvind Anker, *Scenekunsten i Norge fra fortid til nutid,* p. 8.

Solomon, Tobiæ Comedie, and *Susanna.* The latter drama, sub-titled 'a strange play taken from the Book of Daniel about the purity of the upright woman Susanna and her wondrous rescue,' was adapted from the German dramatist Sixt Birch's Latin original by P. J. Hegelund and performed under his supervision in Ribe in 1576. *Susanna,* the first Danish school drama to appear in print, is a representative example of this genre. Written in five acts with a prologue and an epilogue, its form follows classical comedy. Its didactic tone and episodic structure are, however, obvious inheritances from the medieval period. The story of the chaste Susanna follows closely the biblical original. Two scoundrels, after watching her bathe and unsuccessfully attacking her, accuse her of indecency. Brought to court, she is tried in vivid and dramatic detail and sentenced to be stoned to death. At the very last moment the young prophet Daniel intervenes and unmasks the false informers. Susanna's unsullied virtue receives its just recognition, deep-dyed villainy its appropriate punishment. The vilifiers are themselves stoned at the end, with devastating results—'see how their brains are running down over their eyes', comments one observer.

A single dominating principle, the power of a moral exemplum, constitutes the aesthetic of these school dramas. In virtually all of them, the emphasis upon a moral correspondence between biblical and contemporary phenomena is primary. This didactic, moralizing stance is particularly evident in the morality play or religious allegory, several of which survive from this period. The anonymous *Dødedansen/The Dance of Death,* published in the 1550s in an edition illustrated with woodcuts, treats the medieval pictorial-choreographic theme of the *danse macabre.* Death appears with his scythe and orders people of all ranks and classes to obey his command to follow him along 'an unknown road.' One by one they move toward him with a few dance steps, and are taken into his castle. In the *Comedia de Mundo et Paupere* a poor man, Pauper, decides to serve Lady Mundus, the world, in spite of better advice given him by two angels. Rewarded with riches he becomes emperor and marries the daughter of Lady Mundus. In the midst of the nuptial festivities and dancing he is taken ill. None can help him, and he dies. After being judged before the throne of

23

Heaven, devils carry his soul to Hell. Although no specific performances of *The Dance of Death* are recorded, *Mundo et Paupere* was acted in Randers in 1607 under the supervision of school-master Peder Thøgersen, who probably adapted the play from an unknown source and is referred to in the text as 'ludimoderatore.'

Distinctly native dramatic traditions, independent of foreign sources, also grew up during this period. In Sweden, Uppsala professor Johannes Messenius declared his ambitious intention of illustrating the entire history of his country in fifty plays to be 'exhibited publicly' by his students. Only six of these plays, based on Nordic sagas and legends, were actually completed and four were acted. More significant, however, is Messenius' special vision of a nationalistic drama devoted to 'the strange and glorious old stories of his fatherland'[3]—a vision to which Strindberg was to return nearly three centuries later. Messenius' *Disa,* subtitled 'a merry comedy about the wise and renowned Queen of Sweden Lady Disa,' became Sweden's first national history play when it was performed in 1611. Replete with comic episodes, music, dances, processions, and lively depictions of folk customs, *Disa* soon acquired considerable popularity both in Sweden and in Germany, where performances were seen far into the eighteenth century. The Swedish professor and ecclesiastic Andreas Prytz continued in the historical vein with such dramas as *Olof Skottkonung,* performed at the wedding of Gustav II Adolf in 1620, and *Konung Gustaf Then Första,* acted the following year at Uppsala University to commemorate the anniversary of Sweden's liberation by Gustav Vasa. Although no corresponding body of plays based on national history emerged out of the scholastic theatre in Denmark, H. T. Stege's *Cleopatra, eller en historisk Tragoedia om [den] sidste Dronning i Ægypten, ved Navn Cleopatra, og M. Antonio, en romersk Kejser* ('a historical tragedy about the last queen of Egypt, Cleopatra by name, and M. Antony, a Roman emperor') represented in 1609 the first Danish attempt to utilize classical history as tragic subject matter. Like the Swedish history plays, Stege's drama is irrevocably yoked to the didactic aesthetic of the Humanist stage. Whether nationalistic, classical, or biblical

---

[3] See Claes Hoogland and Gösta Kjellin, eds. *Bilder ur svensk teaterhistoria,* p. 52.

in subject, the moralistic and instructional tenor of these plays never varied.

The legend of Pyramus and Thisbe afforded promising raw material for the creation of Sweden's first secular drama of love, Magnus Olai Asteropherus' *Thisbe* (1609), acted by students in Uppsala and Karlstad in 1610. A free and original treatment of legendary material is also seen in the Södertälje headmaster Jacob Rondeletius' dramatization of the story of Judas Iscariot, entitled *Judas Redivivus* (1614). Perhaps the most successful of all Scandinavian school dramas from this period is, however, Hieronymus Justesen Ranch's delightful character comedy *Karrig Niding/Niding the Niggard*. Ranch's play—a conscious attempt to create a Danish counterpart of Terence and Plautus—is preserved in an edition from 1633, but evidently dates from 1598. It was performed on a double bill with Plautus' *The Pot of Gold* (*Aulularia*) in Randers in 1606. Both of these comedies ridicule the foibles of a miser, but here the resemblance ends. Ranch's *Niding* transcends the tradition of classical imitation to become a thoroughly original artistic creation. The wealthy but niggardly Niding, obsessed by the idea that he will one day find himself in need, compels his household, including his wife Jutta and his children, to dine on mouldy bread and rancid pork. Meanwhile, appetizing delicacies (the favourite subject of conversation in the first act) are kept under lock and key, to be eaten by rats. Taking the keys to the larder with him, Niding and his servant Meagre-cole set off on a begging expedition, and in their absence two tramps, Jep Skald and his boy, arrive on the scene. Plying the ravenous Jutta and the others with food from his well-stocked beggars' sack, Jep succeeds in usurping the absent husband's conjugal prerogatives. Plotting with the servants, the tramp lays a trap to catch the miser. The locks are changed, Jep dresses in the husband's best clothes, and when Niding returns, distressed by a dream in which a tramp had usurped his own place beside his wife, no one seems to recognize him. The confusion is compounded, his keys fail to fit, and he is soon convinced that his memory of himself as master of the household must all have been a dream. The reversal is complete when, delirious with starvation, Niding begs for shelter for the night, is royally feasted by Jep, and even begins to entertain lecherous vagabond-thoughts about Jutta. Revived by food and drink, the chastened miser sets out in search of his true wife and home, and, as the climax of his comic humiliation, gratefully accepts Jep's gift of his tattered beggar cape.

Performances of these school dramas were usually given in the mild months of May and June or at Shrovetide. Like the medieval religious dramas, they were presented in whichever location seemed convenient, either indoors or outdoors. In rainy Bergen, a long-standing tradition of performances in the town hall seems to have persisted. In Elsinore, the town hall is also known to have been at the disposal of student actors both in 1572 and 1574. Performances within the church were as a rule frowned upon by the Protestant authorities, although a number of such instances are recorded. Considerable official consternation resulted when the minister of the town of Slesvig directed a production of Terence's *Andria* in his church, featuring the boys of the local Latin school in such rôles as a midwife and a courtesan who gives birth, evidently directly before the high altar. The cleric's enthusiastic plan of following up his success with a church production of Terence's *The Eunuch* was firmly squelched, and the performance was relegated to the town hall.

In general, however, outdoor productions appear to have been more usual than indoor ones. The main squares of such Danish towns as Odense, Ribe, and Viborg could accommodate large crowds and were admirably suited for theatrical purposes. The local churchyard, its stone wall forming a convenient perimeter, was also an excellent playing area. In 1562, the Norwegian humanist A. P. Beyer utilized the churchyard in Bergen to enact 'with great effort and expense' a play about 'the Fall of Adam.'[4] Similarly, Swedish students from Örebro School presented Johannes Rudbeckius' *Rebecka,* an adaptation of Nicodemus Frischlin's Latin original, in the cemetery adjoining their school in 1616. On the following day, the audience was treated to Terence's *Andria* in Latin in the same surroundings. The performances, which took place in the afternoon and lasted until six o'clock, began with a colourful procession of the costumed players from the headmaster's house, where they dressed, to the 'theatre.' Admission was free, and the spiritual

[4] H. J. Huitfeldt, *Christiania Teaterhistorie* (Copenhagen, 1876), pp. 17–18.

edification of the plays was followed by a meal during which cast and spectators consumed fifty-three courses of food and quaffed fourteen barrels of beer.

As this suggests, these scholastic performances were important civic events often subsidized by local town councils, normally in the form of a subvention for the supervisor. The court frequently shared the bourgeoisie's lively interest in this genre. Although Sweden's Gustav Vasa was not very favourably disposed toward the theatre, the sons who succeeded him to the throne were otherwise inclined. Johan enthusiastically recruited student players while still residing in Åbo, and Erik similarly decorated his brilliant ducal court at Kalmar with stage performances. The wedding of Prince Johan and Princess Maria Elizabeth in 1612 was marked by the production of Johannes Messenius' second play *Signill* at Stockholm Castle, acted by no fewer than forty of the master's students from Uppsala, four of whom were themselves members of the nobility. In Denmark, the Humanist stage flourished during the reigns of Frederik II and Christian IV, and school dramas were acted both at court and as part of the festivities connected with royal progresses around the country. At the christening of Christian IV in 1577, students from the University of Copenhagen, directed by two of their professors, were invited to entertain the royal guests at the castle with performances in Latin and German. During the festivities of 1589 surrounding the significant union of Princess Anna, daughter of Frederik II, and James VI of Scotland, England's future monarch, university students acted Plautus' *The Pot of Gold* at Copenhagen Castle. When King James, who was married by proxy, arrived in Denmark the following spring, Christian IV again mounted an impressive array of festivities for his brother-in-law which included 'Latin and Danish comedies for the entertainment of their high lordships,'[5] presumably performed by student actors.

The stage on which such school plays were acted continued to utilize the venerable medieval principle of mansions. Through their study of contemporary editions of classical plays, the author-directors of these scholastic dramas had undoubtedly become familiar with Humanist reconstructions of

[5] N. Slange, *Christian den Fierdes Historie* (Copenhagen, 1749), I, p. 33.

the antique stage. Among the illustrated Renaissance editions of Terence, that of Jodocus Badius (Lyon, 1493), with its conjectural depiction of a platform stage backed by a columned, curtained façade forming a series of entrances or 'houses' for the characters, was particularly influential. Such editions not only suggested staging techniques but also popularized the use of a descriptive classical terminology. Hence, such terms as 'proscenium,' 'scena' and 'theatrum' come into general use in the Scandinavian play texts of this period. In most cases, however, an open platform backed by a curtained enclosure—usually called a 'Pallads' in the records of the time—would be insufficient unless supplemented by mansions designed to meet the requirements of a particular play.

The text of Hegelund's *Susanna* clearly makes reference to a relatively simple stage. In addition to the house of Joachim, Susanna's husband, two other localities are needed, the garden of the maltreated heroine and the courtroom where she is tried. Joachim's house was probably indicated by a simple curtained entrance, but the garden and the bath were conceived by the author in far greater and more 'realistic' detail:

Part of the stage is covered with greensward, in which herbs and flowers are planted and around which shady foliage is woven so that it resembles a garden. As large a basin as possible is filled with water, or else water is poured from a pitcher from above, as if a spring were flowing.

Other school dramas could, however, call for a far more complex staging plan than this. The Uppsala production of *Holofernis och Judiths Commoedia* required a large number of localities, including the Temple, Judith's house, the city walls with a gate, a house to which Judith is taken, and the tent of Holofernes, from which Judith emerges dramatically with the severed head. The *mise-en-scène* for the Danish *Tobiæ Comedie* included two characteristically medieval mansions. God appears surrounded by the heavenly hosts in an elevated Paradise, from which Raphael, Tobias' angel in need, descends to earth. Placed at the farthest possible remove from this was the Hell of the play's two devils, Asmodeus and his helper. Between these metaphysical extremes stood such localities as the house of Tobias' parents, the distant and fateful bridal chamber of

Sarah, where the devils make off with the unfortunate girl's bridegrooms, and the intervening River Tigris, in which Tobias catches the remarkable fish. That exoticism was not meant as the principal feature of the latter locality is suggested by the archangel Raphael's observation that the water reminded him of the local Viborg Lake!

More elaborate still was the production of H. J. Ranch's *Allegiance to Solomon,* 'a new merry and instructive comedy derived from the legends of King David and King Solomon' which was performed in Viborg in 1584 as an allegorical homage to Frederik II (King David) and his son, the newly elected crown prince Christian (King Solomon). Among the cast of over sixty players, the author himself appeared in the medieval guise of the Fool, in this case called Crow. The prologue introduces us to some of the mansions which confronted the royal family and the citizens of Viborg:

> This building is called Jerusalem,
> Here King David holds house and home,
> Look now there at lovely Zion,
> Here stands Israel's regal throne. . . .

Ranch's lively stage picture also afforded examples of simultaneous action: thus a sumptuous third-act banquet continued on through the following act, irrespective of activity going on in other mansions, although the participants were specifically admonished not to upstage the main action with excessive jollity and noise-making.

Inspired by the study of classical theatre, Humanist dramatists frequently introduced musical and choreographic passages in their plays. Songs often introduced and concluded each act, and solo or choral musical numbers were sometimes incorporated directly in the dramatic action. H. J. Ranch's *Samsons Fængsel/Samson's Prison* (c. 1599), termed the first Danish operetta, contains nine songs, each of which contributes to the dramatic tension or characterization. Dalila lulls the strong-man to sleep as her maids sing love songs and a pastoral ballad. The melodies of merry millers are heard, and Samson himself sings of fickle fortune, 'so like the wheel and grinding mill.' Choreographic sequences and full-scale balletic spectacles occasionally

29

gave these school productions the character of a Renaissance *ballet de cour*. In 1607, a performance in Randers of Terence's *The Eunuch* included three intermezzi—'The Four Seasons,' 'Hercules and Omphale,' and 'The Four Ages'—presented as pantomimic character dances by allegorically dressed figures. Similarly, at the climactic moment in *Allegiance to Solomon* when Solomon is acclaimed, Ranch sought in typical Renaissance fashion to recreate the singing and dancing chorus of classical drama. The text describes a formation of 'twelve angels in the outer circle, seven planets in the inner. . . . All sing and dance.' At the centre of this universe knelt the chosen sovereign, surrounded by the whirling planets and protecting angels.

In a scene such as this, the Humanist stage came closest to the spirit and style of the elaborate royal festivities of the Renaissance which amalgamated music, ballet, song, declamation and pageantry in a splendid allegorical homage to the ruling house. By the middle of the seventeenth century the vogue of school drama in Scandinavia had waned, and new forms of theatre predominated, represented by these lavish court festivities and *ballets de cour* on the one hand and by the visits of itinerant professional troupes on the other. Indicative of a declining popularity is the fact that Uppsala's energetic student actors were invited only once to appear at the court of Queen Christina, where they gave a performance of Seneca's *Hercules Furens* in 1648. Apparently no student players were recruited to grace the magnificent wedding festivities held by Christian IV for his son in 1634, although two dramatic allegories were contributed by Sorø professor Johannes Lauremberg. The Uppsala students were once again able in 1665 to delight their monarch, the eleven-year-old Charles XI, with a performance of the versatile Urban Hiärne's powerful and sanguineous Seneca pastiche *Rosimunda,* but by this date the popularity of the Humanist stage had passed its zenith. A belated epilogue to its history in Sweden is formed by the six seasons from 1686 to 1691 during which a group of student actors from Uppsala gave public performances at the court theatre of Charles XI in Stockholm. In almost every sense, however, the features of the older school drama had now altered. The young student amateurs, dressed in costumes borrowed from the royal wardrobe, performed on a fully equipped perspective stage in Lejonkulan, a disused lion's den located beside the palace wall. With Isaac Börk as their *primus motor,* they mounted a series of imitative heroic plays whose very titles—*Apollo, Darius, Philomela, Hippolytos,* and the like—suggest the new classical-mythological emphasis in their subject matter. Struggling to live up to the ideals of French classicism and offering a rather pale reflection of the baroque splendour of contemporary court theatricals, Lejonkulan's seventeenth-century student productions represent—their quality notwithstanding—a note-worthy milestone, denoting both an early step in the direction of a permanent native troupe and a last vestige of the vigorous Humanist stage tradition in Scandinavia.

CHAPTER THREE

Renaissance Festivities

During the sixteenth and seventeenth centuries, the courts of Scandinavia glittered with a series of pageants, processions, and court ballets which deserve to stand as worthy counterparts to the more internationally familiar Renaissance festivals of Europe. A royal wedding, a burial, a coronation or a christening became the traditional occasion for an opulent display of regal largesse and taste. Gradually the mummings, disguisings and courtly revels of the sixteenth century developed into the spectacular festivities and stunning *ballets de cour* which hall-marked the important events at the courts of Christian IV, Frederik III and Queen Christina. Sometimes extending over a period of days or even weeks, these 'compliments of state', as Samuel Daniel liked to call them, would incorporate the central ceremony into a rhythmic and coordinated round of jousts, tournaments, fireworks, masques and triumphal processions. Insubstantial as these pageants may have been in the eye of history, something of their splendour continues to radiate from the very full descriptions which remain.

A delight in dramatized spectacle and emblematic representation permeated the sixteenth century and clearly underlies the significant public events of Frederik II's reign in Denmark (1559–88). No instance better illustrates the essentially theatrical conception of such a public action than the ceremonial oath-taking of the Slesvig vassals at Odense in 1580. A 'pallads', or curtained stage, decorated with an elaborate framing arch and exhibiting a clearly theatrical lineage, was erected in the public square. The king made his entrance surrounded by one hundred halberdiers, preceded by heralds wearing 'the Danish coat-of-arms, richly and artistically embroidered and worked with gold and pearls.' The monarch having taken his place on the stage, with the Privy Council at his feet, the royal vassals, marshalled on horseback under a blood-red banner, drew up their ranks in attack formation and rode about the platform. Dismounting, they ascended to the king and swore their allegiance. Frederik II seized the banner of blood, while the dukes of Slesvig grasped its staff, and conferred the fiefdom upon them. He then threw the banner to the crowd, which 'according to ancient custom and usage tore it to pieces.'[1]

The splendid coronations of Christian III in 1537 and Frederik II in 1559 were but a prelude to the spectacle of Christian IV's official assumption of the Danish crown in 1596. Particularly popular on such occasions were the *Trionfi,* or regal processions, which evolved during the Italian Renaissance and which afforded a rich opportunity for the princes of the realm to masquerade in the guise of the gods, heroes and generals of antiquity. The chief participants were then joined by a cavalcade of elaborately constructed pageant cars, presenting allegorical and fantastic groupings and appropriately termed 'inventions.' Dragons, camels, rolling mountains, stately temples, ships under full sail—all rumbled past the gaping spectators.

Nor was the tone necessarily one of self-conscious solemnity. On the sixth day of this particular festivity, the procession which preceded the traditional contest of riding at the ring was led by the young Christian IV in the guise of Pope Sergius VI, riding jauntily in a sedan chair under a canopy. Flocks of cardinals, bishops, Swiss guards and monks swinging smoking thuribles completed this barbed travesty of the papal court. On the following day, the newly crowned monarch disguised himself as a woman in an 'invention' representing the Mount of Venus, complete with four choir-boys as cupids.

Along the route of such a Renaissance cavalcade, triumphal

[1] Quoted in Otto Andrup, 'Hoffet og dets Fester', *Danmark i Fest og Glæde,* eds. J. Clausen and T. Krogh, I, p. 316.

arches often added to the spectacle. On its return from the coronation ceremonies, Christian IV's procession encountered such an arch, several storeys high and supported at each corner by 'a giant with a gilded shield in his left hand, a scimitar at his side, and a gilded helmet on his head.'[2] As the king passed through the arch, an angel descended to place a crown on him, the four giants nodded with 'appropriate reverence', and a roll of kettledrums blended with trumpet fanfares from the musicians grouped atop the structure (Plate 8).

[2] Quoted in Torben Krogh, *Musik og Teater,* p. 3.

8. Enlarged detail from the royal procession celebrating King Christian IV's official assumption of the Danish crown in 1596

The princely passion for masquerade and spectacle which these examples of Renaissance pageantry represent was most fully satisfied in the great *ballets de cour,* a genre which grew from the Italian *intermezzi* and spread across the courts of Europe during the sixteenth century. The form of the genre crystallized in the celebrated *Ballet comique de la Reine,* performed in Paris in 1581. Three component parts remained more or less constant: *'l'ouverture',* an exposition in song or recitative; *'les entrées',* a succession of related episodes, usually no more than five in number; and *'le grand ballet',* the extended closing dance in which the courtly spectators joined. It seems hardly surprising that Christian IV, brother-in-law of James I of England, at whose elegant court the masques of Inigo Jones and Ben Jonson flourished, should take a particular interest in this type of theatrical entertainment.

Outshining all other Renaissance festivities in Denmark was the thirteen-day celebration held by Christian IV in October of 1634 to seal the union of his eldest son Prince Christian with Princess Magdalene Sibylle of Saxony. *Trionfi* (which included the king and his son in the heroic guise of Publius Scipio Africanus and Lucius Scipio Asiaticus), grand balls, banquets, tournaments, fireworks, and theatrical entertainments all contributed to the pomp and circumstance of the occasion. A high point in the programme was the performance on the third day of Scandinavia's first full-scale *ballet de cour,* created by the court dancing-master Alexander von Kückelsom and scored by the able composer Heinrich Schültz, an avid champion of the new Italian musical style of Monteverdi.

In traditional fashion, von Kückelsom's untitled ballet paid allegorical homage to the royal house. Neptune (Christian IV) has cleansed his realm of all monsters and has silenced the fierce goddess of war Bellona. In the most striking of the entrées, Orpheus and the animals and trees which dance to his sorrowful music are torn to pieces by furious bacchae and she-devils. Grieved at this atrocity, the gods decide 'harmoniously to create a new world and love from Orpheus' ashes.'[3] Cupid wounds Neptune's son (Prince Christian) and the goddess of wisdom Pallas Athena (Magdalene Sibylle). Descending in a

[3] Quoted in Torben Krogh, *Hofballetten under Christian IV og Frederik III,* p. 19.

35

cloud, the gods arrive to bless the union of this pair and join in 'le grand ballet', which in this case spelled out in intricate dance patterns the names of the prince and his bride.

This noble display, performed largely by the court amateurs themselves, took place in the castle ballroom. Although the printed programme prepared by its author is explicit concerning the action, however, less is certain regarding the staging. The festivities of 1634 represented a remarkable mixture of Renaissance and medieval traditions, as seen in the presentation on this occasion of the medieval morality, *The Tragedy of the Virtues and the Vices*. The simultaneous staging technique of the morality, discussed previously, was undoubtedly carried over into the indoor court performances as well. The *ballet de cour* seems to have made use of at least two distinct, free-standing localities, supplemented by rolling scenery, such as the hill on which Orpheus sings his plaintive monody as he is drawn around the hall, a flying machine for divine transportation, and a backcloth, called a 'tent', to facilitate exits and entrances. The problem of clearing such a curtainless open area was handled adroitly. Following the scene in which the bacchae tear Orpheus and the local flora and fauna to shreds, for example, four angels appeared to 'bear the dead Orpheum away' and three Pantalones 'collected the dead animals and cleared the ballroom.'

The technique of simultaneous staging is even more clearly operative in the first of two German allegorical plays by Johannes Lauremberg which were performed for Christian's wedding guests. This obvious and, under the circumstances, rather uncomplimentary allegory, performed on the fourth day of the celebration, presents Aquilo, rude ruler of the North, who complains to Jupiter of the intemperate climate of his realm and his own lack of a wife. To solve his problem, he is transformed by Venus into an attractive youngster who easily makes off with the lovely and amorous Orithyia. Two contrasting mansions, called 'Theatrum' in the text, were seen—the snow-covered and forbidding 'winter theatre' of Aquilo and the luxuriant and inviting 'summer theatre' of Orithyia. The neutral forestage could change its character from scene to scene.

36   In contrast to *Aquilo*, Lauremberg's second play, enacted on

the eighth day of the festivities, decidedly required a perspective stage for its production. This erudite allegory about King Pineus and the savage harpies (*Wie die Harpyiæ von zweyen Septentrionalischen Helten verjaget, und König Phineus entlediget wird*) called for rolling waves as well as for a view of sirens who disappear in water up to their waists and sing in Neptune's honour. Before the production, contracts had been issued both for the construction of a perspective stage and for the painting of a backcloth displaying a view of Kronborg and Elsinore. The latter drop undoubtedly provided an effective touch of local colour in Lauremberg's septentrionalian fable.

Due to the enormous expense involved—and some estimates have placed the costs of the wedding celebration of 1634 at the equivalent of over £1,000,000—such festivities were as infrequent as they were extravagent in the Denmark of Christian IV. Not to be outdone by such Danish revels, however, the court of Queen Christina of Sweden soon carried the art of the *ballet de cour* to its highest peak of development in Scandinavia. Christina, surrounded by some of the ablest statesmen and keenest minds in Europe and imbued with a delight in magnificent entertainments that the younger nobility eagerly shared, created around her an atmosphere of opulent splendour which dazzled even the ambassador of the Sun King Louis XIV himself.

Beginning with *Le ballet des plaizirs de la vie des enfans sans soucy,* staged by the French ballet-master Antoine de Beaulieu and presented in 1638 by the Countess Palatine Catharine to amuse the twelve-year-old queen, the Swedish court ballets grew steadily in scope and munificence. Homage to the ruling house, always the traditional function of the *ballet de cour,* was the undeviating purpose of *Le Monde rejovi,* 'occasioned by the commencement of Her Royal Majesty's happy reign' and danced at Stockholm Castle on New Year's Day 1645. The opening section shows the rejoicing of Heaven as Virtue, in the name of Christina, ascends the throne and Mercury is dispatched to proclaim the glad tidings. Subsequent sections depict the resultant jubilation in the sea and on the earth, as Christina's praises are sung by all, including 'the four winds', which promise that they will look after her armies at sea.

The elegant lyrics of court poet Georg Stiernhielm have

raised the printed programme texts for several of these Swedish *ballets de cour* to literary as well as theatrical importance. Stiernhielm's celebrated ballet *Then fångne Cupido/Cupid Captured* was performed at Christina's newly erected court theatre in November 1649, and featured the queen herself as Diana and Duke Adolf as Apollo. So delighted was the queen dowager that she conferred two properties on the ballet-master de Beaulieu for his choreography. For the royal birthday the following month, Stiernhielm provided the Swedish lyrics for the elaborate *La Naissance de la Paix,* celebrating the Treaty of Westphalia which ended the Thirty Years War in 1648. No less a figure than René Descartes, residing in Stockholm at this time as Christina's tutor, seems to have been responsible for the actual composition of this trenchant piece of anti-war agitation. The customary allegorical figures are juxtaposed with a vision of grim reality: Mars and others praise the glories of war, until 'some soldiers appear as proof that war is no pleasure' and ruined peasants are seen contemplating their burning farms. Earth and the other three elements deplore Mars' bellicose attitude, while Justitia, Pallas, and Pax grieve over the fact that Peace has no homeland. At last, the gods agree that war must end.[4]

All previous spectacles paled in the brilliance of Christina's formal coronation in October of 1650. For her ostentatious royal entry into Stockholm, the queen rode in a chariot covered in rich brown silk brocade, embroidered in silver and gold and drawn by six white horses decked out with plumes and gilded harness. For an entire intoxicating week wine flowed from the public fountains. For two and a half months the round of balls, tournaments, processions, fireworks and ballets continued, crowned by the production of Stiernhielm's effective theatrical tribute, *Parnassus triumphans,* on the first day of 1651. This stage extravaganza, designed to pay homage to the queen as the protectoress of art and learning, had been intended for performance on the coronation day itself, but the colossal staging and costuming problems it created caused its postponement.

With Queen Christina's abdication and departure in 1654, the

[4] Gustaf Ljunggren, *Svenska dramat intill slutet af sjuttonde århundradet,* p. 434f.

Swedish worship of French culture subsided for a time and the most hospitable climate for the great *ballets de cour* again became the Danish court, presided over by Frederik III and his pleasure-loving queen Sophie Amalie. Reports of Christina's luxurious entertainments had reached the Danish king through his ambassador Peder Juel, and no doubt fired Sophie Amalie's fertile theatrical imagination. During the 1650s, the two Scandinavian courts vied with one another in the elaborateness of their *Wirtschaften,* a popular form of courtly masquerade which imitated the life in and around an inn or a market and allowed the courtly participants to cavort in pastoral surroundings dressed as soldiers, pilgrims, hunters, shepherdesses or the like. In general, the court ballets of Frederik III tended to differ perceptibly from those seen during his father's reign. The previous unified emphasis upon the allegorical figures of antiquity was splintered. The aim now became the presentation of a baroque variety of characters, among which pastoral types were in high favour, in a loose and non-sequential framework, appropriately referred to in France as a *ballet à entrées*.

The stage-struck queen herself led the eager court amateurs in the performance of these mid-seventeenth-century ballets. In a grandiose work entitled *Unterschiedliche Oracula,* a loosely organized ballet-masquerade written by the court poet A. F. Werner to celebrate the acclamation of crown prince Christian in 1655, Sophie Amalie delighted the spectators in no fewer than five separate rôles. Among the multitude of characters who solicit the oracular reply of the Sibyl in the thirty-five *entrées* of this ballet, the queen impersonated Fame, a peasant girl, the Muse of War, a Spanish lady, and an Amazon. In his observant description of the production, the gallant Spanish ambassador Count Bernardino de Rebolledo eulogizes her 'comely decorum and charming grace.' As the Muse of War, 'dancing and swinging a banner with such extraordinary agility in time to the music', she 'transformed the surprise of the spectators to speechless amazement'.[5] The 'indescribable charm' which Rebolledo discovered in Sophie Amalie's enactment of a peasant girl is still to be discerned in a contemporary painting by Heimbach which, in all probability, is a depiction of the queen in this very rôle (Plate 9).

[5] R. Nyerup, *Efterretninger om Kong Frederik den Tredie*, p. 419f.

9. Queen Sophie Amalie as a peasant girl in A. F. Werner's
ballet-masquerade *Unterschiedliche Oracula*, 1655. Painting
by Heimbach in De danske Kongers kronologiske Samling,
Rosenborg Castle, Copenhagen

In addition, this painting clearly suggests a perspective stage
with painted scenery. Rebolledo's account confirms the fact
that the Italianate perspective stage, with its painted wings and
borders, had firmly established itself in the Scandinavian court
performances. When the curtain rose on *Unterschiedliche
Oracula,* 'a large stage with bushes on either side was revealed'
and 'a perspective which ended in the cave of the Sibyl' was

seen in the background. The illusion, Rebolledo's account assures us, was 'so natural that even the keenest attentiveness would be baffled.' Adroit stage lighting enhanced the effect. 'Through the bafflingly natural sky, covered with reddish and transparent clouds, illumination from countlessly many lamps shone, without anyone being able to detect how it was done.' The visible or *a vista* scene change, a technique which lay at the heart of the wing-and-border system, was also seen in this spectacular court ballet when 'toward the end the stage was suddenly transformed, and two enemy camps were seen facing one another.'

Unterschiedliche Oracula was, of course, not the first ballet to apply modern Italian staging principles to the portable stages erected in the ballroom of Copenhagen Castle. The second of Lauremberg's festival plays in 1634 had required perspective scenery; a painter's invoice for *Das weiblichen Geschlechts Preisz und Ruhm* (1649), a *ballet de cour* whose conceit is the praise of womanhood on the basis of episodes from Roman history, also mentions 'two cloths' painted with perspective views. Aided by a significant number of such invoices and accounts from the period, Torben Krogh has convincingly reconstructed the salient features of the perspective wing stage at the court of Frederik III.[6] A proscenium arch, painted to resemble stone blocks and with an ornate frieze at the top, framed the stage. For the floor in front of the proscenium arch, a painter's invoice for Werner's ballet *Vergnügung und Unvergnügung/Les contents et mécontents du sciecle* (1650) mentions 'five cloths and four boards' painted to resemble grey and yellow stone tiles. A similar 'tiled' forestage is clearly in evidence in Heimbach's painting of Sophie Amalie, which also contains a hint of the matching steps (the 'four boards' in the painter's bill) that led down from the stage to an open dancing area on the ballroom floor. A railing may have been erected to separate this open playing area, or 'orchestra', from the crowd of surrounding spectators.

The programme for the *Ballet des 4 Elémens,* performed in 1653 to celebrate the christening of Prince George of Denmark, is remarkable for the examples it offers of typical seventeenth-century stage décors. The work, 'a musical play and ballet',

[6] *Hofballetten,* p. 90f.

depicts the festive rejoicing ordered by Jupiter to take place in each of the four elemental spheres to mark the christening of the infant prince (the relationship to *Le Monde rejovi,* the homage to Queen Christina, seems unmistakable). One of the most indispensable settings in these *ballets de cour* was a garden, with flowers, fountains, and shady paths all painted in illusionistic perspective. Characteristically, such a garden did duty as 'Earth' in the allegorical *Ballet des 4 Elémens:* 'In the play the perspective changes to a garden, in which the Five Senses are presented.'[7] A sea décor was another highly important piece of inventory in this genre, and as early as the festivities of 1634, rolling waves had been seen in the second of Lauremberg's plays. Twenty years later, when the *Ballet des 4 Elémens* turned to acquatic matters the nautical illusion was considerably more sophisticated: 'The perspective is changed to a sea, on which the royal navy is seen. Neptune comes forth with the other water divinities.'

In the air, the *Ballet des 4 Elémens* did its best to emulate the spectacular cloud machines and flying feats with which the 'Great Sorcerer' of Italian stagecraft Giacomo Torelli had stunned Parisian audiences at the Petit Bourbon. Hence, in the opening section Pax and Fame were seen 'out in the clouds' and other gods appeared 'out in the perspective' while Jupiter arrived, as he is wont to do, 'from above, riding on an eagle'. In contrast, the ballet offered its audience a chilling version of the mandatory Underworld setting: 'In the play the perspective is changed to Hell, where Tantalus and Titius are seen in their suffering and torment. Cerberus lies before the gates of Hell, howling in his bonds'. An invoice for the production, which reveals that the scene also utilized a 'Hell-mouth' in the form of 'a large devil's-head', is, moreover, a vivid reminder of the long persistence of medieval conventions on the perspective wing-and-border stage.

The princely penchant for elaborate *ballets de cour* and related festivities in which cavaliers capered at the great courts of Scandinavia remained strong throughout the seventeenth century, and the reigns of both Christian V of Denmark (1670–99) and Charles XI of Sweden (1660–97) offer notable instances of this tradition's survival. Poet and politician Erik

[7] Programme quoted in *ibid.,* p. 98f.

Linschöld's ballet *Den stoora Genius/The Mighty Genius,* staged for Charles XI's fifteenth birthday in 1669, recalled the lyric spirit of Stiernhielm's tributes to Christina. In *Certamen equestre,* the ornate pageant which marked Charles' coronation three years later, the young monarch made his appearance on horseback dressed as a Roman warrior and followed by his courtiers masquerading as Roman foot-soldiers. Similarly, the Lord Chamberlain U. F. Gyldenløve's celebration of Christian V's birthday in 1683 took its place in the long tradition of Renaissance and Baroque festivities with the performance of a ballet-opera composed for the occasion by the noted poet and hymnist Thomas Kingo in the accepted allegorical vein, depicting the visit of the legendary King Dan to Christian's realm.

In one sense, these princely toys and 'transitory devices', so much a part of court life during the sixteenth and seventeenth centuries, represent a stylistic terminus, a form of theatre which perished and is incapable of resurrection. In a far more meaningful sense, however, their subsequent influence has proved to be profound. In terms of stagecraft, they embody the transition from the medieval conventions to the Renaissance principles of perspective staging. The future development of both opera and ballet was shaped by their example. In cultural terms they constitute a significant espousal of theatrical art by the royal houses of Scandinavia, an initial response which grew into the enthusiastic protection which has characterized and moulded the Scandinavian theatre. Nevertheless, in the evolution of a broad popular theatre a second, co-existent tradition, represented by the activity at this time of itinerant foreign professional troupes, played a far more dominant rôle.

CHAPTER FOUR

Royal Troupes and Strolling Players

Among the most important factors in the development of the Scandinavian theatre during the seventeenth and eighteenth centuries is the influence exerted by the bands of strolling players which visited Denmark and Sweden for more than a century. Functioning as ambassadors of theatrical style, they performed under royal patronage and were occasionally invited to take up residence at court for extended periods. The acting of these foreign troupes, often of a high professional calibre, created a favourable climate for the subsequent growth of a native theatre. The establishment in Denmark in 1722 of the first permanent national playhouse in Scandinavia can be viewed as the direct outgrowth of the activities of one such company.

The warmth of the welcome accorded such theatrical troupes depended entirely upon the views and tastes of each reigning monarch. As early as 1579 we find evidence that Frederik II of Denmark took a company of English comedians into his service, in which they remained for seven years, performing at the newly constructed Kronborg Castle in Elsinore for the glory of his majesty and the pleasure of the numerous sea-captains returning with bulging coffers from their long ocean voyages. In the summer of 1586, a second troupe of English players, numbering such illustrious Shakespearian comics as Thomas Pope and Will Kemp, entered the king's service for a short time before moving on to the court of the Elector of Saxony. That Shakespeare himself might have been among the English strollers at Kronborg is an attractive but highly unlikely notion.

It is improbable that these small bands of comedians, numbering about five members, would have performed actual plays. Players such as these, referred to expressly as 'instrumentalists', offered a mixture of dance, song, gymnastics, clowning, and declamation in their performances, and the term 'English comedians' subsequently came to be applied to similar Swedish and German strollers commanding the so-called English arts of fencing, vaulting and rope-dancing. Although the long and shining reign of Denmark's Christian IV (1588–1648) saw more attention paid to music and courtly festivities than to professional dramatic performances, English troupes, including those of Thomas Sackville and John Green, continued to visit the country. Sackville's celebrated company of comedians and acrobats, numbering eighteen members, was sent to Denmark by their patron, Duke Henry Julius of Brunswick, to contribute their share to the spectacular festivities marking the coronation of the Duke of Brunswick's brother-in-law, Christian IV, in 1596. Similarly, that greatest of all Renaissance festivities in Denmark, Christian IV's munificent celebration of the marriage of Prince Christian to Princess Magdalene Sibylle of Saxony in 1634, was also enlivened by an invited band of English actors who no doubt appeared in Lauremberg's German plays as well as in *The Tragedy of the Virtues and the Vices*.

In Sweden at this time, a comparable interest in things theatrical led King Gustav II Adolf to complement his fully equipped court orchestra with a professional troupe of players in 1628 under the leadership of Christian Thum. Thum, who thus became Sweden's first court theatre director, was given not only an annual stipend of 400 silver dollars but also the privilege of requisitioning all necessary costumes from the royal wardrobe. In 1640, he was accorded an additional sum of money for the construction of a public theatre in the Södermalm district of the capital, where he was to present plays for a popular audience when not appearing at court, but nothing more is known about its history.

With the succession of the young Queen Christina to the

throne, the Swedish court soon became one of the most resplendent in all of Europe, dazzling those present with a steady
array of *ballets de cour* and similar entertainments. Determined
to rival the court of the great Louis himself, Christina decided
in 1647 to equip a room in the castle as a theatre, patterned on
French models and supervised by the Italian architect Antonio
Brunati. Seven years later, Brunati created a still larger and
more sophisticated perspective stage in the palace, measuring
more than fifty feet in depth and affording Swedish audiences
their first real taste of the wonders of changeable baroque
scenery. A contemporary description of this court theatre tells
us that it was painted in imitation marble with grooved Doric
pilasters, and presented a proscenium arch flanked by columns
with niches containing statues and topped by an emblematic
frieze. The stage curtain was hung on rings attached to a rod
and was drawn aside. In addition to amateur courtly theatricals,
Christina's elegant playhouse accommodated performances of
Italian opera and *commedia dell'arte* given by a professional
troupe of Italian actors and singers, under the direction of
Vincenzo Albrici, which, in good French fashion, she invited to
Sweden in 1652.

The English comedians who had entertained Danish royalty
in the previous century represented a vanguard of the subsequent invasion of German and Dutch wandering troupes
which appeared regularly throughout the reign of Frederik III
(1648–70). In 1662, this self-proclaimed absolute monarch and
theatre enthusiast granted a patent to the Dutch entrepreneur
Andreas Joachimsen Wolf which permitted him to erect the
first permanent theatre building in Denmark, patterned on and
named after Amsterdam's 'Schowburg'. This seventeenth-
century Dutch theatre represents a transition between the
Elizabethan-type raised open stage and the Italianate perspective
stage with its curtain. The royal patent enjoined Wolf to
present something which 'is not common, and has not been
seen by any ordinary comedian'.[1] Eager to oblige, Wolf engaged one of the most outstanding troupes at the time, headed
by the German 'principal' Michel Daniel Treu (or Drey) and
numbering among its members the prominent actor Johan
Velten. The Treu company arrived early in 1663 and was

46   [1] Quoted in Torben Krogh, *Musik og Teater*, p. 38.

allowed to perform 'comedies, tragedies, and other such actions and plays' at the palace tennis-court until Wolf's Schowburg was completed later that same year.

During its brief existence, Wolf's theatre exposed Danish audiences to a brand of theatre which represented the highest professional standards. In addition to Treu's players, Carl Andreas Paulsen's important troupe and Jan Baptista van Fournenburgh's Dutch actors managed to appear at the Schowburg in Copenhagen before the entire enterprise ended in bankruptcy and the theatre was pulled down in 1666.

Following this regrettable event, Treu moved his base of operations to Lüneburg, while the Dutch actors under van Fournenburgh were transferred by the royal yacht 'Green Parrot' to Stockholm, where the regency employed them in the service of the young Swedish king Charles XI. In the royal palace's Lejonkulan, originally constructed to house Queen Christina's pet lion, the cages in the den were dismantled and another copy of the Dutch Schowburg was erected for their use. This playhouse, the first permanent Swedish stage, opened with a Dutch tragi-comedy, *Orondaat en Statira,* in 1667. Meanwhile, Carl Paulsen, joined by his eminent son-in-law Johan Velten, continued to appear at regular intervals in Copenhagen. In 1676, we learn that this troupe consisted of fourteen members, including only two actresses, since female parts were still frequently taken by the younger actors.

The repertoire of these seventeenth-century German and Dutch itinerant players, which provided entertainment not only for the lower classes but for the courts of Frederik III, Christian V, and Charles XI as well, represents a curious mixture. In addition to adaptations of classics by such dramatists as Shakespeare and Lope de Vega, they specialized in the extremely popular and drastically theatrical Haupt– und Staatsactionen, a genre in which elevated heroics were yoked with farcical *lazzi* and which played upon the contrast between the noble and spectacular actions of the main story and the clowning and common-sense reactions of Hans Wurst or Pickelhering. Usually, of course, the main play was capped by a broadly farcical *Nachspiel.*

An interesting document offers at least some idea of the titles performed by such a troupe. When Treu left Denmark for

Lüneburg in 1666, he petitioned the authorities there for permission to perform and, happily, supplemented his application with a list of the plays he had presented while in the service of the Danish monarch. Treu's list[2] includes twenty-five regular plays, in addition to an unspecified number of 'various lovely pastorals'. His flair for scenic effects is suggested by the very first item, a chronicle of the destruction of Jerusalem 'presented naturally on the stage with the help of special inventions'. Biblical, mythological, and particularly historical subjects (including plays about the death of Cromwell and the restoration of Charles II) recur frequently in the repertory. In addition to adaptations of Calderón and Lope de Vega, a rich inheritance from the earlier English troupes is evident in the form of such titles as Marlowe's *Doctor Faustus,* Kyd's *The Spanish Tragedy,* and Shakespeare's *King Lear.* The version of the latter play which Treu performed in Copenhagen, entitled 'The History of King Liar of England, being a Matter in which children's disobedience towards their parents is punished and obedience rewarded', is obviously of special interest. Research by Torben Krogh has uncovered a later programme describing the action of this seventeenth-century German *Lear.* In it, the Fool was absent and the ending was considerably altered. Both Regan and Goneril stab themselves to death on stage, the latter because she 'cannot have Edmund'. More emphatic yet is the death of the bastard: Lear orders that Edmund shall 'an 4 Ketten in die Luft hängen, und also sein Leben beschliessen'. A comforting reunion followed these horrors, however, as Lear in the end 'rejoices over his daughter Cordelia's obedience'.[3]

In the France of Louis XIV the art of acting had reached an unequalled peak of excellence, and the courts of Europe competed to secure French companies, more permanent than the essentially itinerant English, German, and Dutch troupes, which could bring them something of the splendour of Versailles. Frederik III engaged a company of French actors under the leadership of Jean Guillemoys du Chesnay Rosidor in 1669, but their activities were abruptly halted by the death of the Danish king the following year. In 1681, Christian V and his courtiers

[2] Discussed *ibid.,* pp. 39–40.
[3] *Ibid.,* pp. 41–2.

determined to secure a new French troupe for the Danish capital, where, with interruptions and changes of personnel, the company continued to perform until 1694, when the last of the French actors returned home. Little definite is known about their repertoire or playing conditions. Although its membership changed frequently, the normal size of this troupe seems to have been twelve performers, probably eight actors and four actresses. Their presentation on the king's birthday in 1683 of the festive five-act comedy *L'Inconnu,* a demanding *pièce à machines* written by Thomas Corneille and de Visé and first produced by Molière's company less than eight years before, suggests a good deal about their technical ability and range. In 1686, a group of new troupe members arrived which we assume included René Magnon de Montaigu, the son of Molière's friend, dramatist Jean Magnon, and subsequently the founder of Denmark's first national theatre.

In general, the reign of Christian V saw a considerable broadening of the range of theatrical culture in the Danish capital. In addition to the installation of a highly trained French troupe at court, the opening of Copenhagen's first opera house took place under his aegis in April 1689. The initial production was an allegorical representation of warring gods by theologian P. A. Burchard, entitled *Der vereinigte Götter-Streit.* Unhappily, however, during the second performance of this uplifting spectacle later the same month, Christian V's wooden opera house burned to the ground; a new opera, built this time of stone, first rose from the ashes under the rule of his musically enthusiastic son in 1703.

The crowning of this son, King Frederik IV of Denmark, in 1699, and the succession of his bellicose cousin Charles XII to the Swedish throne two years before, ushered in a new era, a new century rich in theatrical developments and conducive to the eventual establishment and growth of a native theatre in Denmark and Sweden. In 1699, the court architect and passionate theatrical collector Nicodemus Tessin the Younger convinced his young sovereign to do credit to Sweden's position as one of the great powers of Europe by inviting a permanent French troupe of twenty-three actors, singers, and dancers to Stockholm. For their public performances this company, headed by Claude Rosidor, a son of the former leader of

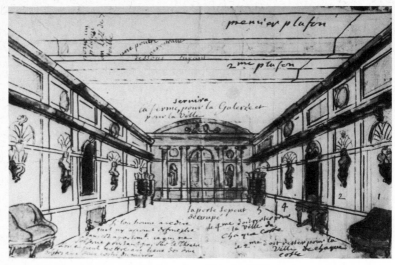

Seventeenth-century stage design: three Bérain-d'Olivet
designs for King Charles XII's French troupe in Stockholm.
10. A formal hall ('La galerie')

11. A street ('Le village')

Frederik III's troupe, was given permission to equip and operate Bollhuset—the palace tennis-court—as a theatre, at its own expense. For court performances, however, a second play-house was needed. Fire had destroyed Stockholm Palace and the stage in Lejonkulan two years before, and Tessin therefore set out to create a new court theatre in the great hall of the Wrangel Palace. The resultant plans and sketches for this project rank today among the most informative pieces of iconographic evidence concerning seventeenth-century European stage design. Tessin requested no less an artist then Jean Bérain himself to forward the necessary scenery from Paris, and under his supervision three basic settings were created by Jean St-Hillaire d'Olivet, one of Bérain's collaborators at the Paris Opéra, tested on the stage of the Hôtel de Bourgogne, and promptly shipped to Stockholm. These three Bérain-d'Olivet designs could be combined in various ways to allow for a total of six distinct décors; with their ingenious permutations, they provide a complete range of the timeless scenic environments needed for the classical repertory of Corneille, Racine, and

12. A basic tragedy decor ('Palais à volonté') with an arboreal background added to accommodate 'serious pastorals'

51

Molière. 'La galerie' (Plate 10) could be transformed into 'la place publique' and then into 'le village' (Plate 11) by the swift insertion of new wings into the set. The tragedy décor ('Palais à volonté') could, before the eyes of the audience if one wished, become a setting for 'serious pastorals' simply by opening the back shutter to reveal a new background (Plate 12). There can be little doubt that Tessin's stage in the Wrangel Palace, five wings deep with two sets of wings in each position to permit rapid *changements à vue,* rivalled the theatres of Paris in its display of the very latest techniques of seventeenth-century staging.

Rosidor's players opened the new court theatre on 20 November 1699 with Jean-Louis Regnard's recent Parisian hit comedy *Le joueur,* and followed with a repertoire of Corneille, Racine, Molière, Regnard, Dancourt and other French novelties. Bollhuset was ready for them in February of the following year, having been converted from a lawn-tennis court—painted black to permit the players to see the balls and surrounded by a spectator gallery—to a modern theatre auditorium. This new public playhouse, accommodating 800 spectators, consisted of a standing pit and three tiers of boxes, furnished with blue upholstered benches, with the royal box in the first tier near the stage. Unlike the court theatre, admission was charged: those choosing the better seats paid one caroline for the second level, two carolines for the first, and three carolines for a prominent seat on the stage itself. The latter practice persisted, here as elsewhere, far into the eighteenth century.

The extensive wars of Charles XII eventually suffocated all theatrical activity in gunpowder smoke. By 1706 the war effort had undermined the economy to such an extent that the actors' salaries could not be met, and the last of the troupe turned homeward. During the period that followed in Sweden, a variety of itinerant companies performed without any particular regularity.

Although his adversary on the battlefield, Frederik IV resembled Charles in his desire to brighten his court with a new French troupe of players. These actors, arriving in Copenhagen at the end of the year 1700, actually included some of the members of Rosidor's gradually dissolving company. The Danish court troupe, organized by the able René Montaigu and consisting of twelve members, seven actors and five actresses, remained in the service of the king for two decades. Montaigu bore the responsibility for every phase of the operation, receiving his orders from the king and his court, casting the parts, supervising preparations, acting, arranging music and choreography, and even contributing an occasional prologue. Each of Montaigu's players was hand-picked, and the ensemble undoubtedly represented a high degree of artistic excellence.

Little is known of the Montaigu troupe's repertory, apart from the fact that it naturally included Corneille, Racine, and Molière. During its twenty-year existence, however, Montaigu was able to travel to Paris four times for the express purpose of informing himself about new trends, choosing new plays for production, and studying the French acting style. A document which he addressed to the king prior to one such journey in 1707 is indicative: 'Je profiterois de cette occasion pour voir, les meilleures comedies nouvelles, et la maniere dont on les joue, afin de les faire representer a mon retour devant Votre Majesté'.[4] Montaigu's French connections have aroused considerable interest precisely because they suggest a demonstrable link between the theatrical culture of the French capital and the imminent development of a native Danish drama.

At the outset, Montaigu's troupe performed on temporary stages erected in various palace locales, often in conjunction with the royal banquet. If the theatre itself on such occasions was somewhat make-shift, however, the settings and staging were in no sense deficient in splendour and complexity. Time and again we encounter the comment that 'the stage was numerous times transformed in great haste and with complete illusion'.[5] For some years after its opening in 1703, the French actors also shared the new opera house with its resident Italian singers, although this building was ultimately converted to other uses in 1720. About 1712, a theatre was created in Copenhagen Castle to accommodate the court performances. This spacious playhouse consisted of fifteen boxes on three levels as well as a pit furnished with benches. It is tempting to surmise that admittance to this court theatre perhaps extended

---

[4] Letter dated 17 April 1707; see Anne E. Jensen, *Studier over europæisk drama i Danmark 1722–1770*, I, p. 21.
[5] Eiler Nystrøm, *Den danske Komedies Oprindelse*, pp. 47–8.

at times beyond the court circle itself to segments of the general Danish public.

During Montaigu's entire tenure at court, German troupes continued to appear in Copenhagen and even gave occasional performances at the palace. Samuel Paulsen von Qvoten, a redoubtable oculist, quack dentist and medicine-man who toured the provinces with an itinerant puppet theatre, gained royal permission in 1718 to present live theatre in the capital itself. Joining forces with him, Etienne Capion, Montaigu's stage technician and designer at court as well as a prosperous caterer, began the following year to present performances by a troupe of 'high German comedians' in one of the admiralty's warehouses (a disused cannon foundry) on Kongens Nytorv. Following von Qvoten's departure for Sweden, Capion continued alone and succeeded, in May 1721, in securing an enviable monopoly on theatrical entertainment in the capital and a patent authorizing the construction of a permanent theatre. Its location was a small side-street off Kongens Nytorv, called Lille Grønnegade (Little Green Street) whose name has become synonymous with the beginning of a national theatre in Scandinavia.

Capion's playhouse, designed by the capable stage technician to rival the glories of the court theatre, rose during the autumn of 1721. By the kind of coincidence upon which such historical developments sometimes depend, Frederik IV chose to dismiss Montaigu and his French actors that same Fall, replacing them with Johan Kayser's German opera company. Hence, when Grønnegadeteatret opened in January 1722 it offered performances by René Montaigu's formerly royal comedians. A partnership between the jobless theatre director and Etienne Capion was inevitable. Montaigu's new scheme, the formation of a popular Danish language theatre in Capion's playhouse, lacked only one ingredient—native plays—and Ludvig Holberg was waiting eagerly in the wings to provide them.

CHAPTER FIVE

Holberg
and the Danish Comedy

The vogue of the French court troupe in Scandinavia was by no means over following Frederik IV's dismissal of Montaigu and his company. The intermittent presence of similar troupes at the courts of various Danish and Swedish monarchs during the eighteenth century continued to constitute an important aspect of the theatrical climate. During this century of enlightenment, however, the focus of attention shifts to the emergence of a national popular theatre and a corresponding native drama. It needs hardly be emphasized that Ludvig Holberg was the century's overwhelmingly predominant playwright in Scandinavia. Less clearly evident perhaps is the pattern of development undergone by the theatre during this period. The first steps toward a truly national theatre, taken by Montaigu's actors at Grønnegadeteatret in the 1720s, led ultimately to the founding of the Danish Royal Theatre in 1748. From the comparable efforts of the so-called Royal Swedish Stage in 1737, a somewhat more indirect path led through A. F. Ristell's Bollhus theatre project in 1787 to the realization of the Royal Dramatic Theatre in Stockholm the following year.

'Dans l'impossibilité de faire à l'avenir éclater mon zèle pour le service de Vostre Majesté en parlant françois', wrote Montaigu to the Danish king in July of 1722, 'je luy demande très humblement la permission de pouvoir établir ici vne Comédie en langue Danoise'.[1] Cut off from performing in

[1] Eiler Nystrøm, *Den danske Komedies Oprindelse*, p. 77n.

55

French by the king's decision, the former court theatre director, motivated more by simple practicality than by patriotic considerations, sought for a means of continuing his work in the national language. Supported by influential officials, Montaigu's plan for 'la Comédie Danoise' received royal approval—but no royal subvention—the following month. During the summer Montaigu assembled his Danish company, consisting of seven actors and three actresses. Although most of the group's members were university students, a seasoned nucleus was formed by Marie Magdalene Montaigu, the director's young wife and former court troupe actress, and Frederik de Pilloy, who was later to convey the original Holberg traditions to the new Royal Theatre. Although Montaigu himself was obviously unwilling to appear on stage in a language which he did not fully command, his life-long immersion in the Molière style of comedy and his outstanding ability to train young actors were powerful assets for the new theatre. Artistically the Danish Comedy began on a solid foundation; financially, however, its position was badly undermined from the outset.

Scandinavia's first national theatre opened in Capion's playhouse on 23 September 1722 with a translation of Molière's *L'Avare*. Thalia came forward in a prologue written for the occasion to proclaim her traditional comic intent:

> I mention neither man nor town nor house nor street,
> But punish without fear what we should hate,
> Wherever I may see it, of whomever it is said,
> For the instruction of all who pay good heed.

Two days later came the first Holberg première, *Den politiske Kandestøber/The Political Tinker*, a play which, as its author records,[2] 'had the good fortune which all good comedies should have, namely that a flock of people became angry over it' but which also 'kept the audience laughing from beginning to end'. It was an auspicious beginning. Fortified with five of Holberg's best comedies in their first season, the Danish actors enjoyed not only popular success but also a patronage by the nobility that included command performances at court of Molière's *Le Bourgeois gentilhomme* and *Le Mariage forcé*. Even

---

[2] In 'Just Justesens Betænkning' (*i.e.,* Reflections), the 1723 Preface to his first five comedies.

before Montaigu's opening, however, Capion had mortgaged his theatre and patent to the hilt, and it became increasingly difficult for the box-office receipts from the 500-seat house to cover the extensive debts and expenses. Holberg's play *Den ellevte Juni/The Eleventh of June,* a debtors' comedy whose title refers to the fiscal date on which instalments and interest normally fall due, had a grim kind of relevance when first acted on 11 June 1723. Shortly after its second performance, Capion himself was hauled into jail for his own bad debts.

Although the financial situation improved temporarily and Holberg continued to turn out play after play for the Danish company, further setbacks were in store for Grønnegadeteatret during the 1723–24 season. A substantial portion of Capion's income derived from profitable bi-weekly 'assemblies' which took place at his theatre, featuring 'gallant music', masquerades, coffee or tea, and some discreet gambling. When these frivolities, which form the colourful background for much comic indignation in Holberg's *Maskarade,* were outlawed as a source of youthful corruption in February of 1724, Capion sought desperately to counteract the loss by supplementing the actors' bi-weekly performances with a band of rope dancers. Outraged, Montaigu succeeded in wresting control of the playhouse from the patentee: ownership passed into the hands of creditors, and the wily Etienne Capion decamped permanently in the summer of 1724, apparently taking a troupe of Danish actors on tour to Norway. Continued efforts by Montaigu to stave off an inevitable financial collapse were fruitless, however, and his Comédie Danoise, faced with dwindling attendance, closed in bankruptcy in February 1725.

One year later, the embryonic Danish national theatre was temporarily resuscitated when Montaigu's players resolved, 'despite the harsh fate which for some time has befallen the Danish plays', to resume their performances 'at their own risk'.[3] The actors, who now rented the theatre for each performance and then divided the proceeds, chose *Tartuffe* for their reopening (in spite of Holberg's rather narrow view that Molière's play was written for a Catholic audience and would have no relevance for a Danish public). Throughout 1726, the surviving playbills make it clear that Montaigu's troupe bent

[3] Nyström, p. 101.

every effort to attract a following, performing three times a week and occasionally offering as many as four plays on a single bill. Audiences were treated to displays of perspective staging reminiscent of Montaigu's court theatre. Molière's *Amphitryon*, popular from the theatre's earliest period, could boast of Mercury seated on a cloud in the prologue, Night in a chariot drawn by horses, and the majestic descent of Jupiter at the conclusion in a specially designed machine. In Nicolas Boindin's *Le Port de Mer*, an afterpiece which opened as *Toldboden* on 20 May 1726, spectators were promised 'a complete view of the Copenhagen Roadstead as it looked in those days, with numerous men-of-war, three-masters, other smaller vessels and barges rowing here and there in the water'.[4] Song and dance became an added major attraction after the arrival in June of the notable French ballet-master Jean Baptiste Landé and his wife. Recruited from Stockholm by the Danish actors, Landé had been the Swedish court's dancing master. In 1721, his staging of a ballet divertissement and two Regnard plays acted by court amateurs on King Fredrik I's birthday had met with royal approval, and he was subsequently permitted to form a French opera troupe, called l'Académie royale de musique, under the Swedish king's protection. At Grønnegadeteatret, Landé's talents were utilized to create the Polichinelle interlude in Molière's *Le Malade imaginaire* and to enliven Holberg performances with interpolated harlequinades such as 'the Italian Night of Harlequin and Scaramouche'.

New plays were added steadily in an effort to strengthen the repertoire and stem the financial ebb tide. Holberg's *Banquerouteren eller Den pantsatte Bondedreng/The Bankrupt or The Pawned Peasant Boy* armed Montaigu with yet another popular intrigue comedy. The production in May of *Le Menteur eller Løgneren* very likely introduced Danish audiences not to Pierre Corneille's comedy but to a version of Richard Steele's *The Lying Lover*, a free adaptation of Corneille originally transferred to Scandinavia by the Swedish playwright Carl Gyllemborg. Steele's play exposed the Danish theatre to its first taste of sentimental drama. The timely arrival of Holberg's *Den Stundesløse/The Fussy Man* in November once again rescued the

---

[4] From the theatre's playbill, reproduced and commented in, *e.g.*, Anne E. Jensen, *Teatret i Lille Grønnegade 1722–1728*, pp. 156, 158.

actors from the public's indifference, but the flurry of interest was brief. Audiences shrank, a particularly ill-attended performance had to be called off. Just before the end, Montaigu made a desperate excursion into the motley world of the *commedia dell'arte* with Le Noble's *Les deux Arlequins,* found in Gherardi's *Le Théâtre Italien.* No amount of effort or ingenuity seemed able, however, to exorcise the twin demons of insolvency and indifference. Bowing to the inevitable, the Danish Comedy died in bankruptcy on Shrove Tuesday 1727.

A brilliant resurrection seemed possible when Montaigu's tireless campaign to win royal subsidy finally bore fruit in February 1728, and the Danish actors were raised by Frederik IV to the status of a court troupe with an annual subvention of 1500 rix-dollars. Performances by the now Royal Players commenced at court and at Grønnegadeteatret in April, but the revival was short-lived. The theatre's owner, General H. J. Arnoldt, had decided to hire Landé to form a *commedia dell'arte* troupe whose repertory would be taken from Gherardi's *Le Théâtre Italien*—a move which Montaigu, whose company had also begun to draw upon the same goldmine of harlequinades, naturally opposed. The general proved implacable, and at one point even threatened his theatrical tenants with eviction at the hands of a subaltern and six musketeers. The dispute dragged on into the Fall, but on 20 October 1728 fate settled it permanently. The great Copenhagen fire gutted two-fifths of the city, razing 1670 buildings including the University and Town Hall, and pious minds saw in the calamity a punishment of godless activities. High on their list stood playgoing. The dark mood which followed the catastrophe swept away any thought of continuing the Danish Comedy, and with the succession of Christian VI to the throne two years later, a reign of pietism (1730–46) effectively stifled all theatrical activity in Denmark and Norway.

Although the duration of Scandinavia's first national theatre was brief, its six-year existence is historically significant in many respects. Abiding traditions were established, not the least of which was the novel phenomenon of professional performances given on a regular basis in the vernacular for a popular audience. A living link, in the person of Montaigu, connected the court theatre tradition of Frederik IV and the new stage in Lille Grønnegade. The repertoire of the latter theatre was almost exclusively comic and offered generous helpings of the best of French classicism, including at least sixteen comedies by Molière and five by his disciple Regnard. Enjoyment of these French pieces, formerly the privilege of the fastidious court audiences, was now extended to a broad public in the form of invariably localized prose translations. In a similar fashion other genres, including the harlequinades of the Théâtre Italien and perhaps the new sentimental drama, were absorbed into the mainstream of theatrical devolopment in Denmark. By far the most remarkable feature of the repertoire of this beleaguered little theatre remains, however, the twenty-one comedies with which Ludvig Holberg created, with astonishing rapidity, a native drama of international stature.

Holberg, born in Bergen in 1684 and appointed a professor of metaphysics at the University of Copenhagen in 1717, had already established a solid literary reputation (under the pseudonym Hans Mikkelsen) with his mock-heroic epic *Peder Paars* when he was approached by 'certain persons' to write comedies for the new Danish stage. Professor Holberg more than satisfied the request: during the first eighteen months of its existence Grønnegadeteatret was able to produce fifteen new comedies by him. The majority of his plays—a total of twenty-seven comedies—belong to the history of this first national theatre. When the Danish Royal Theatre was founded in 1748, following a twenty-year hiatus in theatrical activity, the aging Holberg once again came to the aid of the resurrected national stage with six more plays, but these comedies, cast in a more serious, philosophical vein, added little to the measure of his artistic achievement. In 1754, the year of his death, no fewer than twenty-five of his comedies were in the active repertory of the Royal Theatre—vivid evidence in itself of the importance of Holbergian drama as a mainstay of the comic tradition which extends from Montaigu's playhouse in Lille Grønnegade to Frederik V's rococo theatre on Kongens Nytorv.

The five Holberg plays staged during the first Grønnegade season—*The Political Tinker, Den Vægelsindede/The Weather-cock, Jean de France, Jeppe paa Bjerget/Jeppe on the Hill,* and *Mester Gert Westphaler*—are all examples of the genre which the playwright himself termed *comedy of character* and which, with Molière before him as the great model, he considered the superior comic mode. In these and subsequent works such as *Jacob von Tyboe, Erasmus Montanus, The Fussy Man,* and *Don Ranudo de Colibrados,* the foibles of a central figure, generally named in the title, are exposed to ridicule. Throughout the action, dramatic interest remains focussed on the leading character and on the ludicrous situations into which his folly draws him and those around him. As a typical representative of the Enlightenment, a champion of the Age of Reason, Holberg is in all his work distrustful of violent passions or of anything in excess. 'I have made no attempt at tragedy, nor have I any inclination to do so', he remarked, 'for I am repelled by everything which is affected or is placed, so to speak, on stilts' (Epistle 447). In his comedies of character it is precisely that which is 'stilted' which is ridiculed. Eccentricities or foolish quirks rather than grand vices are the objects of his satire.

Herman von Bremen, a muddle-headed tinker obsessed by a vain and foolish ambition to gain power and authority by becoming mayor, is the butt of *The Political Tinker.* Herman is the guiding light of a *collegium politicum*—composed of such eminent local authorities on matters of state as the furrier, the brushmaker, the baggage inspector and others—which convenes regularly to pass judgment on the condition of the world. When some light-hearted men of rank decide to trick him into believing that he has in fact been elected mayor, the greatness so suddenly thrust upon him creates so many practical problems that he is quickly brought to his knees. After a farcical attempt to hang himself, the chastened tinker renounces his political aspirations, returns to his work, and allows his daughter to marry the unpolitical young man whose courtship he had previously opposed.

Both *Jean de France* and *Erasmus Montanus* ridicule equally pretentious but younger fools whose heads have been turned by an acquaintance with the great world beyond their native villages. In the former play, which Holberg in 'Just Justesen's Reflections' called 'a bitter satire' of the bourgeois tendency to corrupt the country with foreign fashions, Jean de France (alias Hans Frandsen) returns from a fifteen-week stay in Paris so absorbed in French fashion and so oblivious to reality that he

61

is an easy victim for various hoaxes. Tricked into wearing his coat backwards and smearing his mouth with snuff in the belief that he is obeying the latest whim of the ever-changing Paris fashions, the gullible snob is at last persuaded to turn his back on his native country for the sake of a non-existent French-woman called 'Mme. la Fleche'. While Jean de France learns nothing from his folly, Erasmus Montanus presents a more complex picture. Rasmus Berg is the peasant student, the great pride of his wondering parents, who returns from the world of the university to his rural village inflated with his newly-acquired proficiency in Latin disputations and syllogisms. (Before his first entrance, we learn that he has three times fallen off the carriage bringing him home in the heat of his learned debates with himself!) Although no one in the village is able to appreciate it, there is in fact nothing wrong with Erasmus' Latin learning, but the inhumanity and conceit with which he flings it in the teeth of his uncomprehending surroundings render it foolish and irrelevant. At the climax of the comedy, the pretentious student suffers humiliation and defeat at the hands of public opinion, in the person of the village deacon, on the crucial question of whether the earth is flat or round. It is, the tormented Erasmus is compelled to concede, 'flat as a pancake', and he promises to mend his ways and abjure further disputation.

While one type of Holbergian character comedy thus ridicules foolish ambitions and pretensions, another group satirizes character absurdities. In *The Weathercock,* the second Holberg play acted at Grønnegadeteatret, the central character is the fickle and unpredictable Lucretia, a capricious female whose ceaseless changes of mind create a veritable wilderness of confusion around her. Lucretia proved a perfect vehicle for the charming Marie Magdalene Montaigu who, according to the delighted author, 'portrayed her habits so nicely that one can say she lacked nothing of what is needed to convey such a personality'.[5] In *The Fussy Man* Holberg created a male counterpart to Lucretia, a busybody called Vielgeschrey who spends his time rushing furiously and aimlessly from one activity to another, accomplishing nothing in spite of all his energy. In

[5] See Hans Brix, 'Holberg og Teatret' in *Komediehuset på Kongens Nytorv 1748,* ed. Torben Krogh, p. 21.

Mester Gert Westphaler the main figure is a compulsively talky barber, while *Jacob von Tyboe* transplants the popular type of the braggart soldier and would-be lover to Danish soil.

As a rule Holberg's character comedies centre around figures set apart from and held up as a ludicrous contrast to the norms of the society surrounding them. Their foibles and affectations both motivate the action and dictate the outcome of the plot. *Jeppe on the Hill,* Holberg's most celebrated play, employs a different comic pattern. In this version of the fable of the peasant made king for a day, based on a tale in Jacob Biederman's *Utopia,* the main character, a good-natured and witty soul with a predilection for sleeping his cares away and drowning serious concerns in the bottle, has no special quirk or pretension. The story of the play is that of a practical joke. Jeppe is discovered one day by the local baron sleeping off his intoxication on a dunghill. He is carried into the baron's manor, dressed in the nobleman's best clothes, and placed in his bed, after which he is informed that he is the master of the house and his hallucination of being a poor peasant must be attributed to a bad dream. Jeppe plays his new rôle with gusto, shows himself something of a tyrant, and soon becomes drunk again on the fine wines which are served to him. The joke culminates when Jeppe, back on the dunghill, is once more plucked from his repose, accused this time of impersonating the baron, and executed in a mock hanging—after which he is allowed to return to life, and goes off once more to have a drink! The focus of this comic *tour de force* never deviates from the earthbound reactions of Jeppe to the amazing experiences which befall him. The impact of the play lies not in the unmasking of folly but in the development of a character portrait so rich in comic charm and humanity that *Jeppe on the Hill* holds a unique place in Holberg's production.

In this group of comedies Holberg, as he remarks in 'Just Justesen's Reflections', strove consciously to draw original central characters which other dramatists 'had not worn too thin'. In many instances, however, the collection of figures surrounding them re-appeared from play to play. This principle of a permanent gallery of familiar figures became the predominant one in Holberg's *intrigue comedies,* plays which depend not upon a particular main character but upon a succession of tricks, disguises, bewildering misunderstandings, and confusions of identity for their effect. As in the *commedia dell'arte*, the cast of characters with their distinctive characteristics remains largely unchanged: only the situations vary. In his comedies of intrigue Holberg drew his inspiration from the scenarios in Gherardi's *Le Théâtre Italien* and from Roman comedy. Plautus was a professed favourite. At the head of the list of Holberg types stands the indefatigable and roguish servant Henrik, who made his first entrance in *The Political Tinker* munching a sandwich and, as always, fully in command of the situation. The first in an illustrious series of Henrik actors was the Grønnegade troupe's Henrich Wegner, also the creator of Chilian, the first recorded Danish Harlequin, in Holberg's madcap parody of Haupt- und Staatsactionen *Ulysses von Ithacia*. Henrik's equal in wit and feminine charm is the maid Pernille. Together, these two manage much of the intrigue and unite the somewhat pale and less interesting young lovers Leander and Leonore, whose affairs of the heart provide the nucleus of the plot in *Henrik og Pernille, Pernilles korte Frøkenstand/Pernille's Brief Ladyship,* and *De Usynlige/The Invisible Lovers*. A far more vigorous character than the lovers is Jeronimus, the *senex* whose stubborn paternal opposition to the world in general and to any kind of youthful mirth in particular motivates the action in many of Holberg's plays.

In the two *parody comedies* which Holberg wrote for the Grønnegade stage, grossly distorted proportions are the source of the humour. *Ulysses von Ithacia* crams the eventful action of both *The Iliad* and *The Odyssey* into its wildly farcical five acts. In *Melampe,* a 'tragi-comic' travesty of the highly charged psychological conflicts of French classical tragedy, the title figure around which the action revolves is none other than a lap dog.

The essence of theatre in Holberg's view was the festive spirit, 'the soul of comedy' which brings a play to life on the stage. 'A comedy must possess *festivitas,* gaiety, and the ability to make people laugh', he declared in 'Just Justesen's Reflections', the first important piece of comic theory in Danish. It is not enough for the comic playwright to study 'the ridiculousness of humanity' and to be able to 'chastise faults so that he amuses as well', he insisted in this dramatic manifesto.

In addition to fulfilling the dual Horatian purpose of pleasing and instructing, the comic dramatist must envision the effect which his play will have on the stage: 'sometimes the comedy which is wittiest to read is the least amusing on the stage' if it lacks 'that which cannot easily be described but which is the thing that makes a theatre live'.

An underlying requirement of Holberg's comic theatre is the exaggeration or heightening of individual characters. Not, however, to the extent that they appear to be madmen. Such exaggeration must be contained within the bounds of artistic decorum 'so that the audience will be able to believe that it is real'. Decorum can, moreover, be defined only in terms of what is acceptable and comprehensible within the context of local customs and fashions. Hence certain kinds of characters and environments are foreign to Holberg's audience, just as certain subjects must be regarded as unfamiliar and therefore unsuitable. Thus, he is led to reason, 'highly romantic and amorous plays are very inappropriate here and have not had the same acceptance as in England and other lands where people hang themselves for the sake of love'! Understandably, this emphasis on the element of audience self-recognition caused Holberg to make a strong plea for a native drama and for localized comedy. Furthermore, it provided him with a welcome excuse to bait Molière, his prodigious and more popular rival in the Grønnegade repertory: for every negative point singled out in Molière's comedies, a positive counterpoint is selected from his own work.

In Holberg's view, Molière's plays held a distinct advantage over his own when these were first produced at Grønnegade-teatret. For the performance of Molière rôles, a tradition of interpretation, movement and gesture existed beforehand and was communicated by Montaigu to the young Danish actors. By contrast, Holberg's new works had 'only their own intrinsic merit to recommend them'. That they succeeded was due, the Danish playwright insisted, to the fact that they afforded, even to inexperienced actors, a veritable blueprint for character physicalization. The figures in Holberg's classically comic universe, each with his particular dominant trait or attitude, are vividly delineated in terms of appearance, speech, and manners and are armed by the playwright with a battery of

65

opportunities for effective *lazzi* and pieces of comic stage business. Each character is related to a distinct, localized milieu which, while obviously in no sense naturalistic, adds colour and concreteness to the classic simplicity of the comic design.

'Machines, displays, masquerades, and other such things which attract more spectators than the comedy itself' evoked Holberg's displeasure in a play such as Molière's comedy-ballet *Le Bourgeois gentilhomme*. Nevertheless, a specific group of his own comedies depend upon animated tableaux and visual displays of local customs and festivities for their effect. *Barselstuen/The Lying-in Room* sketches a lively picture of the popular custom of visiting women in childbed that adroitly accentuates the tormented husband's (unfounded) doubts about his own paternity. *Julestuen/The Christmas Party* is an afterpiece which focusses on the Yuletide socializing and merrymaking of the period. Like *Maskarade,* in which the festivities of the Carnival season form the context for a love intrigue and a masquerade interlude is staged between the first and second acts, it was written to satisfy the Montaigu troupe's desire for comedies incorporating visual appeal. (The Danish actors had first commissioned Holberg's less successful fellow dramatist J. R. Paulli, whose intrigue comedy *Den seendes Blinde/The Blind Man's Vision* had been acted in 1723, to write a play on the theme of the Christmas party and the masquerade, but his awkward effort, entitled *Jule-Stuen og Maskarade,* failed to please Montaigu. It remained for Holberg to realize the subject matter's potential by reorganizing it into two separate 'display comedies.')

The technical demands created by this type of Holberg comedy range from the relative simplicity of the staging in *The Christmas Party* to the complexity of the tableaux in *Kildereisen/ The Healing Spring,* in which the object of the therapeutic pilgrimage to the spring 'suffers' from a feigned disease that renders her unable to express herself except in operatic arias. The entire second act of this play is a complicated pantomimic interlude in two parts. In the first part, 'a road to the spring' crowded with streams of wayfarers is seen: 'the same ones can hurry out on one side and come in from the other in order to give the impression of many', advised the practically inclined playwright. The scene culminates in two processions accompanied by music, one comprised of a group of gaudily costumed peasants celebrating springtime and the other consisting 'of old crones, all wearing different deformed masks and walking with crutches in time to the music. . . .' Following this grotesque display, the stage opens to its full depth to reveal a picturesque representation of the healing spring itself, framed by small tents. 'The spring is a small hole in the floor from which some constantly scoop water, others use pitchers, still others use their hats', reads the stage direction. Real water undoubtedly added to the illusion of this colourful folk scene, which was further enhanced by continual noise and movement: 'Some shout, others talk, still others swing and crack their whips, and crones fight to be the first at the spring. A blind man enters with a violin, after which the peasants dance'.

In his later years Holberg grew progressively more bitter concerning the taste of audiences which, in his opinion, no longer cared whether a play was 'well or poorly written but only whether it ends with song and dance' (Epistle 360). Yet even corrupted taste has its usefulness in the world, he added coldly, since it helps to support the theatre. Several of his later *philosophical comedies,* influenced by the moralizing currents which prevailed at mid-century, were made more palatable by catering to the 'corrupted' popular taste through the incorporation of singing, dancing and scenic effects. In 1751 *Plutus* provided the new Royal Theatre with a particularly elaborate scenic spectacle that featured splendid processions, magnificent costumes, special lighting effects, and gods in flying machines. In the opinion of the delighted author no play had ever achieved greater success: 'that which contributed to it were the various splendid displays which please both the mind and the eye because they flow naturally from the action itself'.[6]

Holberg's reputation as a dramatist rests, however, on the series of comedies which he wrote for the embryonic national theatre in Lille Grønnegade. Its closing in 1727 was solemnized by the performance of his grimly farcical playlet *Den danske Komedies Ligbegængelse/The Interment of the Danish Comedy,* written when the theatre's economic crises had driven it into

---

[6] Torben Krogh, *Studier over de sceniske Opførelser af Holbergs Komedier,* p. 62.

bankruptcy in 1725. Accompanied by drum rolls, a funereal procession of actors and actresses which included even Montaigu's children marched three times around the stage, as the sorrowing creditors followed the deceased Comedy—an actor in a wheelbarrow preceded by a drummer dressed in black and two men bearing marshals' batons with crepe streamers—to the grave. As the once-vital corpse was lowered through a trap in the stage floor, Henrik threw himself grief-stricken into the grave. At last Thalia, who less than four and a half years before had stood on the same stage to proclaim the beginning of halcyon days, now came forward again in the person of the lovely Madame Montaigu to pronounce the eulogy over the Danish comedy.

CHAPTER SIX

Rococo Playhouses: from Kongens Nytorv to Drottningholm

The middle decades of the eighteenth century comprise a transitional era of vigorous growth and restless activity in the Scandinavian theatre. The surge toward the establishment of a native popular theatre might be temporarily balked, but it was not ultimately to be denied. By mid-century the first truly national theatre in Scandinavia stood—where it continues to stand today—on Kongens Nytorv in Copenhagen. Equally strong at this time was the parallel influence exerted by the tastes of the aristocratic court theatres. Under the festive aegis of such theatre-mad royalty as Sweden's Lovisa Ulrika and Denmark's Frederik V, the enjoyment of French drama and Italian opera remained the hallmark of an enlightened mind. To compartmentalize unduly these two types of theatre, popular and courtly, would be to distort the interplay of styles and crossing of currents which characterized the theatrical climate of this period.

With the succession of the pietistic Christian VI to the throne, Danish theatre perished. The official death certificate, dated 21 March 1738, decreed that 'no play actors, rope dancers, conjurers, or those who run so-called games of chance shall be found in Denmark or Norway, nor shall their plays and routines anywhere be performed or exercised'. Although comparable anti-theatrical sentiments were entertained and voiced by the clergy in Sweden, the results there were far less damaging. Throughout the 1730s itinerant German troupes continued, as they had done for a century, to perform their customary motley repertory of Haupt- und Staatsactionen, farcical afterpieces, acrobatics and rope dancing. One year before the edict abolishing Danish theatricals, a group of Swedish students and young civil servants obtained permission to enact the story of 'the unfortunate but thereafter happy Tobias' at the 'Royal Theatre' in Stockholm (*i.e.,* Bollhuset) on the occasion of the king's birthday. The enthusiastic response to this enterprise, reminiscent of the scholastic tradition of the previous century yet clearly moved by the same spirit which animated the Grønnegadeteater endeavour, swelled the impetus toward a native Swedish theatre. Four performances of the Tobias play to crowded houses provided the encouraging basis for the formation of the Kongliga Svenska Skådeplatsen, the Royal Swedish Stage. Montaigu's counterpart in the Swedish Comedy was the experienced French troupe actor Charles Langlois.

The new vernacular theatre opened in early October, 1737 in the refurbished Bollhus with the production of Carl Gyllenborg's original five-act comedy *Svenska Sprätthöken/The Swedish Fop.* Young Count Quick returns, a la Erasmus Montanus, from his schooling in France with a profound distaste for the Swedish language and customs. The fop's salvation is the spirited girl who agrees to marry him on the strict condition that he abandon his folly and become a good Swede again. Gyllenborg's pointedly topical satire enjoyed the fate prescribed by Holberg for 'all good comedies': 'a flock of people became angry over it' and audiences were delighted.

Like the Danish actors at Grønnegadeteatret, Langlois' company performed twice weekly in a varied repertoire that combined originals and translations with the traditional burlesque afterpieces and harlequinades. The Royal Swedish Stage was not, however, an exclusively comic theatre. New native plays such as Erik Wrangel's *Fröken Snöhwits Tragœdia/ The Tragedy of Snow White,* Modée's comedy *Fru Rangsiuk/ Lady Snob,* and Olof von Dalin's pseudo-classical verse tragedy *Brynilda* alternated with older as well as more recent works by Molière, Corneille, Holberg, and Voltaire. Hence the versatile Petter Palmberg could be seen both as Count Quick in Gyllenborg's comedy and as Brutus in Voltaire's recent tragedy *La*

Mort de César. During the first two years alone, twenty new plays were presented, half of which were Swedish originals.

Unfortunately, neither the variety of its repertoire nor the skill of such performers as Palmberg, Petter Stenborg, and the popular harlequin Petter Lindahl could apparently rescue the Royal Swedish Stage from that fatal cycle of public indifference, financial crises and internal strife. The aging King Fredrik I seemed far more interested in the joys of Bacchus and Venus than in the attractions of Thespis. A single visit by the cosmopolitan Lovisa Ulrika, a true product of the French enlightenment transplanted to Sweden in 1744 as the future King Adolf Fredrik's betrothed, sealed the theatre's doom: 'I found so little enjoyment', she wrote in 1746, 'that I shall never in my life return. The vulgarities lasted for four hours. No possibility of escaping because of the mob which blocked the passage'.[1] In 1753, the new régime cancelled Langlois' patent and subsequently evicted the Swedish company from Bollhuset in favour of a new French troupe. A segment of the original company under Petter Stenborg was granted permission to continue performing in the capital, but it now became their own responsibility to find a suitable stage. Stenborg's theatre, moving from one hastily improvised playhouse to another and falling steadily deeper into public disrepute and artistic disrepair, continued its fitful existence for nearly two decades before Gustav III again raised the Swedish-language stage to grace and dignity.

Simultaneous with the demise of the Royal Swedish Stage, however, the desire for a native national theatre which had animated both the Langlois and the Montaigu companies achieved its fulfilment in Denmark. Following the death of the stern Christian VI in 1746, the new monarch Frederik V lost no time in reviving the performing arts. Long before the prescribed period of mourning was over, the Danish ambassador in Paris received the following court news: 'Les plaisirs seront rapellés à la cour, le roy a dejà témoigné qu'il désiroit avoir une comédie françoise; il a paru à la vérité balancer entre ce spectacle et celui d'un opera italien. . . .'[2] In fact, the king

---

[1] Claes Hoogland and Gösta Kjellin, eds. *Bilder ur svensk teaterhistoria*, p. 108.
[2] Anne E. Jensen, *Studier over europæisk drama i Danmark 1722–1770*, I, p. 195.

chose both. No fewer than six separate theatres were authorized by Frederik during the first years of his reign. A pall had lifted, and theatrical activity flourished as never before.

The traditional French troupe, *de rigueur* for any civilized court, was soon installed in a theatre in Nørregade. Queen Louise, daughter of England's George II and a personal pupil of Händel, naturally encouraged the establishment of Pietro Mingotti's Italian opera company, which she had enjoyed in Hamburg on her honeymoon, in the new playhouse which was fitted up in Charlottenborg Palace. (During the 1748–9 season their conductor was no less a personality than C. W. Gluck.) In the meantime, S. P. von Qvoten, the quack dentist and medicine-man who had obtained a theatre patent in 1718, turned up with his son Julius Heinrich to claim his rights. The younger von Qvoten, in partnership with the formidable General Arnoldt, the former patentee at Grønnegadeteater, was allowed to open a German-Danish theatre located in Store Kongensgade in 1747. During the single season he endured, Heinrich von Qvoten presented a fascinating potpourri which drew upon the modern Scandinavian drama, including Olof v. Dalin's tragedy *Brynilda* and seven comedies by Holberg, upon the contemporary international repertory popularized by J. C. Gottsched through Caroline Neuber's renowned German troupe, and upon the venerable traditions of the harlequinade and the Haupt- und Staatsactionen. When von Qvoten abandoned the theatre in 1748 to return to his family calling of oculist, hernia surgeon, and 'tooth-breaker', an era had ended: Danish audiences had seen the last of Pickelhering's antics and the *lazzi* and heroics of the vigorous Haupt- und Staatsactionen.

Hence the competition facing Carl August Thielo, the organist and composer licensed by the king in 1746 to re-create a Danish national theatre 'along the lines previously laid down by our beloved Ludvig Holberg', was substantial. Like Montaigu before him, Thielo turned to the university for his company. Frederik de Pilloy, the sole connection to the Montaigu style and the traditions of Grønnegadeteatret, took charge of casting, rehearsing, costuming and training the new actors. Baron Holberg himself, though unwilling to assume an official post in the enterprise's management, clearly functioned behind the scenes as the adviser and protector of the new Danish stage.

The top floor of Christian Berg's public house in Læderstræde was hastily equipped with a small provisional stage and a gallery, and Thielo's company, following Holberg's advice, opened its embryonic Danish Royal Theatre on 14 April 1747 with *The Political Tinker*. A dozen Holberg comedies followed, including the first Danish productions of *Erasmus Montanus* and the harlequinade *The Invisible Lovers*.

The small, temporary theatre in Berg's public house remained in operation only eight months. Fortified with their newly won experience and ambitious to acquire their own playhouse, the Danish actors, having deposed Thielo, sought a collective license to erect a permanent theatre on Kongens Nytorv, on the site of the disused cannon foundry (Lille Gæthus or Tjærehuset) where Capion and von Qvoten had staged performances thirty years before. The coveted royal patent was granted to the actors in December, 1747; while preparations for the new Royal Theatre went forward, they moved their base of operations first to Tjærehuset and then, when the site was cleared for construction in June, to the playhouse in Store Kongensgade just vacated by the ruined Heinrich von Qvoten. Court architect Niels Eigtved's noble and harmonious rococo theatre rose with remarkable haste. On 18 December 1748 the Danish Royal Theatre, today one of the oldest functioning playhouses in Europe, opened with a prologue hailing the generosity of the royal family, seated in its brilliantly decorated box in the middle of the first gallery. The main attraction was Regnard's comedy *Le joueur,* the perennial favourite with which Rosidor had opened in Stockholm half a century earlier and which the Danish actors now presented as an implicit challenge to the competing French troupe in Nørregade. Taken loosely as a moral satire of the gambling mania, Regnard's play could also serve as a perfect expression of the eighteenth-century view of drama which the new theatre's motto stated with such determination:

... When in our plays, as in a mirror, you observe the ways of the world, the evil and the good, and laugh at humanity's frailty, wickedness, and vice; then learn thereby to know your own, to correct it, to improve and change from impropriety to decency, from evil to good, from vice to virtue.

[3] Robert Neiiendam, 'Hvordan det gik til' in *Komediehuset paa Kongens Nytorv 1748*, ed. Torgen Krogh, p. 50.

At the outset the theatre on Kongens Nytorv shared many of the characteristics of its modest forerunner in Lille Grønnegade. Holberg's House remained essentially a comic theatre. The small initial company, consisting of eight actors, four actresses, and three dancers, appeared twice weekly in a repertoire based squarely on the classical comedy of Holberg, Molière, and Regnard and the light-hearted *lazzi* of the *commedia dell'arte*. Eigtved's building, which was drastically altered and expanded in 1772, originally accommodated 782 spectators in three tiers of boxes and a pit—dandies of the day were no longer allowed to buy seats on the stage, as they had done at Grønnegadeteatret and in Berg's public house. Capacity houses were infrequent, however, and the financial situation was often precarious. Balls, at which the actresses served coffee and tea, were held in the playhouse in order to swell its coffers, and the actors' slender incomes were supplemented by their right to take home the candle stubs left after each performance. In 1750, control of the debt-ridden theatre passed from the actors to the less-than-enthusiastic Copenhagen city fathers. It was not until 1770 that the Danish 'Royal' Theatre actually came under the economic shelter and administrative aegis of the monarchy.

Jacopo Fabris, a Venetian designer and technician of international format, equipped both the opera house in Charlottenborg Palace and Eigtved's public theatre with the latest in machinery and appliances for a modern wing-and-border stage. Fabris' six principal settings—a room, a wood, a street, a garden, a hall, and a sea décor—formed a fully adequate basic framework for the Royal Theatre's comic repertoire. Within this framework, impressive scenic displays and mechanical coups were the order of the day. The aerial manoeuvres of Mercury and Night and the majestic descent of Jupiter in his 'Gloria' naturally made Molière's *Amphitryon* a popular selection for the first season at Kongens Nytorv. Holberg's free-wheeling parody *Ulysses von Ithacia,* revived in 1750, also relied confidently on Fabris' flying machine for the scene in which Queen Dido whistles for her dragon, which obediently descends, bears her aloft, and subsequently returns to carry off her terrified servant Rasmus. In Harlequin's world, such scenic legerdemain was an even more indispensable ingredient. The theatre's dragon re-appeared in Le Sage's *Le Monde Renversé,* an entertaining example of the so-called Théâtre de la Foire which was staged by the Danish actors in 1751. Harlequin and Pierrot, having served Merlin the magician, are rewarded by being sent to a utopian world of milk and honey where everything is topsyturvydom. At the start of their adventure the two clowns are seen high in the air astride the sprightly monster, which 'circles the stage two or three times'; toward the end, audiences could watch the mighty Merlin 'descending from the air in a car' drawn by 'two vultures'.[4] Probably the favourite harlequinade of all at the Royal Theatre was Regnard and Defresny's *La Baguette de Vulcain,* a sensation when first produced in Paris in 1693 and a staple afterpiece in the Danish company's repertory from 1748. In this selection from Le Théâtre Italien, Harlequin's bat is no longer a slapstick but a magic wand bestowed on him by Vulcan. The most striking of the play's many tricks and transformations must be said to be the technically demanding scene in which Harlequin battles a fearful, bearded giant and succeeds in hacking off his head and limbs, only to see the amputations 're-unite themselves with the body, yet in a different shape, giving Harlequin the occasion for a new battle'.[5]

Even before Holberg's death in 1754, however, new dramatic styles and tastes were emerging. Serious neoclassical drama, represented at von Qvoten's theatre by Dalin's alexandrine tragedy *Brynilda,* first came to the Royal Theatre in 1752 with Gottsched's adaptation of Addison's *Cato,* a lavish production in which careful attention was paid to the correctness of the Roman costumes and accessories. Sentimental comedy, the antithesis of the laughing, festive comedy of Holberg and Molière and the avowed anti-sentimentality of the Théâtre de la Foire, began to appear in ripples that would soon become a wave. Steele's transitional comedy *The Conscious Lovers* (1722), with its appeal for 'a joy too exquisite for laughter', first appeared at Kongens Nytorv in 1761 in a thoroughly localized version that failed to draw. A decade before, however, the national theatre, following the lead of the French troupe in Nørregade, had established the vogue of lachrymose comedy with its performance of Destouches' *Le dissipateur,* a typical

[4] Torben Krogh, 'Dekorationer, Costumer og Iscenesættelse' in *ibid.,* p. 85.
[5] *Ibid.,* p. 85.

dramatization of the obligatory moral conversion in which a young girl rescues her lover from prodigality. The staging at the same time of Voltaire's *L'Enfant prodigue* and *Nanine,* his version of Richardson's sentimental novel *Pamela,* further strengthened the trend towards sensibility, which in the 1760s took on added impetus with a rash of Goldoni and Diderot productions and a series of native Danish counterparts by Charlotta Dorothea Biehl.

Regardless of such new currents, however, Harlequin and Henrik, Holberg's ubiquitous servant figure, retained their supremacy for the generation during which Gert Londemann reigned as the Danish theatre's unchallenged comic virtuoso. Masked and clad in the familiar patched costume, Londemann was the embodiment of Harlequin for eighteenth-century Royal Theatre audiences, and, with his death in 1773, the genre seemed inconceivable without him. Versatile and unpredictable in his improvisations (as Sganarel in Molière's *Don Juan* he dashed out through the audience in fright during his master's duel!), a master of comic mimicry, the archetypal clown with a hint of the marketplace buffoon about him and more than a trace of melancholy and sadness behind the grinning mask, his *lazzi* became institutions. Wessel's miniature elegy captures something essential about Londemann's art: 'We sigh because he is no more,/Recalling what he was, we roar'.

A company of gifted comic performers surrounded Londemann at the Royal Theatre. His opposite in type and temper was Clementin, the tall, refined, and dryly humorous embodiment of Jeronimus, Holberg's *senex,* and the miserly Harpagon. Anna Materna v. Passow, whose moral comedy *Mariane* became the first Danish play to be acted after Holberg, was the company's dignified and cultivated female lead until her resignation in 1753. Caroline Thielo, daughter of the original patentee, was the scandalous epitome of piquant rococo charm until her death, possibly at the hands of her lover, at the age of nineteen. Elizabeth Bøttger, Holberg's protégé, succeeded her as the theatre's leading lady, but her imitation of the style of the French troupe drew critical fire. In serious parts she had two expressions, we are told, 'a weeping tone with limply hanging or imploringly outstretched arms when she was unhappy; loud screams and violent gestures when she was triumphant or had the intention of displaying passion'.[6]

The model for Bøttger's misunderstood imitation of serious French acting was Jeanne du Londel, the outstanding talent of Frederik V's French court troupe and one of the great beauties of her day. Her company, led by Pierre de Launai, performed in Copenhagen from 1748 to 1753, first at a theatre in Nørregade and later at the playhouse in Charlottenborg Palace. The troupe's influence upon the style and repertory of the Danish actors was considerable, particularly in the propagation of Destouches and the new sentimental comedy. In 1753, de Launai and most of his company, including the delightful du Londel, moved on to Stockholm, where they provided royal entertainment for the court of Adolf Fredrik and Lovisa Ulrika for nearly two decades. Thus, while the Danish popular theatre was now solidly established, the so-called Royal Swedish Stage was evicted from Bollhuset and Stenborg was left to his own devices. If, however, the playhouse on Kongens Nytorv represents the initial culmination of the impetus toward a native national theatre in Scandinavia, a parallel and no less significant highpoint in the courtly theatre's development was reached at the festive and theatrical court of Lovisa Ulrika at Drottningholm.

Lovisa Ulrika, sister of Frederick the Great of Prussia and a true product of the enlightenment eulogized by Voltaire himself, typifies an age for which, as Taine remarked, life itself was an opera. This champion of French culture who was repelled by the 'vulgarity' of the Swedish plays at Bollhuset quickly transformed Drottningholm, the seventeenth-century summer palace which became her personal Versailles when she married the crown prince in 1744, into a centre for lavish theatrical entertainments reminiscent of the Renaissance festivities of the past. Supported by the elegant Carl Gustav Tessin, 'le Lucullus suédois', and the court poet Olof von Dalin and surrounded by a distinguished circle of eager court amateurs, Lovisa Ulrika lit up Drottningholm's Salle des noces with a brilliant succession of performances. The repertoire of these courtly dilettantes, embracing a wide selection of popular French dramatists (Racine,

---

[6] Thomas Overskou, *Den danske Skueplads i dens Historie,* II, p. 309; see also Torben Krogh, *Christian VII's franske Hofaktører,* p. 2.

Molière, Regnard, Voltaire, Marivaux, Destouches, and others), included the very same titles which drew cavalier and citizen alike to the Copenhagen theatres of Frederik V. Such pieces as Destouches' *Le Glorieux,* de Boissy's *Le Français à Londres,* and especially Saint-Foix's contrived and spectacular afterpiece *L'Oracle,* Holberg's pet dislike, were becoming favourite attractions at this time both at Kongens Nytorv and at the French theatre in Nørregade. In 1749, Lovisa Ulrika's aristocratic Drottningholm audience could join with their Danish counterparts in the exquisite enjoyment of the conversion of Ariste, the dissembling philosophical misogynist in Destouches' most popular sentimental comedy *Le Philosophe marié.* The French ambassador to Sweden gallantly permitted himself to doubt that it could have been done better in Paris.

Soon after the birth of the future Gustav III, the first Swedish-born heir to the throne since Charles XII, in 1746, children's performances became an established pastime for the young prince. In his participation in court theatricals and ballets from an early age, he followed in the footsteps of the great Louis himself. At six he led a chorus of pages clad as mandarins in an oriental homage to the queen which introduced a week-long festival of pageants and entertainments. That same evening, the Drottningholm audience could watch a ballet requiring three hundred dancers, an opera and a drama in sixteen acts which employed thirty-two scene changes. Johann Pasch's design for a mountainous waterfall with gliding swans below evoked particular admiration. At two in the morning, the court was ready for the lively ball which followed.

Adolf Fredrik, crowned in 1751, lost little time in supplementing these extravagant spectacles and elegant amateur theatricals with the customary foreign troupes. De Launai's company of French actors arrived from Copenhagen and was joined in 1754 by an Italian opera company under the direction of the talented composer and conductor Francesco Uttini. Handsome court theatres were equipped for them at Drottningholm and Ulriksdal, and the Swedish actors were obliged to surrender the Bollhus stage to their French colleagues. The accomplished du Londel quickly conquered the hearts of the Swedish aristocracy in such plays as *Le Philosophe marié.* That the king seemed especially enchanted by her delights caused endless comment. Appearing in Anseaume and Duni's *opéra-comique, Le Peintre amoureux de son modèle,* her provocative rendition of 'Quand j'étais jeune, j'étais un morceau, digne d'un roi' drew an injudicious reaction from an incensed Lovisa Ulrika, and the knowledgeable court audience giggled.

A fire (of another sort) from which the royal family narrowly escaped laid Drottningholm Theatre in ashes in 1762. A second and larger Drottningholm, world-renowned today as the most perfectly preserved eighteenth-century court theatre in existence, was designed by the court architect Carl Fredrik Adelcrantz and opened in 1766. The 350-seat auditorium, decorated by the French court painter Adrien Masreliez, is designed to blend with the equally large stage to form a single harmonious interior. The spacious stage of this ideal rococo playhouse, measuring sixty-two feet in depth (twice that of Eigtved's Royal Theatre) and eighty feet in width, was the responsibility of the Italian theatre technician Donato Stopani. The machinery and technical devices which he designed for this typical wing-and-border theatre, with its characteristic fly-gallery and elaborate understage equipment for operating the traps and wing chariots, are still to be seen in actual use. Although Lovisa Ulrika's French players continued their performances at the second Drottningholm for five years following its completion, however, the period of greatest activity in this theatre's history occurred after Gustav III's succession to the Swedish throne in 1771, a date which ushered in not only a new government but also a new cultural and theatrical spirit.

Few theatrical developments have taken place in one Scandinavian country which have not had their parallels or repercussions in another. Christian VII came to the Danish throne in the year in which the second Drottningholm Theatre opened and, not to be outdone, promptly summoned a French troupe led by Mariane Belleval to his court, much to the irritation and concern of the supporters of the public theatre on Kongens Nytorv. Following the example set not only by the Swedish monarchy but also by numerous German princes during this period, the Danish king built a court theatre for his so-called 'Comédiens François ordinaires du Roi' above the stables at Christiansborg Palace. Its model seems to have been the lovely theatre of Charles-Theodor in Schwetzingen, near Heidelberg;

79

one remarkable feature was an auditorium floor that could be raised to accommodate masquerades and lowered to suit stage performances. Professor Jardin's Christiansborg theatre, which still exists, in a far less perfectly preserved form than Drottningholm, as a museum, was inaugurated by the French actors on 30 January 1767 with a production of Monsigny's much-admired operetta *Le Roi et le Fermier*, followed by a balletic homage to the king.

The modern portion of the Belleval company's widely ranging repertory brought the newest Parisian fashions and styles to the Danish capital. Together with Lovisa Ulrika's court players, they introduced the genre of the *opéra-comique*, popularized by the lively and unpretentious melodies of Monsigny, Grétry, and Philidor, to the Scandinavian theatre. The most recent excursions into the new bourgeois drama, including Beaumarchzis' *Eugénie*, Falbaire de Quingey's *L'Honnête criminel*, and *Béverlei*, Saurin's verse adaptation of Moore's *The Gamester*, were seen for the first time by Copenhagen audiences at Christian VII's court theatre. The troupe's versatile leading man Henry de la Tour, seconded by Mlle. Le Clerc and later by the highly emotional Marie Cléricourt, created a whole gallery of the heroic figures from Voltaire's verse tragedies that were taking Paris audiences by storm: Tancrède, Mahomet, Arzace in *Semiramis,* Gengis-Khan in *L'Orphelin de la Chine,* Egiste in *Mérope,* Orosmane in *Zaïre.*

An impression of de la Tour's tragic style is conveyed by the humorously vivid description left by Clemens Tode, the theatre's doctor. 'He often stood in conversation as if sawing a piece of wood,' insisted Tode, 'or rather, like the Roman gladiator in the Royal Gardens. The upper part of his body and his left leg had a vertical direction, the right leg was perpendicular: thus in some ways his figure, particularly when his hands were crossed over his chest, resembled a country well or a toll-bar standing open.'[7] One is reminded at once of the highly accentuated poses and mimetic actions of Lekain and Clairon as they appear in the numerous and frequently reproduced gouache rôle pictures from the 1760s by Foech-Whirsker and others. The report of another member of the Danish court audience suggests that the Frenchman's powerfully emotional-

[7] *Dramatiske Tillæg til Museum og Hertha. Kritik og Antikritik,* p. 62.

ized alexandrines occasionally elicited an unforeseen response. Christian VII's dog Gourmand, its black head leaned against the royal box as it watched the ballets and listened to the plays 'with such rapt attention that people were ready to burst with laughter', sometimes 'began to speak in the theatre in such a manner that even the furious la Tour himself had difficulty in being heard'.[8] Such testimony notwithstanding, however, it is reasonable to view de la Tour and his successor Le Boeuf—known specifically as an imitator of Lekain—as accomplished exponents of the new style of emotionally charged and continually modulating acting advocated by Voltaire to express 'those outbursts of nature which are represented by a word, by an attitude, by silence, by a cry which escapes in the anguish of grief'.[9] As Clairon realized, moreover, 'the truth of declamation requires that of dress',[10] and there is little doubt that the French costume reforms brought about after the middle of the century and disseminated through the illustrations of Foech-Whirsker were carried to Scandinavia by the Danish and Swedish court troupes of the 1760s.

The life of Christian VII's Christiansborg court theatre was brief, despite its effect on the Royal Theatre's subsequent repertory and its less positive influence on some of the more impressionable of the Danish performers. The young king sank deeper into the madness which had become evident early in his life, and the royal physician Struensee was quick to see his way to power as the weak monarch's representative. After a palace revolution mounted in 1772 had cost the lives of the bold Struensee and his accomplice Enevold Brandt, *maître de plaisir* and head of the court theatre, the French troupe's ascendancy collapsed. Several of its members, including de la Tour and Mad. Cléricourt and her husband, would turn up again at the court of the young Gustav III. In April, 1773, the theatre at Christiansborg, the final in the series of rococo playhouses erected in Scandinavia during the middle decades of the eighteenth century, resounded with the last performance of the French actors.

[8] Letter from Sophie Reventlow Gramm, quoted in Krogh, *Christian VII's franske Hofaktører,* p. 9.

[9] A. M. Nagler, *Sources of Theatrical History* (New York, 1952), p. 296.

[10] *Ibid.,* p. 295.

CHAPTER SEVEN

The Gustavian Age

During the early 1770s, the theatre entered a new era in all three Scandinavian countries. The Danish national theatre on Kongens Nytorv, now officially 'Royal' and relieved of the threat of competition from Christian VII's French players, began in earnest to cultivate the new vogue of the *singspiel* and the drama of sensibility. In Norway—still a Danish possession wholly dependent on itinerant provincial strollers for its theatrical entertainment—a first, fumbling gesture toward the establishment of a native professional company was made in 1771 by Martin Nürenbach. His troupe staged three Holberg comedies in Christiania (Oslo) and was therefore granted a licence 'to perform Danish plays given by Norwegian subjects',[1] but this primitive venture soon vanished without a trace. In dazzling contrast, the succession of Gustav III to the Swedish throne in 1771 marked the beginning of one of the most luminous and unusual periods in the history of the eighteenth-century European theatre. While virtually every branch of Swedish arts and letters achieved a new life and national identity under the enlightened absolutism of Gustav's rule (1771–92), the stage remained the abiding passion of this remarkable actor-king. Earlier monarchs have, as we have seen, exercised a profound influence on the course of theatrical development in Scandinavia. In a far more direct sense, however,

82   [1] Øyvind Anker, *Scenekunsten i Norge fra fortid til nutid*, p. 10.

Gustav III, participating at every step in the selection, casting, performance and writing of the plays and operas he wanted performed and devoting himself even on the battlefield to his grand theatrical design, literally planned and called into being a native Swedish theatre and drama.

Less than three weeks after the death of Adolf Fredrik, the new king sent a dispatch from Paris dismissing the French court troupe. Petter Stenborg, the indomitable leader of the ragged descendants of the defunct Royal Swedish Stage, sensed that the moment was ripe for action and petitioned Gustav for permission to use once again the vacated Bollhus for productions in the vernacular. The young monarch granted Stenborg a single demonstration, and on 11 March 1772 the unpolished Swedish actors played Regnard's popular comedy *Les Ménechmes* and Legrand's afterpiece *L'Ami de tout de monde* to an enthusiastic audience. An opening plea to the king, delivered by Stenborg's youngest son Carl, assured the royal spectators that 'under an Augustus' the languishing native drama could 'win such respect that a French Clairon and an English Garrick would in time find worthy rivals in Sweden'.[2] Gustav was convinced, however, that a far more elaborate and sophisticated framework was needed to accustom Swedish audiences to hearing their own language on the stage. A national opera, combining all the resources of the stage and forming in reality a continuation of the tradition of lavish court ballets and theatricals so much a part of Gustav's youth, seemed a logical, if somewhat extravagant, place to start.

Progress was swift. The aging Bollhus theatre underwent a thorough and elegant face-lifting. The spacious royal box, patriotically decorated in blue with gold crowns, was moved to the centre of the first balcony; the amphitheatre or *balcon noble* beneath it, the standing pit, and the three tiers of boxes could now accommodate about 500 spectators. Gustav himself selected the subject matter for the inaugural production, and his choice, the story of Thetis and Pélée with which Mazarin had entertained Louis XIV, was a revealing one. The glories of the fabled court of the Sun King had long exercised a magnetic appeal for the Swedish nobility. Court counsellor and poet Johan Wellander was invited to write a libretto on Gustav's

[2] Nils Personne, *Svenska teatern*, I, p. 89.

chosen theme and Francesco Uttini, the former director of Lovisa Ulrika's Italian opera company, composed a pleasing score for Sweden's first opera. Although experienced performers were obviously scarce, Carl Stenborg and Elisabet Olin, wife of a prominent official and overnight Sweden's first star, formed a talented nucleus around which to build. On 18 January 1773, barely ten months after Stenborg's initial move toward a vernacular theatre, the newly founded Royal Opera presented the first of twenty-eight successive performances of Wellander and Uttini's popular *Thetis and Pélée*.

In its mythological subject matter, the tale of King Pélée and his love for the sea goddess Thetis, the opera differs little from the wealth of baroque forerunners dedicated to that particular kind of allegory described by Agne Beijer as 'the illusion that the imaginary phantoms moving on the stage are nothing more than the idealized mirror-images of the courtly society which followed the spectacle from their boxes'.[3] In its vivid succession of spectacular descents, ascents, storms and other *coups de théâtre*, however, it exemplifies the trend toward a less static and more illusionistic stage picture. Jupiter and Neptune, Pélée's cosmic rivals for the hand of Thetis, afforded designer Lorens Sundström an obviously attractive variety of entrances and exits. For the sensational first-act curtain, Jupiter, appearing on a cloud, angrily summoned Aeolus to create havoc in Neptune's realm. The stage darkened, storm winds raged, thunder rumbled, and lightning ripped the sky as Neptune and his nautical minions sank beneath the tempestuous waves. Seated in the audience the Tripolitanian envoy, in mute tribute to Sundström's scenic legerdemain, rushed headlong from the theatre to escape the awesome catastrophe!

Its very first year of operation crowned Gustav's new Royal Opera with popular success. Elisabet Olin and Carl Stenborg personified, on the stage and off, the image of the eternal lovers. *Thetis* was followed in May by Lars Lalin's *Acis and Galatea,* a heroic ballet with Händel's music and choreography by the French ballet-master Louis Gallondier, but the year's triumph was yet to come. Gluck's masterful *Orpheus and Eurydice,* staged at the renovated Bollhus in November, chal-

---

[3] *Gustaviansk teater skildrad af Pehr Hilleström,* eds. A. Beijer and G. Hilleström, p. 13.

13. Carl Stenborg and Elisabeth Olin in Gluck and Calzabigi's
opera *Orpheus and Eurydice*, Swedish Royal Opera, 1773.
Copy of scene painting by Pehr Hilleström

lenged and reformed the artificial baroque opera tradition in which *Thetis and Pélée* had been immersed. The production touched off a veritable Gluck fever which continued to rage throughout the entire Gustavian era. In the series of remarkably accurate scene pictures of the period executed by the Swedish painter Pehr Hilleström, one of the most exquisite is his rendering of Stenborg and Olin in the third act of the Gluck-Calzabigi opera (Plate 13). Laurel-crowned and lyre in hand, Orpheus virtually drags his Eurydice from the ugly grotto of Hell. Their expressive stances and gestures suggest the freer and more emotionally charged acting style that had begun to make its way from France to the courts of Scandinavia during the previous decade. Their costumes, while perhaps startlingly inaccurate and exaggerated to the modern eye, have nevertheless undergone a comparable liberation from the obligatory powdered wigs, highly ornate court dresses, and *habits à la romaine* of the older tradition and reflect the efforts of Lekain and Clairon to reform the Parisian theatre in this regard.

Gustav III, his vision of a political theatre devoted to the glorification of Sweden's history and language clearly before him, was determined to have a native spoken drama take its place beside the newly established opera. Following a trial performance by court amateurs of a translation of Voltaire's *Zaïre,* staged in order to test the reaction of sensitive courtly ears to spoken Swedish, the king outlined his plan for a three-act drama entitled *Birger Jarl,* which was transferred to verse dialogue by G. F. Gyllenborg and produced with elaborate care in the summer of 1774. No less cosmopolitan a figure than Carlo Bibiena was invited to design the stage for Gustav's first Swedish historical play, while Stenborg and Fru Olin were again the deathless lovers, Mechtild the fugitive queen in danger and the mighty Earl Birger, once her deadly enemy but ultimately her gallant saviour and spouse.

No outpouring of native writing was immediately forth-coming, but both the court amateurs and the artists of the Royal Opera continued to cultivate a repertory of French classics in Swedish translations or 'imitations', ranging from Racine's *Athalie* and *Iphigénie,* Corneille's *Cinna,* and Crébillon's *Rhadamiste et Zénobie* to Voltaire's *Adélaide de Guesclin, Mérope,* and *L'Orphelin de la Chine.* Gustav, an incurable actor,

included Cinna, Rhadamiste, and Gengis Khan among his
major rôles during the amazing round of private court theatricals held at Gripsholm during the Christmas holidays of 1775.
With somewhat less alacrity, the Bollhus company also incorporated performances of spoken drama in an operatic programme that extended from the charming melodies of Grétry and
Monsigny to the powerful tones of Gluck. The style of performance which characterized these endeavours is recaptured
for us in the paintings of Pehr Hilleström. Voltaire's intensified
and contrasted 'outbursts of nature' are here vividly physical-
ized in the convulsive despair of Admete (Carl Stenborg) in

14. Carlo Bibiena design for a Gustavian opera (c. 1774):
photo of the original setting preserved at Drottningholm

Gluck's *Alceste* (Plate 15), in the dishevelled fury of Christofer Karsten, Stenborg's young rival, as the title figure in Marmontel and Piccini's *Roland* (Plate 16), and in the emotionally electrified attitudes of Marie Louise Baptiste and the grotesquely transformed Karsten as they stand before the magic mirror in Marmontel and Grétry's *Zemire et Azor* (Plate 17).

The first production of the latter opera during the summer of 1778 marked the reawakening to life of the exquisite court theatre at Drottningholm, dormant since the death of Adolf Fredrik and sold by Lovisa Ulrika to Gustav the previous year. Although the king no longer appeared on the stage personally, the playhouse at Drottningholm entered its most brilliant era as the hub of Gustav's theatrical world. During the long summer

Voltaire's intensified 'outbursts of nature' embodied in Gustavian opera. Scene paintings by Hilleström

15. Carl Stenborg as the despairing Admete in Gluck and Calzabigi's *Alceste* (1778)

16. Christofer Karsten as the furious Roland in Marmontel and Piccini's opera (1781)

sojourn of the Swedish court, productions of opera, ballet and tragedy on the indoor stage were complemented by lavish outdoor spectacles reminiscent of the great Renaissance festivities of the past. Two of the most memorable of these pageants, *The Feast of Diana* and *The Conquest of the Galtar Rock,* have been

17. Marie Louise Baptiste and Christofer Karsten before the magic mirror in Marmontel and Grétry's *Zemire et Azor* (1778). Scene painting by Hilleström

18. Pre-romantic gothicism in the Gustavian pageant *The Conquest of the Galtar Rock*, staged in the grounds at Drottningholm in 1779

preserved in all their colour and action in the paintings of Pehr Hilleström. *The Feast of Diana* was enacted on the palace grounds by the lords and ladies of the court in the summer of 1778, shortly after the Royal Opera's command performance of *Zemire et Azor*. The imposing entrance 'to martial music' of Gustav III on horseback, resplendent in a red and white Roman warrior's costume with ermine-trimmed mantle, must have brought to mind the similar appearance of Charles XI in his ornate coronation pageant *Certamen equestre* over a century before—which itself represented the survival of a tradition reaching back to the *trionfi* of the Renaissance. The Gustavian 'carousel' followed time-honoured conventions: as Meleager, the king led his warriors in allegorical combat with Nessus (Duke Carl) and his rapacious fauns in order to defend the virtue of Diana and her nymphs (dressed in the rococo court dress recently proclaimed by royal decree). Despite the mixture of costume styles and the allegorical traditionality of the subject matter, however, these Drottningholm pageants may be viewed as the first examples of a romantic historical drama in Sweden. A pre-romantic fascination with colourful historical— particularly gothic—environments is even more plainly in evidence in *The Conquest of the Galtar Rock,* elaborately staged in the castle park in August, 1779. Although in this case items from Charles XI's 1672 pageant seem actually to have been used, the powerful gothic picturesqueness created by the realistic torchlight assault on the brooding, three-dimensional medieval fortress of Galtar, where fire-breathing dragons dwell and Queen Briolanie languishes in the clutches of the evil wizard Arcalaus, clearly points ahead, prefiguring the vogue of Walter Scott romanticism on the nineteenth-century stage (Plate 18).

A combination of new developments served to make the second decade of Gustav III's reign one of the most significant in the history of Swedish theatre. Behind each development moved the guiding hand of the king. In 1781, Gustav emulated the example of his forebears by summoning to his court a French troupe of fifteen performers under the leadership of Jacques-Marie Boutet, called Monvel, the father of the renowned Mlle. Mars and an intelligent if physically weak Parisian actor. Monvel, expelled from France by the police for unspecified amorous escapades, spent five years in exile in Stockholm in a dual capacity. Besides appearing in the French classics at the summer and winter palaces and later on the public Bollhus stage, he and his company were expected to instruct and encourage prospective native actors in their art. The scheme succeeded admirably. Monvel's trainees numbered several future Swedish stars, the brightest of whom was the versatile and lucid comic actor Lars Hjortsberg, whose long career extended the Gustavian traditions far into the following century.

The new French troupe in no sense distracted the king from his other theatrical passions. Having long recognized the inadequacy of the century-old Bollhus as a suitable opera stage, Gustav commissioned his court architect Carl Fredrik Adelcrantz, the designer of the Drottningholm court theatre, to provide the Royal Swedish Opera with a permanent home. The new opera house opened at the end of September, 1782 with the gala première of *Cora and Alonzo*, an original opera by G. J. Adlerbeth and the distinguished German composer J. G. Naumann based on Marmontel's popular tale 'Les Incas ou la destruction de l'empire de Pérou', and enlivened by exotic mass scenes and spectacular effects. The opening night, however, belonged to Adelcrantz. The acclaim and the diamond-berried laurel wreath which his sovereign bestowed upon him were richly deserved, for he had created a worthy counterpart to his Drottningholm, a theatrical jewel that combined architectural elegance with acoustical perfection.

Simultaneously, Gustav worked vigorously toward the realization of his vision of a native Swedish drama based on national themes—a vision he shared with Messenius and with Strindberg. Following a formidable burst of creative activity during the fall of 1782, his courtly Society for the Improvement of Swedish Speech was ready in the new year to embark on what must surely be a season unique in theatrical history, consisting of six plays written by the king himself. The court was in residence at Gripsholm at this time, where Gustav had equipped a small playhouse which remains one of the most superb eighteenth-century theatres in Europe, combining the Ionic pillars, semi-circular shape, and half-domed ceiling of the neoclassic revival with the changeable scenery, magnifying mirrors, and false proscenium pillars of the baroque period. The court actors rehearsed from ten o'clock in the morning, often dining with the indefatigable king on the stage itself; resumed rehearsals at five; and continued until ten in the evening. After opening with a revival of Gyllenborg's *Birger Jarl*, Gustav's courtiers were ready on 14 January 1783 with his first original play, a five-act 'drama with song and dance' entitled *Gustaf Adolphs ädelmod/The Nobility of Gustav Adolf*. Duke Carl headed the cast as the idealized seventeenth-century monarch Gustav II Adolph in this historical intrigue drama involving the venerable motif of babies switched in the cradle and identities (in this case the 'rightful Lars Sparre') to be sorted out. Far more adroitly crafted was Gustav's next play *Helmfelt,* first performed at the Ulriksdal court theatre three months later and revived with great success on the public stage in 1788. This five-act drama, revolving around the return of the prodigal Helmfelt, now a military hero, to the trembling embraces of his old father the mayor, his deserted wife, and his son, belongs

19. The return of the prodigal son in Gustav III's bourgeois drama *Helmfelt.* Paintings by Hilleström

clearly to the tradition of the French bourgeois drama of sentiment and emotionalism. Hilleström's depictions of the performance (Plate 19) leave no doubt about the fiercely conceived pantomimic pathos of the acting demanded by this genre—nor is it a coincidence that Monvel was the outstanding exponent in Paris of the new sentimental style before carrying it to Gustav's court. To balance the heady emotionalism of *Helmfelt*, the court amateurs presented the charming vaudeville afterpiece *Tillfälle gör tjufven/Chance Makes the Thief*, written by Carl Israel Hallman, a Gustavian comic playwright whose broad parodies were a mainstay of the minor popular theatres which flourished throughout the period. The celebrated lyric poet C. M. Bellman contributed a memorable performance as a mountebank.

Plays and plans for plays continued to flow from the king's prolific pen throughout the year 1783. Following their July production of Gustav's *Frigga*, an arid one-act mythological comedy indebted to Saint-Foix's *L'Oracle* and later converted by Carl Leopold to an equally unsuccessful opera, the court players staged *Sune Jarl*, a new Nordic tragedy by G. F. Gyllenborg in which Gustav almost certainly had a hand, at Drottningholm. Three weeks later Duke Carl and his tireless associates were ready to unveil the king's three-act historical drama of royal romance *Gustav Adolf and Ebba Brahe*, also transformed into a spectacular opera four years later by the gifted poet Johan Kellgren. *Drottning Christina/Queen Christina*, planned by Gustav and rendered in verse form by Kellgren, first reached the Gripsholm stage on Twelfth Night, 1785. The rich scenic environment for this anecdotal, Racine-influenced depiction of the proud and strong-willed Christina's passion for Magnus Gabriel de la Gardie was created by Louis Jean Desprez. Desprez, whom Gustav had met and engaged in Italy the previous year, represents not only a highpoint in the development of stage design in Scandinavia but also ranks as one of the outstanding artists of the European theatre. While Gustav III's plays anticipate by half a century the historical melodrama which culminates with Scribe, Desprez's designs convey a comparable spirit of vehement and atmospheric romanticism that was first matched by Cicéri about 1810. One of his most familiar designs was drawn for the first act of

Queen Christina, depicting the de la Gardie gardens dominated by a splendidly illuminated palace (Plate 20). Using an imaginative device to create an illusion of depth on the shallow Gripsholm stage, the designer makes the foreground appear to be a raised terrace from which the steps descend to a spacious square beyond. The effect of this luminous décor is magically festive, reminiscent in some ways of a mountainous Italian landscape yet evocative of all the atmosphere of a Nordic summer night. The stage setting itself remains preserved at Drottningholm (Plate 21).

Dwarfing all previous spectacles was the production one year later of *Gustav Wasa,* the crowning achievement of the Gustavian theatre. Based on a scenario by Gustav which Kellgren transformed into some of the best dramatic verse written in Swedish, this patriotic 'lyric tragedy' in three acts drew together the foremost theatrical talents of the age. The pace and throbbing vitality of Gustav's scenario and the flow of Kellgren's pliant verse were complemented by the sonorous clarity of Naumann's musical score and brought to life in the picturesque splendour of Desprez's settings. Stenborg as the heroic title figure and the majestic Karsten as the tyrannical Danish ruler Christjern II headed a cast consisting of some 140 rôles. Extolled in countless letters and memoirs of the time and besieged by audiences which had signed up a month in advance, the Royal Opera's initial performances of *Gustav Wasa* were the beginning of a long stage-life for the opera.

The reasons for its popularity are obvious enough. Although the century had witnessed several previous attempts by European dramatists to write Gustav Vasa plays, the most notable of which was Henry Brooke's *Gustavus Vasa, The Deliverer of His Country* (1739), banned under Walpole's Licensing Act, Gustav III and Kellgren's work succeeded in combining a high pitch of patriotic fervour with a succession of thrilling stage actions. The opening scene's sombre castle dungeon, in which the ladies and children of the Swedish nobility languish in chains, offered ample scope for strong emotion in piquantly gothic surroundings. The tyrant Christjern's ghastly visions in the third act, drawing on Shakespeare's *Richard III* for their inspiration, added a degree of psychological excitement. In general, the opera's conventional Augustan conflict of filial

95

20. Design by Louis Jean Desprez in watercolour and gouache:
the first act of *Queen Christina* (1785)

obligations opposed to duty to one's country was thrown in
bold relief against a dynamic and swirling background of historical detail. Unlike its French models, *Gustav Wasa* brought
the actual sights and sounds of war onto the stage. Desprez's
splendid sketch of the decisive victory of the Swedish troops
over the Danish army captures the essential atmospheric
quality of the entire *mise-en-scène,* as we see the opposing
forces sweeping towards each other in a sea of banners and
cannon-smoke beneath the towering architectural monuments
of medieval Stockholm (Plate 22). Small wonder that the first

21. This, a contemporary photo of the preserved setting for
Queen Christina, affords an interesting comparison with 20

audiences cheered and roared to encourage their liberators, and
that loyal guardsmen, recruited to serve as supernumeraries in
the battle and in the subsequent rout of the Danes, gladly
offered their comrades on the Swedish side a schnapps if they
would replace them beneath the hated Danish flag!

Despite sporadic efforts by Gyllenborg, Leopold, and such
comic dramatists as Carl Hallman, Elis Schröderheim, and Olof
Kexél, the remarkable creativity of Gustav III did not succeed
in eliciting the outpouring of native plays for which he had
hoped. Nevertheless, the realization of his grand design for a

97

Swedish dramatic theatre was at hand. A receptive climate, an audience and a trained personnel had been created through the performances of the Monvel troupe, the Royal Opera, and his own court theatre. In 1787, he granted court librarian A. F. Ristell a momentous six-year patent to perform Swedish plays twice weekly at the Bollhus theatre, in alternation with the French troupe. The conditions were far from ideal: free use of the playhouse was Ristell's sole subvention, and only native works were countenanced: translations were strictly forbidden. Actors had to be hired from the Royal Opera company on an individual basis. In June, 1787 Ristell and his overstaffed troupe of twenty men and sixteen women opened with his own

22. Another design by Desprez: the third act of *Gustav Wasa* (1786)

trivial 'imitation' of Poinsinet's *Le cercle* (1764). After ten short months, however, the hapless librarian, unequal to the task of building both an acting ensemble and a repertory from the ground up, was obliged to abandon the venture and flee the country in bankruptcy.

Ironically, his salvation had been closer than he realized. A month before his collapse, Gustav III's newest play *Siri Brahe,* one of the king's most consistently popular historical melodramas of love, revenge, and dangerous intrigue, opened and drew a succession of capacity audiences attracted in no small measure by the substantial physical charms of Fredrika Löf in the title rôle. After Ristell's exit, an association of actor-shareholders banded together, the company was trimmed to twenty-one performers, and their new enterprise—christened the Royal Swedish Dramatic Theatre—was granted a royal patent and a modest subsidy. No time was lost. On 17 May 1788 the Bollhus curtain rose on the first production in Dramaten's long history, the public première of Gyllenborg's Nordic tragedy *Sune Jarl.* The restless movement toward the establishment of native popular theatres that characterized this century of enlightenment in Scandinavia had reached its climax.

Even on the battlefield Gustav was filled with paternal advice and directives for his 'Theatre dramatique que je regarde comme un port tranquille ou on pourra se reposser apres les oragees'.[4] Five of his own plays graced Dramaten's first season. Neither his boundless optimism nor his tireless encouragement could, however, foster enough good native writing to sustain a major theatre. At first, his banishment of translations, reaffirmed in laconic dispatches sent home from the Russian campaign, remained inflexible, but compromise was inevitable. The submission of a version of Sheridan's *The School for Scandal* by Abraham de Broen, the company's gifted and contentious *père noble,* brought matters to a boil. A new set of 'Regulations for the Swedish Dramatic Theatre'[5] granted by the king in May 1789 introduced several important organizational changes. The actors were now entitled to attend bimonthly assemblies which dealt with such questions as casting,

[4] Letter dated 31 October 1788 (French spelling *sic*): E. Lewenhaupt, *Bref rörande teatern under Gustaf III,* p. 52.
[5] Cf. G. M. Bergman and N. Brunius, eds. *Dramaten 175 År,* p. 20.

repertory, budgets, and acceptance of new plays. The tempo of work was stepped up: an actor was responsible for memorizing 40 eight-word lines daily, and the first rehearsal was held 'when half the time for memorizing the longest rôle had elapsed'. In view of the small number of rehearsals usually held in the eighteenth-century theatre, the schedule of fines levied for improper rôle preparation seems reasonable enough. The most significant of these changes was, meanwhile, the regulation easing the irksome ban on translations. Its adoption enabled the new Swedish theatre, sparked by an impressive nucleus of talent that included de Broen, Lars Hjortsberg, Fredrika Löf and the sonorous and stately Andreas Widerberg, to appear in a wider and more excitingly cosmopolitan range of dramatic styles.

New schemes—plans for the expansion of Drottningholm by Desprez, alternative projects for a new playhouse to replace the outmoded Bollhus, proposals for casting a series of French tragedies—continued to fill Gustav's mind until the masked ball of 16 March 1792 marked the abrupt end of all further arrangements. Gustav III's death—he was fatally wounded by an assassin's bullets as he sat in his private box at the Royal Opera House—was in itself a moment of drama and irony that subsequently fired the imaginations of Scribe, Auber, Verdi, and (perhaps most strikingly of all) Strindberg. In a wider sense, it signalled the sudden end of one of the most brilliant and expansive eras in Swedish theatre. A cultural age of iron followed. The French actors were promptly dismissed and the century-old Bollhus theatre was dismantled. The Drottningholm playhouse soon faded into disuse.

Nonetheless, the traditions of a native theatre and drama which Gustav so single-mindedly fostered had firmly taken root. Moved to new quarters in the former Arsenal, which was converted to a 600-seat theatre, Dramaten reopened in November 1793 with the première of the murdered king's last play, a romantically dark and emotional exercise in the *genre sombre* entitled *Den svartsjuke neapolitanaren/The Jealous Neapolitan*. A more timely or symptomatic note could not have been sounded. Intense emotionality in picturesquely forbidding medieval surroundings, a hallmark of this and earlier Gustavian plays and carousels, was quickly becoming the highest fashion.

Kotzebue's abducted virgins, disguised gypsies, and agitated strangers had already begun to weave their spell on the Scandinavian stage. The atmospheric, three-dimensional mood pictures of the gothic style, prefigured both in *Gustav Wasa* and *The Conquest of the Galtar Rock,* drew upon the same piquant ingredients that spiced the novels of Mrs. Radcliffe, 'Monk' Lewis, and Walter Scott: medieval fortifications with walls, towers, moats, drawbridges, and castle spectres, gothic ruins, landscapes shrouded in shadow, graveyards bathed in moonlight, secret grottoes and robbers' dens. The vogue of the so-called *genre sombre,* heralded by Gustav's final play, soon reached fever pitch with productions like A. P. Skjöldebrand's blood chilling medieval spectacle *Herman von Unna* (seen in Copenhagen in 1800 and in Stockholm in 1817), on which the author's knowledge of free masonry and secret orders brought to bear the whole symbolic machinery of glittering daggers and clanking chains, flickering torches and blazing altars, robed figures, oaths and initiative rites.

Extending, then, to the very verge of romanticism, the Gustavian age represents not only a luminous period of growing national (though by no means revolutionary) awareness and cultural identity in Sweden, but also a time of transition throughout Scandinavia from the controlled artifice of the baroque to the unabashed and spectacular theatricality which the new century held in store.

CHAPTER EIGHT

Denmark's Golden Age

At the close of the seventeenth century three distinct directions in the Scandinavian theatre were discernible: performances of school drama in the rapidly waning Humanist tradition, the glittering court festivals and entertainments, and the burgeoning activity of itinerant foreign troupes. By the end of the eighteenth century, however, this picture had altered in every respect: the importance of school drama had passed; the phenomenon of the élite courtly theatre had all but vanished; and the foreign strollers had gradually been replaced by professional companies of Swedish and Danish performers. As popular theatres and audiences multiplied, equipment improved, and the pool of competent native actors expanded, native playwrights also began to increase in numbers and in skill. In Norway, still under Danish rule, the rash of amateur dramatic societies that had begun to spring up throughout the country in the 1780s and 1790s marked the prelude to the emergence of a native Norwegian theatre later in the nineteenth century. In Stockholm, the Royal Swedish Opera and Dramaten were both well established by 1800. The Danish Royal Theatre, having weathered its first half century and housing resident companies for opera, drama, and ballet under one roof, was to become the focal point of nineteenth-century Scandinavian theatre culture. An unexcelled company of actors, headed by such gifted performers as Johan Christian Ryge, N. P. Nielsen,

Anna Nielsen, C. N. Rosenkilde, Michael Wiehe, Ludvig Phister, and, above all, Johanne Luise Heiberg, placed the Royal Theatre among the foremost playhouses of Europe around mid-century. This lustrous era of Danish acting coincided with, and handsomely complemented, Denmark's so-called Golden Age of literature and culture.

This glittering era of artistic achievement had an important prologue. The new romantic ideals which transformed Scandinavian theatre in the early 1800s through the plays of Adam Oehlenschläger had their roots, in Denmark as in Sweden, in the pre-romantic climate that arose in the late eighteenth century. The chief harbinger of Oehlenschlägerean drama is the gifted lyric poet Johannes Ewald, whose unproduced *Adam og Eva,* a Corneille-indebted verse drama focusing on Eve's inner conflict, became the first Danish tragedy when it appeared in 1769. Turning the following year from Corneille to Shakespeare for its model, Ewald's dramaturgy underwent a fundamental change in *Rolf Krage,* a five-act heroic tragedy based on an historical subject from the second book of Saxo Grammaticus. Although this play was never acted, its more stageworthy successor *Balders Død/Balder's Death,* which also draws upon Saxo, established a lasting tradition of 'Nordic gothicism' on the Danish stage. This play, a three-act heroic *singspiel* depicting the fierce and ill-fated love of the demigod Balder for a mortal woman, is a characteristic amalgamation of Racinean passion with the pathos and pity of the new sentimental drama of Diderot, Lessing and their influential Danish spokesman and emulator, K. L. Rahbek. Following a miscarried Royal Theatre première, marred by inappropriate costumes and old sets, in March 1778, *Balder's Death* was revived the next year in a refurbished *mise-en-scène* that offered a foretaste of the picturesquely forbidding gothicism, supernatural wonders, sombre caves and emotional tableaux of high romanticism. Working within the basic eighteenth-century framework of loose sidewings mounted on carriages which could slide in and out, and separate backdrops and overhead borders which could be raised or lowered by means of ropes and winches, the designer Peter Cramer created a convincing stage picture of a spruce forest in the rough Norwegian highlands, surrounded by steep, 103 jagged peaks covered with snow. Among the set-pieces used by Cramer to fill out this perspective wing-and-border framework, a menhir[1] in Odin's honour was a prominent, 'authentic' reminder of ancient times.[2] In the third act, as Balder's desperate rival Hother (played by the idolized Norwegian actor and singer Michael Rosing) sought help in witchcraft, the scene was 'instantaneously' transformed to a sorcerer's gloomy cave. As was often the case in the eighteenth century, this scene change was only partial. The downstage wings, painted as 'wilderness', remained, while the upstage wings and backcloth changed to the cavern; two magic altars—around which a hellish brood of Valkyries cavorted—were drawn onto the stage by ropes. Like the staging, the costuming of *Balder's Death* set the tone for a generation of Nordic tragedies that came after it. No less a figure than N. A. Abildgaard, who together with Jens Juel was the foremost painter of the age, was enlisted, in the cause of 'authenticity', to design the costumes and actually drape the actors. Abildgaard's strong neoclassical sensibility shaped a simple and obviously classical mode of dress for the production from which every trace of barbarism or historical accuracy was expunged.

Ewald's last play *Fiskerne/The Fishermen* (publ. 1779), a three-act *singspiel* in the vigorous eleven syllable verse form that he introduced, abandons historical characters and demigods to explore, in the true spirit of the sentimental drama, the heroism of the common man. Based on a real occurrence, this work depicts a touching domestic drama played against the background of a selfless rescue action carried out by a colony of poor Hornbæk fishermen. (One cannot help being reminded of one of the Scandinavian theatre's wittiest parodies, J. H. Wessel's *Kjærlighed uden Strømper/Love without Stockings*, which only seven years previously had placed the high-flown sentiments of heroic tragedy in the mouths of tailors and artisans—with devastating effect!) In Ewald's play a shipwreck is the dramatic highpoint, and for its enactment in 1780

---

[1] 'Tall, upright monumental stone found in Europe, Africa and Asia. [f. Breton *men hir*, long stone]': *The Concise Oxford Dictionary*. The Danish word is *Bautasten*.

[2] This production is reconstructed in detail in Torben Krogh, *Danske Teaterbilleder fra det 18de Aarhundrede*, pp. 253–67.

23. Gothic interior designed by Thomas Bruun for Samsøe's
Dyveke (1796): 'The Queen's Chamber'

stage manager Christoffer Nielsen constructed a new 'movable
sea' of waves in motion which was so convincing and effective
in operation that its designer was presented with a medal of
honour.

Ewald's plays, in particular *Balder's Death*, fostered a lasting
stage tradition. The intense interest in Nordic subjects spread to
ballet with the performance of Vincenzo Galeotti's *Lagertha*
(1801), based upon the Norwegian playwright Christen Pram's
Saxo-inspired historical drama of unfaithfulness and domestic
retribution. Enhanced by Claus Schall's music and Chipart's
evocative Nordic landscape décor, *Lagertha* became a milestone
in the art of Galeotti, the internationally famous Italian choreo-
grapher who staged half a hundred ballets at the Royal Theatre
and is generally considered to be the creator of the Danish
ballet's illustrious traditions—traditions which his great

successor August Bournonville built upon and renewed in the romantic spirit.

A still more influential, final step in the evolution of the new romanticism is represented by O. J. Samsøe's national-historical tragedy *Dyveke* (1796), a production in which the Royal Theatre bent every effort to create the kind of picturesque historical colouring that throughout most of the next century would continue to be known as Gothic. Samsøe's play, one of the most admired national dramas of this period, is in reality a sentimental tragedy *a la* Lessing; like Emilia Galotti, Dyveke— mistress of the medieval King Christjern II—is a wronged innocent brought to ruin in the courtly milieu into which she is forced. Thomas Bruun's four original stage settings for this drama, in which the talented designer, in Rahbek's estimate, 'proved to be both true to his period and pleasing to our own age',[3] were epoch-making indeed (Plate 23). They remained among those sets most often borrowed and re-used in the nineteenth century to convey the required gothic impression, gracing the plays of Shakespeare, Goethe, Schiller, Oehlenschläger, Hans Christian Andersen, Hertz and many others, and they were still to be found in the Royal Theatre's inventory of active décors in 1873—a scant six years before the world première of Ibsen's *A Doll's House*.

The gothic mode transmitted by such pre-romantic productions as *Balder's Death, Lagertha,* and *Dyveke* is at the theatrical heart of the plays of Adam Oehlenschläger (1779–1850), unquestionably the major figure in Scandinavian drama during the first quarter of the nineteenth century. With his *Poems* 1803 (publ. 1802) Oehlenschläger heralded the conscious establishment of a new movement in Danish literature, aimed at breaking with older traditions and championing the spirit of German romanticism. His powerful keynote poem 'Guldhornerne'/'The Horns of Gold' was a ringing declaration of the renaissance of ancient Nordic culture. Mining a quite different, exotic vein in *Aladdin* (*Poetiske Skrifter,* 1805) he created an imaginative dramatic poem whose central character, the apotheosis of the heroic dreamer, became virtually a hieroglyph for the romantic spirit in Scandinavia. Admired in turn by Heiberg, Andersen, Kierkegaard, Ibsen and Brandes, this masterpiece was so seminal

[3] *Svada* (1796), p. 179f.

that Goethe's inscription in the Danish poet's autograph book read simply 'dem Dichter des Aladdin'. However, Oehlenschläger's main significance as a playwright lies in his formulation, under the persuasive influence of the later classicism of Schiller in *Wallenstein, Maria Stuart,* and *Die Jungfrau von Orleans,* of the Nordic heroic genre with which his name has become synonymous. When the twenty-five-year-old dramatist, staying with Henrik Steffens in Halle, sent home his first stage play *Hakon Jarl* in 1806, a new era dawned.

The author's intimate knowledge of the practical theatre and its conventions, gleaned partly from two years' experience as an actor, was evident in the Royal Theatre production of *Hakon Jarl* in January, 1808, a performance steeped in the gothic style. Many of the sets were borrowed, as was customary, directly from earlier gothic productions, including *Dyveke* (in which Oehlenschläger himself had once acted), and Abildgaard's stylized historicity again influenced the costuming. In the third act a picturesque maritime tableau of the kind that had long delighted eighteenth-century audiences was introduced: for the arrival by sea of Hakon Jarl's adversary Olaf Tryggvesøn, bent on converting Norway to Christianity and destroying Hakon's power, the royal bark—with King Olaf in the bow surrounded by retainers and singing monks—sailed forth from the wings through a painted sea, struck its mainsail and landed on the beach. Much less idyllic was the crucial fourth-act terror scene in which the ambitious and pitiless Hakon sacrifices his son to gain Odin's favour, thereby sealing his own doom. Set in a typically gloomy 'sacrificial grove' dominated by threatening statues of Viking gods, this splendid gothic cameo blended tearful pathos—as the heartless father hesitates to drive home his dagger while little Erling kneels in prayer—with spine-tingling horror. Finally the cruel Jarl leads his unwitting child out of sight behind Odin's icon, from whence were heard screams so unnerving and indecorous that even Oehlenschläger ordered them cut. In a dimly lit and forbidding underground vault where Hakon lies hidden from his enemies, the play reaches its fifth-act climax; slain by his slave as he walks in his sleep, Hakon Jarl remains great in defeat, a 'giant soul' over whom his sometime lover Thora is left to speak one of Oehlenschläger's finest eulogies.

Hakon, the first in a gallery of Oehlenschlägerean heroes 'smelling of seaweed, heathenism and sacrificial blood' (to borrow Bournonville's phrase),[4] was intended as a rôle for the author's former acting teacher, the gifted Michael Rosing, but crippling rheumatism prevented the aging star from attempting this demanding part. With Oehlenschläger's next tragedy *Palnatoke* (1809), a *Wilhelm Tell*-inspired drama which again centres on the historically doomed struggle of ancient Nordic strength against the inroads of the new Christianity, the lack of a persuasive heroic actor was even more keenly felt. Four years passed before the ideal Oehlenschlägerean actor appeared, but with the début of Johan Christian Ryge, a former country doctor who abandoned his practice for the stage, as Palnatoke in 1813, the fiery embodiment of the romantic hero had been found. In a repertoire that made the severest demands on the physical resources and vocal stamina of a performer, Ryge was the perfect expression of Nordic strength, both as a personal quality and as the fulfilment of a specific aesthetic ideal. 'His words', wrote Bournonville, 'rang like sword blows on copper shields, they pierced to the soul like runes carved in granite boulders. His voice resounded like the shrill tone of the lure through the surf of the North Sea'.[5]

Oehlenschläger's fecund and impressionable imagination continued to explore a variety of directions in drama, with varying success. The popular artist-hero of German romanticism is represented in his *Correggio,* lavishly staged with borrowed Renaissance paintings and opulent costumes in 1811. Originally written in German, *Correggio* was also performed with great success in Berlin and Vienna and was widely read in Germany during the first half of the nineteenth century. In a different vein, his *Hugo von Rheinberg* (1814) is a botched attempt to emulate the heady medievalism, poisoned chalices and castle spectres of the deep-dyed terror romanticism popularized by the ubiquitous Kotzebue's *Johanne von Montfaucon* and *Die Kreuzfahrer,* Galeotti's electrifying Bluebeard ballet *Rolf Blaaskæg*, and Skjöldebrand's *Herman von Unna*, the progenitor of the *genre sombre* in Scandinavia. Oehlenschläger's Nordic saga dramas also acquired a new, more controlled tone in *Axel og*

---

[4] *Teatret på Kongens Nytorv 1748–1948,* ed. H. Gabrielsen, p. 67.
[5] Karl Mantzius, *Skuespilkunstens Historie i det 19de Aarhundrede,* p. 56.

Valborg (1810), a twelfth-century tragedy of love and duty based on a folksong motif. Under the influence of French classical tragedy *Axel og Valborg* observes the 'unities' and takes place entirely within the imposing gothic cathedral at Nidaros—a departure that audiences accustomed to a spectacular display of changing scenes in gothic tragedy found difficult to accept. In this play as in *Hagbarth og Signe* (1816), in which Oehlenschläger consciously set out to 'sail even some degrees closer to French classicism',[6] the faithful lovers of the title, parted by hostile circumstances, face their destiny bravely and are joined in death at the end. With the débuts during the 1820–21 season of the dashingly handsome lyrical actor N. P. Nielsen and the stately Anna Brenøe (the future Fru Nielsen), one of the Scandinavian theatre's loveliest romantic heroines, Oehlenschlägerean tragedy acquired the ideal Axel and Valborg to complement Dr. Ryge's ebullient Nordic heroes.

Although by far the most popular foreign dramatists of this period were Iffland, with his touching *Familienstücke,* and Kotzebue, over seventy of whose melodramas were seen by Copenhagen audiences between 1801 and 1825, the new spirit introduced by Oehlenschläger's plays drew with it the first productions of Shakespeare on the Danish stage. Shakespearian drama was seen in the provinces long before it finally gained access to the Royal Theatre and Dramaten in the early nineteenth century. The Swedish town of Norrköping witnessed the first performance of Shakespeare in Scandinavia in 1776, when the remarkable touring theatre manager Carl Gottfried Seuerling presented a version of 'that magnificent bourgeois tragedy' *Romeo and Juliet.*[7] A Swedish translation of *Hamlet* was acted in Göteborg as early as 1787. Odense, where the first professional provincial theatre in Denmark was established, saw a version of *Hamlet* performed by Friebach's German-speaking troupe in 1792—whereas Copenhagen audiences had to wait almost a generation before the first Royal Theatre production of *Hamlet* on 12 May 1813 introduced Shakespeare to the capital. Appropriately, the play's translator, Peter Foersom, who had struggled for a decade to convince the sceptical

---

6 F. J. Billeskov Jansen, *Danmarks Digtekunst,* III, 102.
7 Claes Hoogland and Gösta Kjellin, eds. *Bilder ur svensk teaterhistoria,* p. 146.

management to hazard Shakespeare, was the first Danish Hamlet. His performance marked the highpoint in a modest production put together of older gothic décors borrowed from *Dyveke* and *Herman von Unna* and combined with a minimum of new set-pieces, including five which represented burial mounds, and such new props as a 'death's head' and some 'skeleton bones of wood'. *King Lear,* which followed in September 1816, was a popular fiasco that closed after three poorly attended performances. Ryge's robust attack was ill-suited to the rôle of Lear; it is, the actor stoutly maintained, 'against both my inner and my outer nature to play mad kings when they are not allowed to strike back at their enemies'.[8] The somewhat more successful production a year later of the Schiller version of *Macbeth,* again featuring Ryge in the title part, concluded the Royal Theatre's first round of Shakespearian flirtations.

Dramaten quickly followed suit with the first Stockholm showing of *Hamlet,* mounted at the Arsenal Theatre on 26 March 1819. This production, a major event in the Swedish theatre of this period, typifies in many ways the accepted approach to Shakespeare. The cuts introduced by P. A. Granberg's prose translation, whose running time was three and a half hours, generally followed the lead of traditional English stage versions of the play. Cornelius and Voltimand, those uninteresting ambassadors, were eliminated, as was the dispensable scene between Polonius and his servant Reynaldo. Granberg, like Garrick before him, banished the grave-diggers, and, as in the Bell edition of 1773, he dispensed entirely with Fortinbras, assigning some of the Prince of Norway's speeches to Horatio. The cast boasted two of Dramaten's strongest actors: the noble and authoritative Gustaf Åbergsson was at age forty-four a stately and mature Hamlet, and the resilient Lars Hjortsberg, one of the Swedish theatre's greatest comic actors, was Horatio. This much-discussed production was further enhanced by an original musical score, prepared by the Swiss-born composer and concert-master Édouard Du Puy—a figure whose importance for the development of the musical stage both in Denmark and in Sweden is immeasurable.

Of greatest interest, however, are the actual staging principles at work in the Swedish *Hamlet,* as recorded in Dramaten's

[8] Thomas Overskou, *Den danske Skueplads i dens Historie,* IV, p. 449.

archives—principles which are for the most part still firmly yoked to eighteenth-century methods. Stock settings of the standard wing-and-border variety were used for all five acts. The opening scene utilized five rows of stock forest wings and a background of fortress and battlement pieces borrowed from such familiar gothic favourites as Kotzebue's *Johanne von Montfaucon* and Grétry's *Richard Coeur-de-Lion*. The backcloth was a standard sea drop. The only furnishing on the otherwise bare stage was a stone bench downstage right. As the curtain rose the scene was lit only by the moon, but when the Ghost appeared upstage and moved across a raised, horizontal platform, light was brought up between the wings, disappearing again on the Ghost's exit. Following Hamlet's encounter with his father's spirit later in the act, the grim spectre was seen to sink through the main trap, moving beneath the stage for each 'Swear' and drawing the onstage group after him in symmetrical pattern: first stage centre, then downstage right, then downstage left, and finally down centre for Hamlet's 'Rest, rest perturbed spirit!' In the third act, within a conventional five-wing décor called simply 'Temple of the Muses', the play-within-the-play scene was imaginatively mounted. Blue curtains, hung behind the third row of wings, served as a front curtain for the miniature stage erected in the background. The miniaturization was complete to the smallest detail: the little stage was fitted with two pairs of forest wings, a forest backdrop, and a grass seat for the Player King. Access to this stage was by means of steps placed at either side. (Du Puy devised an elaborate dumb-show which made a telling musical comment: the theme which accompanied the Player Queen as she laments the King's death was repeated a moment later when Lucianus *pretends* to lament with her. Similarly, the theme used to express the Queen's acquiescence to Lucianus' advances was the same one heard earlier to signify the love between the Player King and his Queen.) The act continued in the same décor until after Hamlet discovers Claudius at his prayers. Pages then appeared and carried off the few items of furniture, while another page entered carrying a chair, a table, and a candle; the *changement à vue* to the Closet Scene could now take place.

Although the use of borrowed or incongruously combined settings, clumsy set-shifting techniques, partial scene changes,

111

primitive lighting effects and similar technical inelegancies were being vigorously castigated by the sharp-tongued Rosenstand-Goiske, Denmark's first theatre critic, as early as the 1770s, many of these conventions persisted—as the 1819 *Hamlet* shows—well into the nineteenth century. Nevertheless, the emergence of a new theatrical style throughout Europe, particularly in France and England, was creating profound changes. In 1827 Victor Hugo's preface to *Cromwell* proclaimed a new charter of freedom from the remaining neoclassical restrictions on drama. The English guest performances in Paris in 1827–8 and the productions in 1829 and 1830 of Dumas' *Henri III et sa cour,* Vigny's *Othello,* and Hugo's *Hernani* signalled the decisive breakthrough of romanticism on the Continent. Also in Scandinavia at this time, the more formalized and abstracted theatrical system of the eighteenth century was gradually eroded and displaced by the new scenic goals of 'Walter Scott romanticism', aimed at producing the illusion of living reality in settings, costumes and lighting. However, the realization of these new theatrical ideals—more atmospheric and illusionistic settings, greater emphasis upon local colour and authenticity and the concept of the theatre as 'a living picture-gallery'—presupposed important technical changes.

Eigtved's elegant Royal Theatre had undergone a major rebuilding under the supervision of the architect C. F. Harsdorff, in the course of which the stage was expanded, and the machinery greatly improved, in 1773. Although Harsdorff's theatre continued to function until 1874, when it was demolished to make way for the present Royal Theatre structure, the stage underwent significant alterations and improvements from time to time. Stage lighting obviously played a major rôle in achieving greater scenic illusion, and in 1819 candles and tallow lamps were replaced by more flexible and reliable oil-burning Argand lamps. Dramaten, housed in the Arsenal Theatre since 1793, had in fact anticipated this development five years before. Still greater flexibility was achieved at the Royal Theatre in 1826, when the footlights were made longer and were equipped with more powerful lamps, a mechanism for simultaneously dimming the lamps in the wings was incorporated, and coloured lighting was introduced. Two years earlier the cosmopolitan theatre reformer Gustaf Lagerbjelke, whose term of management at Dramaten from 1823 to 1827 brought the new romantic *mise-en-scène* to Swedish theatre, had already used the novelty of moonlight and other coloured lighting effects in his production of P. A. Wolff's popular lyric drama *Preciosa*. Although gas lighting had been introduced in England in 1817, however, this more sophisticated means of creating such favourite romantic phenomena as moonlight, storm clouds, sunsets and volcano eruptions did not reach Scandinavia until relatively late—first on the Royal Swedish Opera stage (which the dramatic theatre was obliged to share for four decades after the Arsenal went up in flames in 1825) on New Year's Day 1854; next at Det Norske Teater in Bergen in 1856; and finally on Kongens Nytorv in 1857–8.

Changes of scene, which normally took place in full view, were also facilitated in 1826 by the installation of a third set of wing chariots at the Royal Theatre, making it possible to mount as many as three settings at once and thereby reducing the necessity of partial scene shifts. Three years later August Bournonville introduced the box set or closed room of the modern theatre, with its real walls and ceiling, in his ballet *La sonnambula*—an advance carried to Christiania Theatre by designer Troels Lund in 1837 but not commonly employed in Scandinavia until toward mid-century.

Historians have summed up the development of scene design in the first half of the nineteenth century by observing that the backcloth eventually absorbed the side-wings and finally swallowed the whole stage picture. The architect was deposed in favour of the landscape painter, as the architectural formality of the baroque theatre receded before romantic stretches of blasted heath, distant vistas of towns and picturesque views of Mexican burial grounds or Italian village squares. The scene-painter exerted a major influence on the style and appearance of the entire repertoire, and in playbills and reviews his name was often the most prominent one. Aron Wallich, the Royal Theatre's designer for nearly three decades from 1814 to 1842, found in the towns of northern Italy his models for the favourite gothic subjects of contemporary stage painting—murky cathedrals, barren churchyards, vaulted monastery passages and sombre grave monuments. Like his Swedish counterpart Carl Jakob Hjelm, who inherited Desprez's legacy as Dramaten's

113

designer from 1798 to 1827, Wallich combined a predilection for the grandiose lines and deep perspectives of the eighteenth century with a richness of romantic detail inspired by such European masters as Cicéri, Schinkel and Sanquirico. Wallich was succeeded at the Royal Theatre by two scenic artists,

24. Gothic impressions from the sketchbook of Troels Lund, gathered during his travels in Germany, Austria and Italy

Troels Lund and C. F. Christensen. Lund, whose work came to have an important impact upon the developing Norwegian theatre, specialized in historical and architectural designs, bringing the influence of Cicéri and the amazing atmospheric effects of Daguerre's Diorama to bear on his art. Christensen, who remained attached to the Royal Theatre until 1869, was one of the most imaginative and talented scenic artists of the period. While Lund's speciality was architecture, Christensen's strength lay in finely wrought romantic landscapes executed in bright, warm and genial tones (Plate 25). One of his greatest successes was his much-admired Italian décor for Bournonville's exotic ballet *Festen i Albano/Festival in Albano* (1839), a versatile design which like the *Dyveke* sets of old continued to haunt a legion of subsequent romantic stage pictures (Plate 26).

Within the framework of striking pictorialism provided by these designers, a constellation of native playwrights and an exceptional company of actors joined forces during the second quarter of the nineteenth century to create the most memorable epoch in Danish theatrical history. Architecturally as well as intellectually the Royal Theatre dominated the daily life of the Danish capital, and the cultural giants of the age gathered in the stalls each evening. Hans Christian Andersen's lodgings were always within easy walking distance of the playhouse; Oehlenschläger was there every evening; Bertel Thorvaldsen died in the theatre; and the solitary Kierkegaard was a habitual playgoer. At the centre of this glittering circle stood the Heibergs.

P. A Heiberg, whose exile and subsequent divorce had astonished polite society around the turn of the century, rehabilitated Danish comedy with a series of trenchant eighteenth-century satires of fools and double dealers. It remained, however, for his son Johan Ludvig Heiberg (1791–1860) to generate a genuine comic renaissance to balance the serious drama of Oehlenschläger and his imitators. After a brilliant doctoral dissertation in Latin on Calderón in 1817, the younger Heiberg quickly came to dominate Danish intellectual life in a variety of capacities. As a playwright (he has remained second only to Holberg as Denmark's most performed dramatist), publicist, philosopher, theatre manager and unofficial cultural arbiter, Heiberg represented the concept of romanticism as an elegantly

115

25. Exotic landscape designed by C. F. Christensen: a tropical
rain forest

refined parlour game. He was an energetic cultural inter-
mediary who strove to transplant new German and French
developments to Scandinavia. Having spent several years in
Paris, Kiel and Berlin during the early 1820s, he was in a
position to bring the powerful intellectual forces of Europe to
bear on the cultural life of Denmark. From Germany he introduced the contemporary philosophy of F. W. Hegel to Scandinavia—voicing in his Hegelian treatise *On Human Freedom*
(1824) the demand for introspective self-scrutiny and reflective inner freedom which above all else drew Ibsen to
Heiberg. However, his most significant theatrical contribution
remains his systematic domestication of the Scribean vaudeville
116   comedy. His affinity for Gallic culture was strong, and his

espousal of such writers as Prosper Mérimée, Théodore Leclercq, Casimir Delavigne and Scribe himself served to draw Denmark into the mainstream of contemporary Continental theatre. On the basis of the Scribean vaudeville (a type of musical play in which short, topical songs were set to recognizable melodies or arias were interwoven with the dialogue in order to circumvent the monopoly on spoken drama exercised by the Parisian patent theatres) Heiberg created a native Danish counterpart—its hallmarks were realistic topicality,

26. Another Christensen design: his backdrop for Bournonville's ballet *The Festival in Albano* (1839)

recognizable stage settings, the felicitous choice of exactly the right melodies and wide popular appeal. A related effort in his vigorous drive to internationalize and de-Germanize Danish theatrical taste was his translation of some forty contemporary plays, all but a handful of which were modern French pieces and the majority of which stemmed from the prolific dramatic factory of Eugène Scribe.

Heiberg launched his offensive in November 1825 with his vaudeville farce on the theme of mistaken identity, *Kong Salomon og Jørgen Hattemager/King Solomon and George the Hatter*. The grumblings of more conservative elements not-withstanding, the popularity of this genre's light, revue-like mixture of lyricism, jest and satire was immense. 'It was a Danish vaudeville', Hans Christian Andersen later recalled, 'blood of our blood, one felt, and therefore it was received with jubilation and replaced all else. Thalia held a carnival on the Danish stage, and Heiberg was her chosen favourite'.[9] Heiberg's brilliantly polemical Hegelian 'demonstration' of the superiority of the vaudeville to other genres, entitled *On the Vaudeville as a Dramatic Form* (1826), was not only a momentary critical sensation but was still being referred to by Ibsen thirty years later. His early successes drew with them a sparkling cascade of vaudevilles and comedies in the Heiberg spirit. Hans Christian Andersen, versatile as a playwright as well as being the master of the genre with which his name has become linked, made his début as a dramatist with the effective vaudeville parody *Kjærlighed paa Nicolai Taarn/Love on St. Nicholas Tower* in 1829. A few months earlier, the historian and stage director Thomas Overskou had joined the snowballing comic revival with his topical and realistic play *Østergade og Vester-gade/East Side, West Side*. Two other Danish dramatists of considerable note emerged as initial products of the vaudeville rage. Fascinated by the topicality of the Heibergian vaudeville while retaining roots in the character comedy of Holberg, Henrik Hertz came forward as a playwright in 1827 with a five-act satire of amateur dramatics called *Hr. Burchardt og hans Familie/Burchardt and his Family*; *Flyttedagen/Moving Day*, a satire of contemporary apartment-hunting, appeared the following year. Hertz's best play in the comic vein remains,

[9] *Mit Livs Eventyr*, ed. H. Topsøe-Jensen (Copenhagen, 1951), I, 99.

however, his delightful character comedy about a family which mistakenly believes they have hit the jackpot in the lottery, *Sparekassen/The Savings Bank* (1836). In the forties Jens Christian Hostrup delighted audiences with two plays which sprang directly from the tradition of the topical vaudeville-comedy. *Genboerne/The Neighbours* (1844) and *Eventyr paa Fodrejsen/Adventures on Foot* (1848) are festive comedies of Danish student life which combine occasional touches from the fairy-tales of Andersen and the Viennese fairy-tale comedy of Raimund with the revue-like satire and idyllic lyricism of the vaudeville genre. Across the Sound, the liberal politician and novelist August Blanche transplanted the techniques of Heiberg and Scribe to Sweden. *Positivhataren/The Hurdy-Gurdy Hater,* a topical Stockholm comedy that revolves around an innkeeper named Propp who hates the sound of barrel-organs, helped to launch Anders Lindeberg's Nya teatern (later called Mindre teatern), the first private theatre to break Dramaten's monopoly, in 1843. Although Blanche's drama *Läkaren/The Doctor,* acted on the Dramaten stage in 1845, represented an early attempt at serious social drama in a contemporary milieu, his true métier was folk comedy. His best play, a charming adaptation of a French vaudeville about the tribulations of a company of strolling players entitled *Ett resande teatersällskap/A Travelling Troupe* (1848), remains a classic of its kind.

The comic renaissance fostered by Heiberg found its ideal scenic expression at the Danish Royal Theatre in the new generation of talented comic actors that complemented the achievements of Ryge, N. P. Nielsen and Anna Nielsen in the tragic mode. C. N. Rosenkilde brought to the comedies of Holberg and Heiberg a quiet, reflective humour and a formidable sense of comic detail. His temperamental opposite was the great Holberg actor Ludvig Phister, whose début in 1825 revealed a startlingly subtle comic malice which added a new shade to the interpretation of classical and contemporary comedy. The stars in this imposing theatrical firmament paled, however, before the brilliance of the sun around which they revolved—Johanne Luise Heiberg, regarded by many of her contemporaries as unsurpassed by any other actress in Europe. As the roguish and poetically amorous schoolgirl Trine Rar in her future husband's vaudeville *Aprilsnarrene/The April Fools* (1826) the thirteen-year-old Hanne Pätges became the toast of Copenhagen. Her stunning success inspired Heiberg to tailor a gallery of similarly arch ingenue rôles for her; in 1827, the year in which the vaudeville rage was at its peak, she was the romantic Christine in *Et Eventyr i Rosenborg Have/An Adventure in Rosenborg Gardens* and Caroline in *De Uadskillelige/ The Inseparables,* Heiberg's witty satire on prolonged engagements. In these musical plays her remarkably supple physical, facial and vocal expressiveness more than compensated for her lack of a strong singing voice. Out of these lyrical ingenue rôles she created, as Karl Mantzius observes, 'an ideal picture of a young girl such as she felt a young girl should be, and she did so with such an ingenious and confident grasp of contemporary taste that the real young girls—and the men—also felt that they should be such, and at last believed that they really were'.[10] Describing her distinctive blend of 'innocent coquettishness and feminine self-assurance' in Heiberg's vaudeville tour-de-force *Nej/No* (1836), Edvard Brandes conveys a vivid impression of her technique: 'Impossible to re-capture is the wonder of her entrance—her first lines, exchanged with Hammer [the suitor], her sparklingly modest and encouraging smile, the glance with which she caught sight of him in the half-open door all cast a spell which must have finished off both Hammer and the audience'.[11] Quite finished off himself, Heiberg composed a poetic proposal in the form of the rôle of Agnete in *Elverhøj/Elves' Hill*, the folksong-inspired romantic spectacle which, due in no small measure to Friedrich Kuhlau's impressive score, has become Denmark's most frequently performed theatre work. Exploiting the Royal Theatre's unique threefold combination of drama, opera, and ballet to the fullest, *Elves' Hill* was acted for the first time on 6 November 1828 to celebrate the marriage of the popular Crown Prince Frederik (VII). While the theatre's façade was decorated to represent a temple illuminated by thousands of lamps, inside on the stage

---

[10] *Skuespilkunstens Historie i det 19de Aarhundrede;* see also Lise-Lone and Frederick J. Marker, 'Fru Heiberg: A Study of the Art of the Romantic Actor,' *Theatre Research,* XIII, 1 (1973), p. 24.

[11] Edvard Brandes, *Om teater,* ed. Harald Engberg (Copenhagen, 1947), p. 110.

Heiberg's festive royal tribute found its perfect interpretation in Ryge's splendidly magnificent King Christian IV, Nielsen's dashing Ebbesen—determined to defy the King and marry Agnete—Anna Nielsen's impetuous and strong-willed Elizabeth Munk, Rosenkilde's comic castellan Bjørn Olufson—literally bursting to tell his secrets—and, at the centre of the intrigue, the fifteen-year-old Hanne Pätges' lyrical, romantic changeling Agnete (Plate 27).

During the nearly four decades from her acting début in 1826 to her premature retirement in 1864, Johanne Luise Heiberg— known by royal permission as 'Fru' Heiberg on the playbills, instead of the customary 'Madame'—personified the neoclassic-romantic balance of opposites, the period's cult of wonder and strangeness coupled with unblemished idealization as the indispensable counter-weight. Goethe's admonition in his *Rules for Actors* (§ 35) that 'the player must first of all consider that he should not only imitate nature but also portray it ideally, thereby in his presentation uniting the true with the beautiful' touches the very core of Heibergian aesthetics and is re-echoed often in Fru Heiberg's remarkable autobiography *A Life Relived in Memory,* published the year after her death in 1890. 'Is not all art beauty intensified?' she demands in this work. 'All art must elevate and liberate mankind. . . . The human soul can be elevated both by King Lear's tormented outbursts on the heath and by the conflict of [Holberg's] Per the Deacon and the bailiff, for in both cases we are in the realm of fine art; but if art descends to the mere presentation of *reality,* from which the grosser elements have not been strained, we must declare with the poet: Das haben wir alles besser und bequemer zu Hause.'[12]

An obvious and interesting relationship existed between the neoclassic-romantic theatre's preoccupation with harmoniously balanced poses and striking *tableaux vivants* and the arts of painting and sculpture. In a review of her last important rôle as Maria Stuart in Schiller's tragedy, the Ibsen antagonist Clemens Petersen draws attention to a cornerstone of Johanne Luise Heiberg's art: 'a plasticity in movements and positions that reminds one of an ancient sculpture and a keen sense of un-

---

[12] *Et Liv gjenoplevet i Erindringen,* II, 227.

blemished, formal beauty'.[13] Describing the romantic idol
Michael Wiehe's performance as Mortimer in the same play,
Edvard Brandes fastens on the paramount fact that 'he displayed
so great a plastic beauty that had one been able to make a series
of plaster casts of him they would have provided the most
wonderful statues'.[14] Numerous sketches and drawings of Fru
Heiberg, whose legendary performances together with Wiehe
represent the apogee of romantic acting in the Scandinavian
theatre, convey at least some impression of the articulate
plasticity and sculptured grace of her characters. Her talent
for visually pleasing physical characterization was unbounded.
Cast at the age of eighteen as the mute Fenella (a part usually
given to a ballerina) in Scribe and Auber's spectacular opera *La
muette de Portici* (Plate 28) she conveyed, according to awe-
struck critics, 'not what Fenella said but how she heard, not
what Fenella thought but how she felt, not what Fenella did but
what she was like. This was what made Fenella a *character,*
despite the fact that she is deprived of action and speech. Who
can deny that Fenella was the character who *spoke most clearly,*
whose inner self one was best able to comprehend'.[15] The actress
herself was convinced that 'it was not this or that pose, this or
that pantomimic expression which caused the audience to be absorbed in my performance; it was because I succeeded in imprinting the rôle with a personality which fascinated them by
its simplicity and truth' (*Et Liv* I, 118). This acknowledged
mastery of picturesque physical characterization led many
contemporary playwrights to create rôles for her which took
advantage of the rich pantomimic dimension of her art. In his
romantic verse drama *Kong Renés Datter/King René's Daughter*
(1845)—a favourite in the international repertory throughout
the last century—Henrik Hertz designed the rôles of Iolanthe,
the blind princess whose sight is restored through love, and the
manly Tristan, quite literally clad in shining armour, for the
incomparable abilities of Fru Heiberg and Michael Wiehe.
Iolanthe's blindness was delicately evoked through a pattern of
decorously restrained gesticulation and movement; the blind,
the actress reasoned, 'always move with a certain cautiousness,

---

[13] *Fædrelandet*, 30 June 1861.
[14] *Dansk Skuespilkunst*, p. 31.
[15] C. N. David in *Kjøbenhavns flyvende Post*, LXIV (1830), II.

Scandinavia's great leading lady, Johanne Luise Heiberg, in two of her most famous rôles. Engravings by C. Bruun

27. Agnete in her husband's play *Elves' Hill*

28. The mute Fenella in Scribe and Auber's *La muette de Portici*

with their hands invariably slightly in front of their body' (I, 366).

As Fenella in *La muette de Portici* the strikingly exotic, foreign side of her personality had come to the fore, making her seem to Adam Oehlenschläger 'magnificent in her fiery, passionate being, held in check only by grace'.[16] Dark and foreign in appearance, she excelled in evoking a piquant, mysterious, erotic impression delicately balanced by playfulness and lyrical naïvety. The powerful sensual tension between fire and apparent nonchalance created an emotionally charged doubleness that led Danish playwrights to tailor for her a whole gallery of character parts whose duality involved a strong undercurrent of the exotic, the passionate and the demonic. She was Hertz's model for the sensual and demonic Ragnhild in his medievalized drama of runes and spectres, *Svend Dyrings Hus/Svend Dyring's House* (1837)—a play whose masterful modernization of folksong metre and rhyme affords an interesting comparison with Ibsen's *Gildet på Solhaug/The Feast at Solhaug* (1856). She was the strong-willed and fiery Cecilie in *Mulatten/The Mulatto* (1840), Andersen's most successful venture into the ethnographic exoticism that fascinated nineteenth-century audiences. She was the intense and psychologically complex heroine in Oehlenschläger's historical tragedy *Dina* (1842). As the courtesan Ninon, with Michael Wiehe as the Chevalier de Villers, her young admirer and in fact her son, Fru Heiberg created in Hertz's *Ninon* (1848) the true apotheosis of idealized passion, the embodiment, in the words of the wildly enthusiastic Georg Brandes, of 'that beauty which can never age, that nobility which can never be lost, that superior womanly intelligence that is able to guide no less than the earth itself with a light and confident hand'.[17]

Her conception of dramatic character as a synthesis of balanced opposites and contradictions, her espousal of the 'enchanting variety' viewed by the romantics as the reality of nature would inevitably lead Fru Heiberg to Shakespeare (despite her husband's avowed distaste for the 'raw and ugly' side of Shakespeare that merely gave us 'Melpomene's dagger

---

[16] Quoted in Gustav Hetsch, *H. C. Andersen og Musikken* (Copenhagen, 1930), p. 157.

124 [17] Georg Brandes, *Samlede Skrifter* (Copenhagen, 1899), I, p. 452.

transformed into a butcher knife'). Throughout her career, Fru Heiberg was very often implicated in what little Shakespeare there was to be seen at the Royal Theatre. As a young actress of fifteen, her unique lyrical power made her the perfect Juliet. Returning to the same part almost twenty years later, in 1847, her more mature and reflective idealization of feminine youthfulness led Søren Kierkegaard, who perhaps best of all understood the demonic element in her art, to write his lucid panegyric *The Crisis and a Crisis in the Life of An Actress*. Multifaceted emotion and feather-light transitions characterized her comic heroines in the industrious Sille Beyer's free versions of *Twelfth-Night* (1847), *As You Like It* (1849), *All's Well that Ends Well* (1850), and *Love's Labour's Lost* (1853). In a part like Ophelia, which she acted opposite the Hamlet of the progressive reformer F. L. Høedt, the arch foe of the House of Heiberg, in 1851, her intense dynamism was largely misplaced. As Lady Macbeth, on the other hand, Fru Heiberg touched the zenith of her career as a character actress, in a highly individualized performance which crystallizes the neoclassic-romantic aesthetic upon which her art depended. Her careful and imaginative analysis of the rôle is an unrecognized classic of nineteenth-century theatre theory.

The spirit of reconciliation which was an indispensable condition in Heiberg's aesthetics of the ideal became the informing element in Fru Heiberg's untraditional interpretation. Anna Nielsen, her rival and predecessor in the part, had followed established tradition in portraying Lady Macbeth as an older and deliberately evil figure, 'a passionless, icy, calculating yet imposing woman with an ability to make decisions, a power of will, a control even in the most fearful situations'.[18] When Fru Heiberg was persuaded to assume the rôle in 1860, four years after Anna Nielsen's death, she was convinced that a radically different approach was demanded by the text. Her Lady defied tradition as a younger, attractive, fiery creature, recently married and ecstatic with ambition from the outset of the play. Her underlying attitude toward Macbeth and his wife as 'beginners in sin' rather than 'hardened criminals' provided a

---

[18] Clemens Petersen in *Fædrelandet*, 16 January 1860; see also Frederick J. Marker, 'Fru Heiberg as Lady Macbeth'. *Scandinavica*, XII, 2 (1973), p. 130.

dramatically promising clue to their essential humanity, reinforced by the strong emotional upheaval which occurred in Fru Heiberg's portrayal immediately after the murder of Duncan has become a reality. 'From the moment she rushes from the bloody chamber, the transformation is visible', she writes. 'Ecstasy has now given way to the most extreme terror' (II, 258). Clemens Petersen's review recaptures the visual impact of this moment: 'Her eyes are flaming and rolling wildly, without the ability to focus anywhere, her face is frozen in horror, her whole figure totters.' Determined to give her Lady Macbeth a soul, her conciliatory interpretation emphasized overwhelming suffering rather than guilt. As we encounter her in the climactic sleepwalking scene, Lady Macbeth is already in the hell of her own spiritual torment. 'The three famous sighs which issue from her chilled soul during the sleepwalker scene . . . [must] sound like its trembling prayer for eternal mercy and forgiveness,' insisted the actress (II, 261). In performance, the electrifying effect of the scene 'held the audience under an almost demonic spell'.[19] An astonishing technique, perfected as Iolanthe in *King René's Daughter,* of staring vacantly into space without moving her pupils or changing her focus was conjoined by Fru Heiberg with a laboriously acquired ability to utter words without moving the lips or facial muscles in order to produce a harrowing pantomimic portrayal of the spiritually tormented woman. Clemens Petersen's review provides a vivid impression of this final glimpse of Fru Heiberg's Lady Macbeth: 'She wanders forth with stiffened limbs, her face is asleep and expressionless, even the lips remain motionless, so that her words and sighs reverberate as from a grave. . . . She plays [the scene] with a richness, truth, and confidence of artistic expression that will bring this sight to mind, with all its ghostly magic, long after the smile has faded from many another memory that we had carried with us of her art.'

Despite the stature of its achievement, this memorable performance came to be seen only four times. With the unexpected death of N. P. Nielsen, who played Macbeth, in March 1860, the play vanished from the repertory, not to reappear until the

[19] P. Hansen, *Den danske Skueplads, illustreret Theaterhistorie,* III, 83.

close of the century. When Johan Ludvig Heiberg's death followed in August, an era in Danish arts and letters ended. New forces were already making themselves felt throughout the Scandinavian theatre. Heiberg's stormy management of the Royal Theatre from 1849 to 1856, which marked its transformation from a royal to a democratic state theatre under the provisions of the new liberal constitution, had sought in vain to stifle the new demands for ensemble acting and greater stage realism being raised by Frederik Høedt and his converted disciple Michael Wiehe. One result was the famous Christiansborg court theatre season of 1855–6, during which the rebels staged comedies and vaudevilles under the aegis of the energetic Hans Wilhelm Lange, whose popular Casino Theatre became the first private theatre in Denmark in 1848 and whose Folketeatret, started in 1857, is still a major playhouse. At the court theatre, settings resembled real rooms (in a Høedt-influenced production, thought Edvard Brandes, 'it even seems as though the furniture and the set perform a rôle of their own'[20]) and the reformer moved among the furniture and shocked his audiences by turning his back and by puffing on a lighted cigar on stage. Although in a certain sense Fru Heiberg's penetrating psychological rôle interpretations pointed ahead towards the new modernism, she was clearly not impressed by Høedt's display of 'reality in its most coarse features. One sees actors make their entrance on stage with the dirt from the street on their boots because this is so true and is taken from life. They cough, sneeze, blow their noses, scratch their heads, spit across the boards of the floor, all in reverence to truth and nature' (II, 233). 'Truth,' she adds frostily, 'it undoubtedly—unfortunately—is, but not the kind of truth which rises to art'. A vigorous discussion of the director-oriented theatre that would ultimately displace the pre-naturalistic virtuoso—who had hitherto functioned as a sovereign craftsman responsible for developing his own rôle—was already underway at the end of the 1850s. An important article entitled 'On Stage Direction', published in *Berlingske Tidende* (30 January 1858) by (one assumes) August Bournonville, who with Ludvig Josephson introduced a more disciplined *mise-en-scène* to the Swedish Royal Theatre in the early 1860s, calls specifically for a director

[20] *Dansk Skuespilkunst*, p. 36.

who will 'create an ensemble, not only in the actors' blocking but also in the dialogue, so that continuity is achieved and the performance is rounded into a true artistic whole'.

Disillusioned and brought to question the very justification of her art, Johanne Luise Heiberg concluded the luminous theatrical epoch over which she had presided when she appeared, with no hint that this was her farewell performance, for the last time as Elizabeth Munk in *Elves' Hill* on 2 June 1864. During the quarter of a century between her retirement and her death in 1890 she continued to influence the theatre, however, most notably during the period between 1867 and 1874 when she functioned as resident stage director at the Royal Theatre and provided both Bjørnson and Ibsen with a hearing for their early plays. Influenced by the widespread contemporary enthusiasm for 'the young Norway', she vigorously cultivated Norwegian literature and drama, and was an active force in the introduction of the first modern Scandinavian problem play, Bjørnstjerne Bjørnson's *De Nygifte/The Newly Married*, which she directed at the Royal Theatre in 1865. Two years later she directed Bjørnson's *Maria Stuart i Skotland*, which she found more exciting than Schiller's drama because it stresses 'the flood of eroticism suffusing her whole being' (II, 345) as the source of Maria's tragedy. Ibsen was introduced on the Royal Theatre stage by Fru Heiberg's highly successful staging of *De Unges Forbund/The League of Youth* in February 1870. Scribean in construction, this play afforded the serious undercurrent which both she and Heiberg considered a *sine qua non* of the new drama. Her rebuttal of the Royal Theatre's initial rejection of the work was forceful: 'It is a vigorous satire of all the political charlatans and tricksters swarming about us, distinguished by characters consistently drawn and with deep psychological background', she maintained. 'Such serious, psychological genre vignettes are the signposts of the new drama; everything in literature points in this direction.'[21]

One of the most significant productions in Fru Heiberg's directing career was Ibsen's thirteenth-century historical drama *Kongs-Emnerne/The Pretenders*, first staged by her at the Royal Theatre on 11 January 1871. She had read *The Pretenders* when

[21] Quoted in Henning Fenger, *The Heibergs*, ed. and trans. F. J. Marker, p. 169.

it first appeared in print in late 1863 and had been impressed by its technical skill—though her enthusiasm was not as glowing as that which she reserved for *Kjærlighedens Komedie/Love's Comedy*, 'a play perhaps unmatched in any other country'.[22] The multiplicity of scene changes, particularly within a single act, in *The Pretenders* presented, she recalled in her memoirs, 'almost insurmountable difficulties' for the director and the theatre's new designer Valdemar Gyllich. Throughout the course of the nineteenth century the problem of visible scene changes, alluded to earlier in this chapter, grew in step with the continual growth of fuller sets and three-dimensional constructions, leading eventually to the passing of the visible transformation and the lowering of the curtain instead. Determined, however, to eschew the 'unjustifiable expedient which has found acceptance in all foreign theatres' of lowering a front curtain to conceal changes, yet unwilling to destroy the illusion by allowing the audience to 'see walls, trees, and other paraphernalia of the décor glide down helter-skelter from the sky' (II, 347), Fru Heiberg devised her own system, subsequently adopted as the standard practice at the Royal Theatre, of blackouts for each scene change. (Had she thought about it, meanwhile, she might have recalled that, as Dyveke in Hans Christian Andersen's unusual 'flashback' play *Kongen Drømmer/Dreams of the King*, she had seen just such a 'dissolve' technique in use in 1844—in a production evidently supervised by J. L. Heiberg!)[23]

Alert to the theatrical potential of the powerful closing scene in *The Pretenders*, Fru Heiberg had the body of the slain Skule, the anti-Aladdin who is destroyed by his own doubt, borne onstage by his men before the final curtain falls, rather than risking an anti-climax or even laughter by leaving the corpse on the doorstep outside as the stage directions indicate. Characteristically, she also persuaded Ibsen to end his play on Sigrid's line about her brother's 'lawless journey upon earth', thereby eliminating the victorious Haakon's final statement: 'Skule Baardsson was God's stepchild on earth: that was his mystery!' —for in Fru Heiberg's world, if not in Ibsen's, an all-loving and

22 *Ibid.*, p. 168.
23 See Frederick J. Marker, *Hans Christian Andersen and the Romantic Theatre*, p. 113f.

forgiving God would have had no stepchildren on his earth.

Effectively produced and capably performed—particularly by the young Emil Poulsen, whose scheming and manipulating Bishop Nikolas was a major breakthrough for the great Ibsen actor—*The Pretenders* moved theatre audiences as no tragic drama had done since Oehlenschläger's *Hakon Jarl* sixty-three years before. Johanne Luise Heiberg's direction of Ibsen's play was the ostensible occasion for his 'Rhymed Letter to Fru Heiberg', regarded by Brandes as 'one of the finest works of art he has produced'; in fact, however, 'a greater, shining memory' was the true inspiration for his panegyric:

> The memory of a beauty-filled
> Festive spell,
> The memory of a row of hours veiled in time,
> When first I saw you glide—sublime,
> Jeweled, with grace and truth of heart—
> Through the wonderland of art.
> This sight my debt in me instilled.

The debt, Ibsen realized, was a profound one. His first important glimpse of the Heibergian 'wonderland of art' was during his study trip to Copenhagen in 1852 to observe stage techniques at the Royal Theatre; the plays and productions which he saw during his stay had the greatest significance for his future development. Choosing poetry rather than prose for his tribute ('prose is for ideas,/verse for visions'!) Ibsen conjures up the great rôles of Scandinavia's greatest actress—Agnete, Dina, Iolanthe, Ragnhild, Ophelia—as a fleet of proud clipper ships gliding with fluttering ensigns down through the waters of the Sound. It is, in Ibsen's view, the malleable, 'myth-creating' quality of the actress, the ability

> ... to bend
> Your own content, spiritual, rich,
> To whatever form the common eye
> Requires for its own poetry

that ensures securer immortality for her art than for that of 'the rest of us/colour-, form-, and word-poets/architects/and whatever else we're called' who may at any time fall victim to interpretational obsolescence! No inferior literary stylist herself, Fru Heiberg responded with charming theatricality in gratitude for 'the song of a seer about me and to me . . . about a long forgotten time upon which I look back as a ghost looks back on a finished, lived-out life, with its struggles, its sorrows, but also with its joys, its triumphs, with the question whether the latter were deserved, whether they rightfully belonged to me'.[24]

[24] First published by Francis Bull in *Politiken,* 28 October 1949.

CHAPTER NINE

Ibsen Takes the Stage

The story of the nineteenth-century theatre in Ibsen's Norway is to a large extent that of its search for and ultimate achievement of artistic independence, of its development of a distinct theatrical culture, a dramatic repertory and a body of theatre artists able to articulate the country's own language, tastes and ideals. Norway's long cultural and political connection with Denmark, solidified by a relationship that dated back to the Union of Kalmar in 1397 and lasted for more than four centuries, profoundly influenced the evolution of its theatre. At the beginning of the last century, Norway faced the challenge of formidable tasks. New political freedom had been achieved in 1814, when Denmark, paying the price for its ill-advised and casual alliance with Napoleon, was forced to cede Norway as a sovereign territory to the Swedish king. Socially and politically as well as artistically, the period which followed the Treaty of Kiel was one of growing patriotic aspiration and cultural self-assertion. Although theatre performances in Norway can, as we have seen, be traced back to the Middle Ages, a distinct theatrical tradition had not taken root. The initial, basic steps in this direction are marked by the establishment of permanent theatre buildings and professional acting companies during the nineteenth century.

During the latter eighteenth century, Martin Nürenbach's isolated attempt to found a Norwegian theatre had introduced

Christiania (Oslo) audiences to Holberg in 1771. Encouraged by his success, Nürenbach sought and obtained his patent 'to present Danish comedies given by Norwegian subjects in Christiania in Norway' the following year. Nevertheless, the history of his theatrical venture, for which he seems to have enlisted local acting talent of rather questionable artistic quality, was brief. After performances of *Jeppe on the Hill* and *The Political Tinker,* this first attempt to create a Norwegian theatre ended.

During the half a century that followed, professional 'theatre' in Norway was represented by travelling foreign troupes of varying types and uneven merit, performing a repertory that spanned the full range from gymnastic displays, weight-lifting, magic tricks and rope-dancing to the production of comic pantomimes. Side by side with these strollers, amateur dramatic societies catering to a more select audience began to spring up and to become a significant impetus toward the development of a legitimate theatrical culture. Of these relatively small private societies of a few hundred members, each of whom committed himself to active participation in one or more of the productions shown to the membership at large, the oldest was founded in Christiania as early as 1780. Seven years later Christiansand acquired its private theatre company, and by 1789 the vogue had spread to many other towns, including Bergen, to be followed by Arendal (1796–7), Trondheim (1802), Larvik (1810), Frederikshald (1819) and Stavanger (1823). The enthusiastic activities of these amateur groups, which flourished mainly during the first three decades of the nineteenth century, centred on the performance of a varied bill of fare that included contemporary vaudevilles, bourgeois dramas and light comedies—a repertory inspired by, and acquired through, the Royal Theatre in Copenhagen. These clubs did more than help to create a potential audience of enlightened amateurs for the coming professional theatre. Due to their existence many Norwegian towns also came to possess both usable playhouses and technical equipment, including a frequently impressive costume wardrobe. Comediehuset in Bergen, apparently the first permanent theatre in Norway, was opened in this manner by the local dramatic society on 3 December 1800. As it happened, this theatre was destined to occupy a unique place in the

133

history of Norwegian theatre. As the first home of Det Norske Teater from 1850 to 1863, it became the focal point of the distinctly national theatre movement started by the violin virtuoso Ole Bull, and in 1876 it re-opened as Bergen's National Stage. It was in this playhouse, moreover, that Henrik Ibsen and Bjørnstjerne Bjørnson acquired their initial experience in the practical theatre during the 1850s.

The founding of Det Norske Teater, the signpost of a new era in Norwegian theatre art, was a clear confirmation of the general shift of emphasis from amateur to professional theatre that had begun some decades before. From the mid-twenties on, the importance of the private dramatic societies decreased, as Danish and later some Swedish troupes of professional players began to tour the country extensively. At the same time, Swedish-born Johan Peter Strömberg realized a long-cherished dream when he opened Norway's first public playhouse with a permanent company, Christiania Theatre, in January 1827. The members of Strömberg's native troupe of seven actors and three actresses were recruited from among the pupils in the acting school which he founded two years earlier, the first of its kind in Norway. Besides its regular company of actors Strömberg's theatre also boasted a small ballet corps, also drawn from his own pupils, as well as a modest orchestra. Criticism of the artistic standards represented by this assembly of local talent was soon heard, however, forcing Strömberg, whose directorship lasted for only one year, to import more accomplished Danish players.

The keynote for future developments was thereby sounded. Danish actors and a repertory that reflected their tastes continued to dominate Christiania Theatre and to demonstrate a superiority to native efforts for several decades to come. This statement should be qualified, however, by the reminder that Danish performers were not viewed as foreigners in Norway at this time, any more than Danish literature and culture would be so regarded. When, for example, Adam Oehlenschläger visited the country in 1833 he was, as Blanc emphasizes in his history of Christiania Theatre, 'surely not without justification celebrated as the foremost spokesman for the common spiritual interests of both nations', seconded by 'Johan Ludvig Heiberg, whose vaudevilles had overjoyed all of Copenhagen and were bound to exert a similar effect on an audience separated by only half a generation from the time when life in the Copenhagen environment seemed as home-like, and often more home-like, than its own'.[1]

Strömberg's theatre burned down in 1835, but the Christiania theatre company remained active. After an interval of two years, during which the Danish troupe was housed in the play-house of the local dramatic society, a new theatre building opened on the so-called Bank Square in October 1837. Designed and decorated by the Danish-born architect Henrik Grosch and the gifted Danish artist and Royal Theatre stage designer Troels Lund, the capital's handsome new playhouse stood until 1899, when it was replaced by Oslo's present Nationaltheatret, and remained throughout the nineteenth century the stage which, more than any other, set the standard for theatrical art in Norway. In itself, the choice of Andreas Munch's Nordic saga drama of the twelfth century, *Kong Sverres Ungdom/King Sverre's Youth*—from among eleven entries in its competition for the best play with which to open the new building— illustrates Christiania Theatre's ambition to present lavish romantic spectacles in the grand manner of the Royal Theatre or Dramaten. In reality a series of dramatic vignettes in which the variety of picturesque Nordic settings and atmospheric historical tableaux comprises the chief interest, Munch's play quickly faced the new theatre with technical demands it found difficult to satisfy. Stage illusion was somewhat marred on opening night by the sight of the stage manager's feet beneath one of the backcloths, and it was not improved by his sub-sequent appearance in full figure before the audience, dragging along three pieces of scenery!

Critical complaints persisted during the theatre's salad days, but so did its determination. Its initially unsteady control ex-tended to a number of production areas: 'dancing houses, flowing backdrops . . . long intervals with no one on stage . . . tasteless rose-red columns in an enormous yellowish marble hall, and the usual unfortunate bolt of lightning that kills the hero, but which in this case is represented by a kind of kite trailing a slow train of sparks after it' were, for example, only some of the problems besetting a performance of Mozart's *Don*

[1] T. Blanc, *Christiania Theaters historie 1827–77*, p. 109.

135

Giovanni staged, despite popular opposition to the opera's 'frivolity', in 1838.[2] Such production difficulties seem hardly surprising, however, when viewed in the light of the staggering number of productions mounted by the theatre in order to draw audiences in a city of no more than 30–40,000 inhabitants. During its first season, Christiania Theatre presented 101 performances of no fewer than sixty different plays (including short plays and afterpieces) in the course of an eight-month period. French drama, mainly Scribean, predominated with thirty plays; Denmark came next with eighteen plays; Germany was represented by ten pieces; and Norwegian writing accounted for two new plays. The strong popular predilection, here as elsewhere in Europe, for the elaborate pictorialism and evocative local colour of 'Walter Scott romanticism' on the stage is reflected in many of the works chosen for this repertory. Henrik Wergeland's *singspiel Campbellerne/The Campbells*, the second of the two Norwegian pieces acted during the first season, made an obvious bid to appeal to this taste for the recreation of past ages and exotic customs and places in the romantic theatre—a taste slow to disappear in Norway and strongly felt in the early plays of Ibsen and Bjørnson as well. The first act of Wergeland's work featured an exotic East Indian environment, further enriched by orientally flavoured music and an intermezzo of bayadère dancing. In contrast, the second act carried the audience to a Scottish village whose ethnographic appeal was enhanced by effects such as the appearance in a closing tableau of 'a number of Campbell clansmen in national costumes'.

In productions of this kind, in which scenery and costuming played primary rôles in the action, the figure of the stage designer obviously occupied a key position. Troels Lund, Christiania Theatre's first designer, was a painter and scenotechnical expert of cosmopolitan format and training, solidly grounded in the methods of such masters as Sanquirico and Cicéri. As might be expected, his first duty was to furnish the new Norwegian playhouse with a dozen stock utility sets, ranging from a mountainous region, a wood, a garden, and a street to 'rooms suitable for ordinary comedies not requiring

[2] Øyvind Anker, *Den danske teatermaleren Troels Lund og Christiania Theater*, pp. 46–7.

any special elegance'[3]—a selection constituting the theatre's basic supply of reusable décors, to be supplemented by whatever new additions might be required from time to time. Of particular interest is the fact that the far-sighted Lund included a closed box set with a ceiling in his initial stock of settings, many of which were still to be seen by Ibsen and Bjørnson when they first attended the theatre in Christiania. Although Lund's active association with Christiania Theatre ended in 1838, his influence provided the basis for a continuing tradition of Norwegian stage design carried on in turn by his disciple and successor P. F. C. Wergmann, who later collaborated with Ibsen, and by Wergmann's pupil Wilhelm Krogh.

Christiania Theatre's early years were coloured by the heated ideological struggle that was taking shape between ardent Norwegian nationalists, led by the fiery poet Henrik Wergeland, and believers in the higher standard of Danish acting and writing, eloquently championed by J. S. Welhaven. At first, little of a practical kind seemed to result from this clash. Danish traditions continued to dominate the theatre, and in terms of drama little of significance was written by Norwegian playwrights. Although a number of original plays were submitted to Christiania Theatre, few new works were performed and even fewer achieved success. Indicative of the general situation is the fact that when Ibsen's first play, *Catiline,* appeared in print in 1850 under the pseudonym Brynjulf Bjarme, it was the first Norwegian drama to be published in seven years.

Around mid-century, however, the tide of nationalist feeling was again rising, and important changes began to take place in Norwegian theatre. On 2 January 1850 the idealistic Ole Bull launched the first professional Norwegian theatre in Bergen with a production of Holberg's *The Weathercock,* in which Johannes Brun, an outstanding comic actor destined to become Norway's first star, sparkled as the roguish servant Henrik. In the same year, Christiania Theatre accepted its first Norwegian actresses, Gyda Klingenberg and Laura Svendsen—who as Laura Gundersen would become one of the century's first celebrated Ibsen stars as well as one of the most prominent exponents of the new realism in acting. In 1852, the capital moved in the

[3] Letter from Christiania Theatre dated 26 May 1837, quoted *ibid.,* p. 33.

direction taken by Bergen with the establishment of a new theatre staffed by Norwegian performers, known during most of its ten-year existence as Christiania Norske Teater and managed by Ibsen from 1857 until its disappearance in 1862. With its fostering of playhouses, performers, and audiences receptive to native writing, the quickening of Norwegian theatre culture during this period set the stage for the first, crucial phase in the careers of Henrik Ibsen (1828–1906) and his enormously influential contemporary Bjørnstjerne Bjørnson (1832–1910).

Catiline, Ibsen's first play, was politely refused as unsuited to performance when he submitted it to Christiania Theatre, and it had to wait until 1881 for its Scandinavian première, staged by the pioneering Swedish director Ludvig Josephson at his famous Nya teatern in Stockholm. By this time, both tastes and techniques had altered drastically in the direction of greater verisimilitude, and the play proved no success. Nevertheless, Ibsen never lost his personal affection for this youthful work which, as he declared in his preface to the revised edition of 1875, touches on themes that were to recur again and again in his maturer writing: 'the clash of ability and aspirations, of will and probability, at once the tragedy and comedy of mankind and of the individual'. Set in an atmosphere of prevailing darkness (regarded by Ibsen as the unconscious result of the fact that he wrote the play only at night) *Catiline* embodies many of the most characteristic ingredients of the romantic theatre: effectively remote, exotic settings, given an added dash of visual interest by being seen in the sinister gloom of night or by atmospheric moonlight, picturesque tableaux, the passionate portrayal of strong emotions, and a liberal seasoning of the mysterious and the supernatural. The action is seen against the background of a shifting scenic panorama that moves from an evening view of 'a road near Rome' where 'the towers and walls of the city loom up in the background' to the oppressive darkness of a Vestal temple and 'a subterranean vault' in which 'a lamp burns faintly' and, finally, to the threatening landscape of 'Catiline's camp in wooded country. His tent is visible on the right, with an ancient oak tree to one side. It is night. The moon breaks through the clouds intermittently. A campfire is burning outside the tent and there are several more among the trees in the background'. In subject matter and in technique, *Catiline* is obviously coloured by Ibsen's absorbtion in the passionate world of romantic drama, particularly as it was epitomized in the work of Oehlenschläger, one of the very few dramatists for whom he expressed profound admiration. Catiline, a rebellious sturm-und-dranger surrounded by a corrupt, deceitful and self-seeking society, is on the one hand a man of generosity and vision who dreams of restoring the glory of Rome, and on the other a doomed, tormented soul trapped as much by his own tainted past as by the deceptions of the world in which he moves. His ultimate fate is thus inevitably a tragic one. As his past gradually comes to life during the course of the play, in a retributive pattern that will recur many times in Ibsen's later work, it merges with the present to become an ineluctable destiny that crushes his heroic aspirations.

Moved by a spirit far less intense, *Kjæmpehøjen/The Warrior's Barrow*, Ibsen's next play, reflected a different facet of the romantic ambience in its preoccupation with national themes. Written during the period of his stay in Christiania from 1850 to 1852, Ibsen's one-act poetic drama was his first produced play, staged at Christiania Theatre on 26 September 1850, with Laura Gundersen as Blanka, the Southern girl who returns as a conciliatory spirit to the cold but vigorous environment of the Viking chieftain Gandalf to

> Plant Southern flowers there in the pine trees' haunt
> And spread the light of truth throughout the North!

The successful performance of *The Warrior's Barrow* earned the twenty-two-year-old playwright a free pass to the theatre and gave him his first real opportunity to study live theatre by watching a variety of plays that constituted a representative cross-section of the romantic repertory. His reactions to this exposure are recorded in a number of articles and reviews which afford a useful insight into his attitude toward the theatre and culture of his country.

The prevailing mood in the Norway of the early fifties was optimistic nationalism. Swept along in this atmosphere of ardent patriotic aspiration, Ibsen called for the creation of a distinctly Norwegian culture and for the infusion of a national spirit into Norway's theatrical art. This spirit must not, he emphasized, be artificially superimposed on the drama, nor should it consist in the 'tawdry' depiction of happy people in folk costumes. For Ibsen, the truly national author is one who evolves a suitable metaphor to express in concrete fashion 'those undertones which ring out to us from mountain and valley, from meadow and shore, and, above all, from our inner souls'.[4] Side by side with this concern, and echoing the Heibergian principle of aesthetic idealism, is the continual insistence in Ibsen's criticism upon the formal requirement, the necessity for the artist to 'distinguish between the demands of reality and those of art'. To the young Ibsen the fundamental syntax of the theatre was poetic and, as such, drama demanded aesthetic distancing from the banalities of reality. For example, in comparing the relative merits of the contemporary French and German plays performed in Christiania—'Scribe and Co.'s sugar candy dramas' with their sharply focused but schematically one-sided characterization, as opposed to the 'more solid German fare' with its heavy elaboration 'in extenso of character and situation'—he concludes that the German playwright who aims at achieving verifiable reality at the expense of artifice in fact defeats his own purpose. The difference between the German and French modes of drama is, Ibsen declares, the difference between 'a *tableau vivant* and a painting: in the former, figures present themselves in their natural contours and natural colours; in the latter, on the other hand, they only *appear* so to us—which is, however, the only right way. For in the realm of art, reality pure and simple has no place; illusion, on the contrary, *has*'.[5]

Ibsen's initiation into the practicalities of the theatre, during his terms as a stage director in Bergen and later in Christiania, did nothing to alter his view of art as a heightened representation of the ideal. 'People crave only what reality has to offer, neither more nor less', he observed with some bitterness. 'The notion that art should uplift is one that few are able to admit'[6]—

---

[4] Quoted in *The Oxford Ibsen*, ed. James Walter McFarlane, I, pp. 591–2.
[5] Quoted *ibid.*, pp. 600–3.
[6] Quoted in Michael Meyer, *Henrik Ibsen: The Making of a Dramatist 1828–1864* (London, 1967), p. 168.

yet the evaluation of art as a mere reproduction of reality was, to the young Ibsen, utterly absurd. Characteristic in this respect is the tribute which he paid to Vilhelm Wiehe, Christiania Theatre's leading romantic actor during the fifties, for his 'inspired striving, not for crass reality, but for truth, that loftier, symbolic representation of life which is the only thing artistically worth fighting for, but which is nonetheless acknowledged by so few'.[7]

At the invitation of Ole Bull, Ibsen assumed the position of playwright-in-residence at Bergen's Norske Teater, with the obligation of writing a new play for performance each year on the theatre's birthday, in the fall of 1851. At the end of the season he was also offered the job of stage director and was given a travel grant for a three-month visit to Copenhagen and Dresden for the purpose of acquiring, as his contract stated, 'such knowledge and experience as will enable him to assume the position of *Instructeur* at the theatre, which embraces not only the instruction of the actors and actresses, but also the management of everything pertaining to the equipment and properties of the stage, the costumes of the players, etc.'[8] A letter from the Bergen management to J. L. Heiberg, the august head of the Danish Royal Theatre, acquired for Ibsen a free pass and backstage admittance to the playhouse on Kongens Nytorv during the most luminous period in its history. The redoubtable playwright-director-historian Thomas Overskou acted as cicerone for 'the little, hard-bitten Norwegian with the watchful eyes', and Heiberg accorded the guest a cordial reception. The plays and productions that Ibsen saw during his stay in Copenhagen had an immeasurable impact on his future development. During the period between April 20 and June 6 the Royal Theatre repertory offered him a range from Scribe to Shakespeare (*King Lear, Romeo and Juliet, As You Like It, Hamlet*) and from Holberg (four comedies) and Oehlenschläger (*Hakon Jarl*) to Heiberg (two vaudevilles) and Hertz (*King René's Daughter*). In addition, he saw productions at the Christiansborg court theatre and at Casino, whose 'house dramatist', Hans Christian Andersen, recommended the subtle blend of fantasy and realism in the fairy-tale comedies of

[7] *Illustreret Nyhedsblad,* 13 December 1857.
[8] Bent Lorentzen, *Det første norske teater,* p. 102.

Ferdinand Raimund to the young director's attention. In the Royal Theatre performances, Ibsen was dazzled by one of the finest acting companies on the Continent, headed by Johanne Luise Heiberg herself and bringing together the comic talents of Phister and Rosenkilde, the heroic grandeur of Anna and N. P. Nielsen and the romantic lyricism of Michael Wiehe, whom Ibsen remembered years later as the finest actor he had ever seen ('When I recall his performances, it is as though I were walking through a gallery filled with ancient statues. Pure plastique! Pure beauty!').[9] In a very different vein, Ibsen watched Frederik Høedt's realistically toned *Hamlet*, in which Fru Heiberg was Ophelia, but he preferred to see this domesticized attack applied to Scribe. All in all, there seems little doubt that the Royal Theatre in Copenhagen, rather than Dresden's Court Theatre, which he subsequently visited and studied, became the model for Ibsen's management of the Bergen Theatre. Play scripts, musical scores and works on costuming were procured in Copenhagen for use in his new capacity, and the Heibergian taste had a distinct effect on his choice of repertory. Critics have made much of the fact that Ibsen encountered Herman Hettner's newly published *Das moderne Drama,* possibly in Copenhagen rather than in Dresden, and that this work, with its emphasis on the dynamics of character and psychology as the true motivational force in great drama, synthesizes ideas of obvious relevance to the development of Ibsen's drama. Nevertheless, over-emphasis of these lines of theoretical influence should not lead one to underestimate the tangible and immediate impact of Heiberg's personality and Fru Heiberg's penetrating psychological rôle interpretations on Ibsen's growth. Heiberg's refusal of Ibsen's early saga drama *Hærmændene paa Helgeland/The Vikings of Helgeland* in 1858 did not deter the dramatist from commemorating the death of the great Danish cultural ambassador with a moving panegyric to the 'giant' who brought light into the land. For Fru Heiberg's art, whose emphasis on the tension of contradictions within a personality lent a fascinating spiritual depth to every rôle she played, Ibsen reserved the ultimate tribute of his impressive 'Rhymed Letter':

142   [9] Quoted in Meyer, p. 113.

. . . She is like a legend that trembles
Behind the veil enfolding it;
She is like a vision that rises and hovers
Along a secret riddle-path.

The period at the beginning of the 1850s when Ibsen
assumed his directorial duties at Bergen was a transitional era in
the theatre, representing a preparatory prelude to the emergence
of naturalism, with its new principles of *mise-en-scène*, toward
the close of the century. In spite of an increasing concern at
mid-century with the ideal of ensemble acting, however, the
modern conception of a director as the guiding artistic force,
coordinating all aspects of a performance and integrating them
into a unified whole, was not fully formed until the early
1880s. Around 1850, the practical influence of the director was
still governed by the principles and aesthetics of a theatrical
system based on relatively few rehearsals, the observance of
recognized rules and conventions for stage positioning and the
preservation of the individual actor's independence in preparing his rôle. Nor were directorial responsibilities necessarily
vested in one person. In Bergen, the task was typically divided
into two principal parts, stage direction, which was assigned to
Ibsen, and rôle direction, which was the province of Herman
Laading, a well-educated schoolmaster with a strong background in drama. In establishing this kind of division, the
Bergen Theatre was in fact adhering to a pattern proposed by
shrewd theatre men like Heinrich Laube in Germany. The
practical advantage of the scheme was, as a circular from the
management stressed, that 'with two people now sharing the
task of instruction, it is possible to allocate some time to the
general education of the actors and actresses of the company'[10]
—a significant aspect, it would seem, in the development of
artistic standards for a green company such as this one.

Specific regulations demarcated the areas of responsibility
for the two directors at Bergen. Laading's duties of preparatory
play analysis and actor instruction at the initial reading rehearsals were intended: '(1) to remove all obstacles to a rapid
and satisfactory stage rehearsal, both in regard to language and
clarification of vocabulary; (2) to give the players such historical explanation as is necessary, and ensure a correct in-

[10] See Lorentzen, p. 105.

143

terpretation of their rôles; (3) to see that their diction is correct; and (4) to ensure that the players memorize their parts carefully and accurately enough for them to appear at the first stage rehearsal without books or papers'.[11]

As the latter rule, which Ibsen enthusiastically applauded, clearly suggests, the naturalistic concept of an integrated and balanced ensemble, gradually established during the course of numerous stage rehearsals, was not a consideration here. While the rôle director was free to attend stage rehearsals 'in order that—within the limits of his function—he may supervise the observance of the prescriptions he has given to the actors', rôle interpretation and *mise-en-scène* were clearly distinct. As stage director Ibsen was expected: '(1) to organize the scenic arrangements, including the costumes and scenery, of each play, and generally to direct it (groupings, entrances, exits and poses, etc.); (2) to watch the mime and gestures of each player, to ensure that the physical expression is appropriate to the words and the character of the part; and (3) to achieve the necessary coordination and show each of the performers which part, in terms of his various scenes, he is to play in the overall action'.[12] In order for this division of labour to function smoothly, the two directors were urged to reach mutual agreement about casting and rôle interpretation; where differences of opinion arose, the theatre management was to be consulted. In fact, however, after some initial difficulties the collaboration was a harmonious one. Ibsen, who eventually also assumed the supervisory task of stage managing each night's performance, kept the necessary records of sets, floor plans, props and other items needed for each play in a notebook modelled directly on those he had seen in use at the Royal Theatre in Copenhagen. Although his records, preserved in the Theatre Museum in Bergen, also included diagrams of the positions and moves of actors at key moments in the performance, especially when crowd scenes were involved, his contact with actors was limited largely to visual matters. 'There was no question', recalled Lucie Wolf, who acted under Ibsen both in Bergen and in Christiania, 'of his ever giving us instruction as Bjørnson did.'[13]

[11] Quoted *ibid.*, p. 105.
[12] *Ibid.*, p. 106.
[13] Lucie Wolf, *Mine Livserindringer* (Christiania, 1898), pp. 182–3.

Ibsen's preoccupation as a director with the visual effects of setting and costuming and with picturesque patterns of movement and grouping reflects the fundamental character of the romantic theatre as a colourful 'living picture gallery'. The rich pictorial beauty of this style of theatre held a profound fascination for Ibsen the dramatist as well as for Ibsen the director. Although the technical and financial resources of the Bergen Theatre were limited indeed when compared with the Danish or Swedish national theatres, Ibsen's own plays for the Bergen stage are fortified with an ambitious and demanding series of atmospheric stage environments upon which the dramatic action depends. *Sancthansnatten/Midsummer Eve,* a satirical fairy-tale comedy in the Heiberg-Andersen-Raimund vein that was first performed on 2 January 1853, relies on just such colourful and picturesque stage illusion for much of its effect. Moving from an idyllic garden scene in the first act to an atmospherically moonlit forest path leading to the magic Midsummer Hill 'on which the remains of a bonfire periodically flares up' in the following act, Ibsen's play required not only the painting of new scenery but also the accomplishment of such stage legerdemain as the opening up of the magic hill to the sound of 'soft background music', revealing 'a large, brilliantly lit hall' populated by a collection of figures from the fantastic world of Andersen's tales (specifically 'Elves' Hill') and Bournonville's ballets. 'The mountain king sits on a high throne in the background. Elves and mountain fairies dance around him', reads the description of this transformation, brought about by a cunning goblin who bears a strong family resemblance to Shakespeare's Puck. Revolving around the ironic opposition of contrasting pairs of poetically visionary and prosaically commonplace lovers, who predictably realign themselves under the influence of the heady events of a midsummer's night, Ibsen's comedy ultimately pleased neither the Bergen audience nor its own author. It closed after two performances, and Ibsen subsequently refused to include it in his collected works.

Although Ibsen's next Bergen play, a revised version of *The Warrior's Barrow* acted on the theatre's birthday in 1854, represented a much tamer and more static use of the stage, most of the plays written by him during the next ten years reflect a restless experimentation not only with dramatic form but also with the potentialities of theatrical expression. All, with the exception of *Love's Comedy* (1862), are set against a colourful background of national history and folklore. *Fru Inger til Østeraad/Lady Inger of Østeraad,* the first Ibsen play written entirely in prose, was unsuccessful in Bergen in 1855 and failed again when its author directed it at Christiania Norske Teater in 1859. However, the production of the revised version of this intense drama of passion at Christiania Theatre in 1875, directed by Ludvig Josephson and starring Laura Gundersen as Lady Inger, and its triumphant première at Dramaten two years later, with Elise Hwasser in the title rôle, showed the play to be a milestone in Ibsen's dramaturgy. Despite its Scribean net of intrigue, it rises to forceful tragic proportions in the depiction of the Lady Macbeth-like character of Lady Inger, the strong motive power behind the action. Inherent in the conception is the image of an actress like Fru Heiberg. The tension of opposites and contradictions in Lady Inger's personality, ecstatic with the notion of restoring national independence yet tortured with doubts about her own ability to live up to her calling, generates a powerful field of dramatic intensity reminiscent, as critics have realized, of Shakespeare and Schiller. Above all, however, this play affirms Ibsen's vivid theatrical imagination and his ability to exploit the resources of the theatre to underscore theme and mood. Set in the Norway of 1528 but eschewing historical exactitude, *Lady Inger* is steeped in an atmosphere of gloom and darkness. Its sombre gothic interiors are dimly accented by moonlight and the sculptural light from a fireplace (as in Act I) or (in Act V) by a few flickering candles that punctuate the tragic blackness. Ibsen's awareness of the importance of setting, lighting and costuming as dramatic values— large-scale metaphors capable of concretizing the drama's theme and mood—was a significant by-product of his early theatrical apprenticeship. Far from being hampered, as critics have sometimes maintained, by the so-called 'artificiality' and 'unreality' of the theatrical context in which he found himself, Ibsen—who during this period regarded a measure of abstraction as a *sine qua non* of theatrical art—exploited the flamboyantly pictorial and totally theatricalized theatre of the romantic era to the fullest, in an effort to give an extra dimen-

146

sion of dramatic suggestiveness to the performance of his plays. On the other hand, to persist in viewing Ibsen as a single-handed reformer who 'overcame the false perspective' of flat wings in the benighted Scandinavian theatre and 'introduced three-dimensional scenery with walls and solid properties,[14] suggests an almost wilful disregard of the technical and stylistic evolution of the theatre in Scandinavia during the first half of the nineteenth century.

The theatre in Bergen seems to have bent every effort to achieve the kind of colourful picturesqueness required by Ibsen's next play, *The Feast at Solhaug* (1856), a lyrical drama set in the fourteenth century and utilizing an intricate musical weave of folksong patterns similar (though Ibsen furiously denied the fact) to that introduced by Hertz in *Svend Dyring's House*. Produced with new sets and costumes designed by its author-director, *The Feast at Solhaug* became Ibsen's first—and only—resoundingly popular success in Bergen. It was also the first of his plays to be acted outside Norway, first at Dramaten in 1857 and later by Casino in 1861. The framework of this saga drama was, declares Ibsen in his preface to the second edition of 1883, 'the fateful feast [which] . . . became the background against which the action stood in relief, and informed the whole picture with the general atmosphere I had intended'. Margit, who has deceived her true love to marry the rich but weak-willed Bengt, Master of Solhaug, loses her wandering knight Gudmund to her vivacious sister Signe, but the play ends on a conciliatory note well suited to win the applause of the Bergen audience. 'Done supremely well and with rare feeling, it was received in the same way', continues the delighted playwright, who not only took several curtain calls but was also serenaded by the orchestra and his public after the gala opening. Ibsen's effort to follow up this triumph with another lyrical ballad drama, *Olaf Liljekrans,* miscarried the following year, and this medieval tale of romantic complications was taken off the repertory after two performances. Nevertheless, an interesting series of coloured drawings in Ibsen's hand, depicting eight of the characters in his folktale romance attired in picturesque national costumes, testifies vividly to the pictorial consciousness and historical flavour

[14] *E.g.,* P. F. D. Tennant, *Ibsen's Dramatic Technique,* p. 64 *et passim.*

147

29. Henrik Ibsen's own sketches of two characters in his folktale drama *Olaf Liljekrans*, staged by him in Bergen in 1857

that were fundamental to the young dramatist's last Bergen play (Plate 29).

Following the 1856–57 season Ibsen left Bergen to take up a new position in the capital as 'stage instructor and artistic director' at Christiania Norske Teater, the decidedly un-prestigious rival of the 'Danish' theatre on the Bank Square. Located in an unfashionable street and catering mainly for a working-class audience, this playhouse had an artistic reputa-tion which was none too high (Laura Gundersen stated flatly that she would rather beg in the gutter than act there!) and Ibsen's five-year directorship ended with the theatre's financial collapse in 1862. His years there also mark his longest period of inactivity as a dramatist. Between *The Vikings of Helgeland*, which he himself directed in November 1858, and *Love's Comedy*, his vigorous satire on the institution of marriage which was written in 1862 but not acted until Josephson's production at Christiania Theatre in 1873, Ibsen wrote nothing for the stage.

Inspired initially by his absorbtion in the Icelandic sagas, Ibsen's *Vikings of Helgeland* is a conscious attempt to transfer to the stage some of the heroic grandeur and remote starkness of the saga era. Centring on the Medea-like valkyrie Hjørdis and her ruthless pursuit of vengeance, the play's larger-than-life action and elemental characters gradually build up a powerful sense of nemesis, of the inescapable burden of past errors upon the present. Costumes, setting, and lighting further accentuate the underlying vision and atmosphere of a stark, rough Viking age. Moving from a rocky, wintry coastal landscape with a turbulent sea in the background in the opening act, to a banquet hall interior, at first dimly illuminated by a log fire burning on a stone hearth in the centre of the floor, and then (in Act III) lit by daylight, the play returns in the final act to the barren shore. This coast, lit by the sombre glow of torches, a log fire, and the moon 'occasionally seen through dark and ragged storm clouds', is the stern arena for the final tragic events that end with a vision of black horses and the strong-willed Hjørdis riding through the sky: 'the last ride of the dead on their way to Valhalla'. Bold contrasts in the colour and texture of the costumes—described in such unusual detail in the stage direc-tions because Ibsen had hoped to have the play produced at

149

Christiania Theatre rather than under his own supervision at the Norske Teater—lent added force to the visual impact and resonant saga tone of the drama.

Similarly vivid and boldly contrasting stage pictures high-lighted *The Pretenders,* the last Ibsen play to draw upon the colourful pageantry of Norwegian history for its subject matter. Dominated by the towering figures of the two pre-tenders to Norway's throne, Haakon, the unswerving believer in his own heroic destiny and in his strength to carry out his great kingly thought, and the vacillating and reflective Skule, 'God's stepchild on earth', this sweeping five-act historical drama stands in a class by itself among Ibsen's early plays. It was the first of his plays to gain a permanent place in the repertory of the Scandinavian theatre, and its fascinating pro-duction history, bounded by the two celebrated Royal Theatre productions by Fru Heiberg in 1871 and by Edward Gordon Craig in 1926, would in itself form an eloquent chronicle of changing theatrical tastes and styles. The first production of this monumental dramatization of the irresistible power of a great calling, staged by Ibsen himself at Christiania Theatre—where he functioned as artistic consultant—on 17 January 1864, was an immediate success. P. F. Wergmann painted new décors for the production, and the services of a local anti-quarian were secured in order to endow it with an authentic thirteenth-century flavour. Hence Wergmann's designs not only endeavoured to articulate the dramatic and atmospheric values of the play's multiple environments, but also sought to lend them the historical 'appropriateness' and 'authenticity' so dear to the nineteenth-century theatre everywhere. His extant sketch for the last scene of the play, the moonlit convent courtyard at Elgesæter where Skule and his son seek their last refuge, depicts a heavy gate and walls upstage, a cloisters formed of romanesque arches and a correspondingly gothic chapel with lighted windows, which the victorious Haakon enters to be crowned. Wergmann's impressive design for this scene (Plate 30) and his comparable sketch for the courtyard at Nidaros in Andreas Munch's verse tragedy *Hertug Skule/ Duke Skule* (Plate 31) exemplify the vivid and effective pictorial-ism that characterized the theatre in which Ibsen functioned actively until he was thirty-six.

The Pretenders was the last play that Ibsen ever directed, and its production marks the end of his active involvement in the practical theatre. Nevertheless, countless letters to those engaged in producing his plays, dealing with casting, rôle interpretation and even specific staging suggestions, demonstrate that he never lost touch with the living theatre and wrote with concrete performance conditions in mind. The intimate knowledge of the stage and its conventions which he gleaned from his early experiences as a director sharpened his extraordinary sensitivity to the poetry of environment in the theatre. From a purely practical standpoint, these experiences enabled him to develop his truly remarkable ability to write a carefully visualized, highly charged physical *mise-en-scène* into his plays, aimed at concretizing the psychological states and spiritual conditions of his characters as well as at creating a specific mood to enhance and strengthen the spiritual action. Costumes, settings, props and lighting remained throughout his career the syntax of his dramatic poetry.

After leaving Norway in April 1864—and he would not return permanently for twenty-seven years—Ibsen entered a new phase in his development. Both *Brand* and *Peer Gynt,* the first two plays which he wrote after his departure, were conceived as dramatic poems, designed initially for a reading public. Ibsen's burning indictment of the half-hearted spirit of weakness and compromise in *Brand* created a veritable sensation throughout Scandinavia when the play was first published in 1866: 'every receptive and unblunted mind felt, on closing the book, a penetrating, nay an overwhelming impression of having stood face to face with a great and indignant genius', wrote Georg Brandes.[15] *Peer Gynt,* on the other hand, was greeted with considerable hostility when it appeared the following year, and was regarded as a work whose blend of light-hearted fantasy and biting satire lacked any ideal element and, as such, any poetic validity.

It remained, however, for the pioneering Swedish director Ludvig Josephson to uncover the startling theatrical potential within these monumental reading dramas. Josephson enthusiastically accepted Ibsen's proposal to mount a somewhat

[15] *Brand,* translated with an introduction by Michael Meyer (London, 1967), p. 13.

30. Nineteenth-century Norwegian settings: P. F. Wergmann's
design for the Convent courtyard at Elgesæter in Ibsen's
The Pretenders, staged by the playwright himself in
Christiania in 1864

shortened stage version of *Peer Gynt,* with new music composed by Edvard Grieg (who, as we know, found it 'a dread-
fully intractable subject') and the world première of the play
took place at Christiania Theatre on 24 February 1876 under
Josephson's direction. The lavishly expensive production
proved an unprecedented success for Christiania Theatre as
well as a highpoint among the many significant Ibsen performances staged during Josephson's enlightened leadership of
the playhouse during the mid-1870s. A run of thirty-seven
performances of the play was interrupted only because of the
fire which partially gutted the theatre in 1877, bringing with it
the end of Josephson's tenure there. In spite of cuts, *Peer Gynt*
lasted four-and-three-quarter hours in this flamboyantly colour-

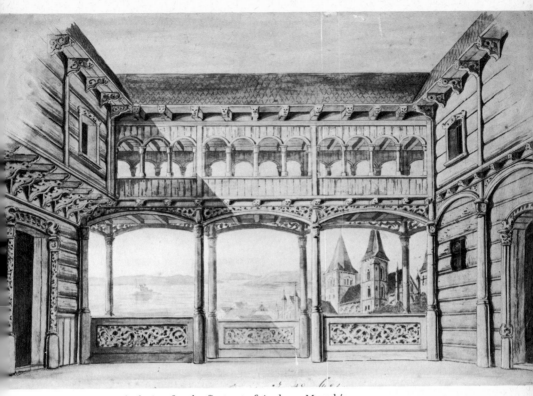

31. Wergmann's design for the first act of Andreas Munch's
Duke Skule

ful production that stretched the theatre's resources to the limit
and which pressed into service not only its own capable
designers, Olaf Jørgensen and Wilhelm Krogh, but also a group
of painters that included the young Fritz Thaulow, to create a
pictorial background rich in local colour and ethnographic
romance. Henrik Klausen was a lyrical and sprightly Peer in a
performance in which—despite the humorously trollish Mountain King of Johannes Brun—the lyrical generally far out-
weighed the satirical. Peer is the liar and cheat who goes round
about, but in Josephson's production he was also the dreamer
of dreams, the realization of which was the dream vision of
Solveig that appeared to him as he slumbered in the desert in
the fourth act. (For the less literal and more simplified and

153

deromanticized approach that such a work seems actually to demand, *Peer Gynt*, like Strindberg's later dream plays, would have to wait until the modern period.)

Although Josephson had told Ibsen of his interest in *Brand* at any early point, it was not until 24 March 1885 that this drama received its first stage production, directed by Josephson at his influential Nya teatern in Stockholm in a marathon performance that lasted six-and-a-half hours. Once again, the experiment was a notable success that crowned Josephson's remarkable management of this theatre—though it set no example, and Ibsen's play would have to wait another ten years after its world première before any producer again attempted the feat of performing it. In Josephson's production, Emil Hillberg's rendering of Ibsen's titanic superman-priest depended on an imposing monumentality and unbending sublimity that ran the risk of unsympathetic indifference. 'The danger inherent in portraying the sublime', commented one reviewer, 'is that it easily becomes uninteresting. Superiority leads to indifference toward human interest, the bond between the hero and humanity bursts, and Ibsen has guarded against this by giving his hero the reformatory zeal and human warmth' that Hillberg's idealized Brand lacked.[16]

By this time, however, changing tastes had already begun to transform the entire tone and fabric of the European theatre, as naturalism, with its accompanying emphasis on contemporaneity, became the dominant mode. Angered by the criticism of *Peer Gynt,* Ibsen determined to move with the times: 'If I am no poet, then I shall try my luck as a photographer. . . . One by one I shall come to grips with my contemporaries in the North', he wrote to Bjørnson from Rome (9 December 1867). *The League of Youth* (1869) pointed the new direction, and with the completion of the behemoth *Kejser og Galilæer/Emperor and Galilean,* depicting the clash of paganism and Christianity in fourth-century Byzantium, in 1873, Ibsen's 'poetic' period ended. During the period that followed, his transformation of the apparently neutral language and settings of the realistic mode created a new kind of dramatic poetry that redefined the nature of drama itself.

[16] Hellen Lindgren in *Ny ill. tidning* (25 May 1885), quoted in Georg Nordensvan, *Svensk teater och svenska skådespelare,* II, p. 361.

The dramatist who in the first instance contributed most significantly to preparing the way for these new trends in Norwegian drama and theatre was, however, not Ibsen but Bjørnstjerne Bjørnson, the playwright who, next to Ibsen and Strindberg, was most responsible for the rise of Scandinavian drama to world prominence during the late nineteenth century. Bjørnson, a popular leader, lecturer, journalist, novelist, director, and theatre manager as well as a dramatist, began his luminous career—as Ibsen did—steeped in the tradition of Nordic romanticism and historicism at mid-century. His first play, *Mellem slagene/Between the Battles,* a one-acter set in a moment of peace during a bloody twelfth-century civil war, was successfully produced at Christiania Theatre in 1857. The two saga plays which followed, *Halte-Hulda/Limping Hulda* (1858) and *Kong Sverre* (staged by Ibsen at Christiania Norske Teater in 1861), again reflected the popular interest in history and folklore and in national figures and landscapes. Their impact was not nearly as great, however, as that created by the sweeping verse trilogy *Sigurd Slembe/Sigurd the Bastard* (1862), a brilliant pilgrimage drama which won a legion of admirers throughout Scandinavia, including Ibsen, and which made its mark upon the theme and characterizations of *The Pretenders.*

It was, however, his plays on contemporary themes which earned him a wider reputation as a dramatist, established by the overwhelmingly successful problem play *The Newly Married,* which was performed simultaneously in Copenhagen, Stockholm and Christiania in 1865. This play, whose subject is a young married couple's period of adjustment, emphasized, interestingly enough, not the Ibsenian liberation of the woman but rather the dilemma of the man, who is treated, as Bjørnson expressed it in a phrase that was to catch on, like a doll. Bjørnson, who throughout his career as a director as well as a dramatist was a step ahead of Ibsen in the sense that he was more directly attuned to contemporary cultural and artistic trends, had already begun in his theatre criticism from the period 1854–60 to voice the demand for a drama more responsive to contemporary modes of thought. Pointing to Musset, Augier, and Dumas *fils* as better models than Scribe, he called for a re-evaluation of the goals of the contemporary

155

theatre. 'People are delving more deeply into human nature from every angle, in science as well as in art,' he insisted.[17] 'We investigate each minutest trait, we dissect and analyse . . . the smallest flower, the least insect. . . . And in art this current of naturalism reveals itself in theatrical terms in a strong demand for individualization,' he added in this 1855 article, which touches a theme to be repeated frequently and even more forcefully by such leading Scandinavian spokesmen for modernism as Georg and Edvard Brandes. For Bjørnson as for this whole new generation of writers and critics, the enemy was not only romanticism, with its emphasis upon beauty and ideality, but also the Scribean well-made play, with its involved complications, startling reversals, and improbable distortions of psychology. Instead, Bjørnson proposed to introduce 'truth' into the theatre, through a drama in which the characters 'are no longer marionettes moved by invisible strings but human beings, men and women with the pain of life on their faces'.[18]

Bjørnson's energetic campaign to chart new courses in the theatre bore fruit not only in his criticism and playwriting but also in his contributions to the practical theatre. His earliest experience as a stage director was gained in Bergen, where he succeeded Ibsen, between 1857 and 1859. However, his tenure as artistic manager and stage director at Christiania Theatre during a two-and-a-half year period from 1865 to 1867 was an era of far greater importance in the history of the Norwegian stage. On the one hand, he presented his Christiania audiences with an impressive range of contemporary Danish and Norwegian drama (including Ibsen's *The Feast at Solhaug* and *The Pretenders* and his own *Sigurd the Bastard, Limping Hulda, The Newly Married,* and *Maria Stuart*) and a French repertory that reached from Molière to Musset. In addition, he also staged several of Shakespeare's plays, who until then had occupied a very inconspicuous place in the Norwegian repertory. As a director Bjørnson possessed a remarkable ability to inspire and influence his actors, and hence the overall performance, with his ideas. 'He has', commented Clemens Petersen, 'an almost incredible, almost magical ability, even during a walk down the street, to paint a character in such a way that it ends up

[17] *Morgenbladet,* 9 December 1855.
[18] Quoted in Meyer, p. 140.

walking along right beside you'.[19] His efforts at Christiania Theatre heralded, therefore, the future emergence of the dominant figure of the director in the theatre. His Shakespearian productions also offered an opportunity for him to experiment with new theatrical techniques. In *A Midsummer Night's Dream,* which he mounted in April 1865 in Oehlenschläger's translation and with music by Mendelssohn, he boldly introduced a somewhat baffled Christiania public to the radically simplified concept of Shakespearian production, championed by Tieck. By drastically reducing the heavy pictorial illusionism and multiple scene-changes that normally accompanied a performance of Shakespeare in Scandinavia—or in England—at this time, Bjørnson's method allowed, as he maintained, 'the text to speak with its own power, neither submerged by inventiveness nor pushed aside by movable scenery'. For those who objected to the paucity of visual and pictorial effects in the production, he had a ready reply: 'It takes a truly petty soul to sit and worry about the moon while Shakespeare speaks to us through Oehlenschläger's mouth and Mendelssohn adds the music'.[20]

As a playwright, however, Bjørnson remained firmly committed to the illusionistic, representational theatre. His attempt to bring 'truth' and life-like 'reality' to bear in *The Newly Married* was continued in *En fallit/A Bankruptcy* and *Redaktøren/The Editor,* plays set in contemporary environments and examining modern problems in an essentially critical spirit. Both were produced for the first time at Stockholm's Nya teatern in early 1875, and *A Bankruptcy,* by far the more effective of the two works, was chosen as the inaugural production of this modern new 1150-seat playhouse on 19 January 1875. 'They were the signal rockets which rose towards the heavens and broke out into salvos whose echoes we have not yet forgotten,' recalled August Strindberg.[21] Dramatic breaches in the hitherto solid romantic tradition, these plays answered Georg Brandes' impassioned demand in 1871 that literature should not embroider on memories of the past—it should enter

---

[19] See Blanc, *Christiania Theaters historie,* p. 195.
[20] *Ibid.,* p. 197.
[21] Quoted in Barrett H. Clark and George Freedley, eds. *A History of Modern Drama* (New York and London, 1947), p. 48.

into the struggles of its times, working actively for new ideas. However, while 'taking up problems for debate' in the Brandes spirit, neither *The Editor,* an attack on the stifling effects of unscrupulous journalism on family life and human happiness, nor *A Bankruptcy,* the story of a wealthy family which is ruined by dishonest commercial practices but which regains its happiness under more modest living conditions, dealt with really explosive issues. The particular strength of *A Bank-ruptcy,* Bjørnson's most popular international success, lies in its creation of a specific and richly detailed milieu, radiating the atmosphere of a particular home in which the characters seem to live a life of their own. Just such a close interaction of character and environment, giving the audience the illusion that they were watching actual episodes taken from life, was to become the basic tenet of the new stage naturalism.

By focusing more outspokenly on character as the victim of its social environment and of the narrow, dogmatic restrictions imposed by society on the individual in the name of truth and morality, Bjørnson, like Ibsen, was drawn into the public controversies and clashes that frequently followed in the wake of the new drama. His two 'women' plays, *Leonarda* (1879), which portrays the noble struggle of a divorced woman to find a place for herself in society, and *En Hanske/A Gauntlet* (1883), an open attack on the double standard of sexual morality in contemporary society that takes for its basic theme the idea that women are judged by other laws than men are, were met with outrage and were denounced by many critics as offensive and immoral. If these plays ultimately failed to come to grips with the questions they raised and were overshadowed in this respect by Ibsen's modern dramas, part of the explanation lies, as many contemporary critics realized, in an unfailingly con-ciliatory and innately optimistic attitude on Bjørnson's part. Ameliorism in Bjørnson's plays tended to rob their conflicts of dramatic intensity and their overly light-hearted conclusions of trenchancy. His energetic and positive outlook did not share Ibsen's profound sense of the disintegration of a whole universe of spiritual and moral values. Nor did he possess his great contemporary's unique gift for transforming the stifling at-mosphere of contemporary prejudices and moral hypocrisy

158 into a metaphor for an all-enshrouding tragic fate.

A Doll's House burst like a bomb on the contemporary scene, sounding, as Halvdan Koht put it, 'the crack of doom on prevailing social ethics'. 'No Doll's House discussions here' read the placard which graced the walls of many Danish homes whenever guests were entertained in the months following the world première of Ibsen's revolutionary play at the Royal Theatre in Copenhagen on 21 December 1879.[22] At once, Ibsen belonged no longer to the Norwegian theatre but to the theatres of the world. In the history of the Scandinavian stage, however, our interest understandably focuses on the rapid evolution of a style of production capable of articulating Ibsen's mature work effectively. During the 1880s Ludvig Josephson was joined by a new generation of naturalistic directors who perfected the new style. August Lindberg, who collaborated frequently with Josephson at Nya teatern, was a celebrated Ibsen actor-director whose series of Ibsen productions includes his pioneering first production of *Ghosts* in Scandinavia in August 1883. Bjørnson's eldest son Bjørn Bjørnson, the first head of Norway's Nationaltheatret introduced the new methods (including electric stage lighting) to the Norwegian capital during his dynamic tenure as actor-director at Christiania Theatre from 1885 to 1891. Above all, the gifted Danish director William Bloch established a naturalistic tradition in the Scandinavian theatre fully comparable to the more widely publicized, 'revolutionary' advances being made elsewhere in Europe. Approaching the colourful and complex history of later Ibsen productions in Scandinavia in a necessarily selective way, however, two of the most notable performances in that history may be taken as representative: the epoch-making world première of *Et dukkehjem/A Doll's House* in 1879 and William Bloch's famous naturalistic production of *En folkefjende/An Enemy of the People* in 1883.

The Royal Theatre première of *A Doll's House* enjoyed what even the dramatist himself regarded as 'unparalleled success' (reflected in the exceptional total of twenty-one performances during the first season) and it established Betty Hennings, the

---

[22] See Frederick and Lise-Lone Marker, 'The First Nora: Notes on the World Première of *A Doll's House*', *Contemporary Approaches to Ibsen*, II, ed. Daniel Haakonsen (Oslo, 1971), pp. 84–100.

world's first Nora, as an actress of international repute. The critical reaction to the play itself in performance did not, as is sometimes assumed, centre either on the question of female rights or on the validity of Nora's accusations in the celebrated discussion scene to which Shaw later attached so much importance. Instead, the burning issues in the ensuing debate became the psychological motivation for Nora's actions, including her abrupt 'spiritual metamorphosis' from songbird to

32. From the world première of Ibsen's *A Doll's House* at the Danish Royal Theatre, 1879: the tarantella scene

new woman, and the dramatic justification for Ibsen's joylessly bleak open (and unchanged) ending. Critical sympathy was almost unanimously on the side of Helmer. Viewing the play as a dramatization of a moral and ethical dilemma, a number of its first reviewers drew a parallel with *Samfundets støtter/The Pillars of Society*, which had had its world première at the Royal Theatre two years before, and compared Nora's moral actions to those of the selfish and unscrupulous Consul Bernick. 'I ask you directly', demanded the most hostile of the critics, 'is there one mother among thousands of mothers, one wife among thousands of wives, who would behave as Nora behaves, who would desert husband, children, and home merely in order to become "a human being"? I answer with conviction: no and again no!'[23]

Much of the difficulty lay in the fact that, as that tough-minded spokesman of modernism Edvard Brandes realized, both the critics and the audience harboured the views and sympathies of Helmer, particularly as he was portrayed in the production by the brilliant Emil Poulsen. Equally at home with the twilight melancholy of Holger Drachmann and the intellectual reality of Ibsen, Poulsen created a gallery of memorable Ibsen portraits that extended from his early Bishop Nikolas in Fru Heiberg's production of *The Pretenders,* through the philistine Bernick and the arrogant Helmer, to a restlessly grieving John Gabriel Borkman (1897). His authoritative and boldly underscored portrayal in *A Doll's House* made the rôle of Helmer far more than the colourless supporting figure it has sometimes become in subsequent productions. 'Every speech displayed understanding, and the irony in his characterization was incomparable', stated the demanding Edvard Brandes, who went so far as to assert that Emil Poulsen alone stood on a level with Ibsen's composition.[24] His acting of Helmer afforded, maintained Vilhelm Topsøe in *Dagbladet* (22 December 1879), 'the right touch of vacillation, half educated, half likeable, a little arrogant, and cleverly ordinary'. And the 'short-sighted, self-satisfied playfulness with his tormented wife, the intensified champagne mood which turns first to indignation and then immediately to vapid jubilation, and at the very end all the

23 M. W. Brun in *Folkets Avis,* 24 December 1879.
24 *Ude og Hjemme,* 4 January 1880.

161

shifting moods of the closing scene, in which he must deliver the cues for Nora's divorce proceedings, were each clear and finely drawn details in his carefully executed overall presentation', added the conservative critic Erik Bøgh, who as the Royal Theatre's play reader flatly rejected *Ghosts* two years later.[25] Brandes was alone, however, in recognizing the character of Helmer for what he is, 'the intellectual aristocrat without intellect, arrogantly conservative partly through conviction and partly through pragmatism, indifferent, but possessing all the opinions of good society. . . . It is he who felt insulted by *The Pillars of Society* and who decried *Leonarda* as scandalous.' Yet Brandes' prediction that the shared philistine sympathy for Helmer would cause the play to fail proved far from accurate.

Whatever ethical or dramaturgical objections were raised by the first reviewers of *A Doll's House,* these were totally overshadowed by their boundless admiration of the production, particularly of the stunning performance given by Betty Hennings as Nora. Her acting of the part was hailed at once as 'a performance which will stand among the theatre's greatest memories'. Her Nora, like Fru Heiberg's Lady Macbeth, seemed to her contemporaries the veritable personification of the dramatist's literary creation. Novelist, actor and critic Herman Bang, in a memorable analysis of her acting style, maintained that she transformed 'even readers to spectators because, after we have but once seen her, she follows us from scene to scene, we see her and not Nora, even as we read. And we do so because we constantly place the stress where Fru Hennings has placed it, because, influenced by her, we hesitate where she hesitates, we close our eyes where she closes them'.[26] Convincing evidence of the format of her success is the telegram sent by the Royal Theatre management to the anxious Dr. Ibsen in Munich on the day following the world première: '*Enormous* success. Interpretation generally excellent. Nora wonderfully created by Madame Hennings; she brings to the part an intelligence, a grace, an art beyond compare. My sincere congratulations.'[27]

[25] *Dagens Nyheder,* 22 December 1879.

[26] Bang's analysis appears in his *Kritiske Studier* (Copenhagen, 1880), pp. 220–8.

[27] Quoted in Robert Neiiendam, *Det kgl. Teaters Historie,* III, p. 65.

At twenty-nine Betty Hennings, whose characterization so profoundly affected not only the reception but also the comprehension of Ibsen's play, was the period's ideal of the charming and graceful ingenue. Her Nora was the embodiment of frivolous youthfulness, unconcerned gaiety and childish caprice, and her attack thus served to direct the principal dramatic emphasis to the first two acts, filled, as *Berlingske Tidende* (22 December) notes, with scenes in which 'the sun-drenched comfort and happiness of the "Doll's House" are depicted, and in which the lark cavorts with her children, decorates the tree, and plays hide-and-seek'—moments which, in this reviewer's opinion, belonged to 'the most charming pictures ever to be imagined on the stage'. The Royal Theatre production was concentrated around a succession of visually effective moments in these two acts—the children's game and Krogstad's sudden appearance in the doorway (considered by several critics Fru Hennings' best scene), the tree-trimming punctuated by Nora's mimic reactions to Helmer's recital of Krogstad's background, the tarantella rehearsal (Plate 32)—each of which seemed, in the opinion of *Dags-Telegrafen*, (23 December) 'to stop in a tableau for an instant, imprinting its picture indelibly on the mind of the spectator and then moving on again in the inexorable progress towards the fateful consequences of the conclusion'. Betty Hennings, who as a former ballerina had been the toast of contemporary poets and the pride of August Bournonville, possessed a supple plastic grace and a remarkable pantomimic ability which were ideally suited to make such choreographic moments as these, rather than the subdued and chilling encounter of the final act, the peaks of her performance. Her transition to this sombre last act created a sharply defined break with Nora's previous personality, a break which the play's first reviewers found both gloomy and unprepared in the writing itself. Although Brandes criticized her lack of authority in the confrontation with Helmer, however, most of the reviews were unreserved in their praise for Fru Hennings' handling of her controversial 'transformation', as she rises, in Vilhelm Topsøe's words, from confusion and disappointment 'to become what she must become, the greater of the two, completely superior to her husband'. The deep sense of loss and oppressiveness which the closing moments of the play imparted to its first audience is another manifestation of the powerful dramatic impact exerted by her particular approach to this undeniably difficult transition.

Although the conservative and uninspired H. P. Holst (whose principal fame as a director seems to have rested on his propensity for falling asleep in his seat in the auditorium during rehearsals!) was nominally in charge of the first production of *A Doll's House,* one would search in vain for a director's prompt-book containing detailed blocking instructions and line readings. Such matters were still at this point largely the responsibility of the individual performer. The clearest illustration of the actor's artistic independence in the prenaturalistic theatre remains the limited number of collective rehearsals regarded as necessary for any given performance. Although the première of *A Doll's House* took place at a time when naturalism was just on the verge of becoming the dominant theatrical style in Scandinavia, an examination of the Royal Theatre's daily journal[28] reveals that the rehearsal schedule for this production did not differ significantly from the traditional nineteenth-century pattern: two general blocking rehearsals and only eight further rehearsals were held prior to the sole dress rehearsal on December 19th. It is thus not unusual that Betty Hennings, in developing her characterization of Nora, sought (unsuccessfully) to persuade her former coach Frederik Høedt—the progressive theatre man who had endeavoured to introduce a more realistic style after mid-century—to suggest an approach to the part.

In terms of style, the world première was in fact a transitional production that combined features of rehearsal practice and performance style directly related to the conventions of the actor-oriented romantic theatre with other aspects of staging clearly influenced by the growth of naturalism, with its emphasis on the interaction of character and environment. In its creation of a photographically realistic environment of solid walls, lighted lamps and three-dimensional furniture, the Royal Theatre production endeavoured to follow both the explicit and the implied directions of the playwright to the letter. The unit setting corresponded closely to the printed stage directions,

[28] Det kgl. Teaters Journal, 16 August 1869—2 June 1880, manuscript in the Royal Theatre Library.

and the aesthetic atmosphere of middle-class cultivation in the Helmer household was underscored by a number of more or less subtle touches. The room was decorated with such items as flowering plants and bouquets, chairs with flowered seat covers, a bust of Venus on the bookcase, a bust of Holberg atop the stoneware oven and, paradoxically enough, a reproduction of Raphael's Madonna with child on the upstage wall above the piano. A decidedly naturalistic penchant for detail is exemplified in the care with which Helmer's offstage study and the outside hallway were furnished. In contrast to such naturalistic features of the setting, however, one senses in the ground plan a strong flavour of earlier staging traditions in the neatly symmetrical arrangement of the furniture along the walls, leaving most of the playing area open and uncluttered. A somewhat more curious reminiscence of older practices is the fact that the set was borrowed almost entirely from *The Pillars of Society*, which was still in the repertory at this time.

The property list for this production suggests a discernible pattern of physical action centring on specific objects during the first two acts. The entrance of Nora and the delivery boy, overloaded with presents, dress material, decorations and a Christmas tree, Nora's display of her purchases to Helmer, the game of hide-and-seek underneath the round table, the contrasting scene in which Krogstad wields the forged document and the brilliantly conceived tree-trimming all contributed to the pattern of predominantly pleasant domestic pursuits which established the tone of the first act. A well-stocked sewing basket on the round table and a wood box placed beside the practicable oven afforded added opportunities for the actors to 'live' within the stage milieu, although the emphasis on this kind of subsidiary physical business seems less marked than in, for example, the later, more minutely detailed naturalistic productions of William Bloch. In the second act, Nora's unpacking of 'a large carton containing an Italian peasant girl's costume, silk stockings and a tambourine', Fru Linde's efforts to mend the disintegrated costume, the skilfully motivated business with the flesh-coloured stockings in the scene with Doctor Rank and the final hectic tarantella rehearsal were actions which sustained the sense of forward movement and mounting tension. By contrast, the pattern of business in the

165

final act becomes noticeably more subdued as the play approaches the disenchantment of the 'static' discussion scene. Scraps of paper proliferate. The threatening atmosphere of bleak and depressing dissonance which affected so many of the play's first reviewers was evoked in theatrical terms by other means: costume changes, as Nora lays aside her masquerade costume to appear in 'ordinary clothing with a small valise', and sound effects—the distant music and voices from Consul Stenborg's party, soft steps heard on the stairs, the punctuating slam of the street door below.

A little more than three years later, William Bloch's renowned production of *An Enemy of the People* in March 1883 became a theatrical milestone of another kind, a brilliant crystallization of the new naturalistic concepts. 'The care with which Bloch had brought out even the minutest detail, had polished the smallest facets,' wrote Sven Lange, 'created a theatrical phenomenon whose parallel had not been seen in any Scandinavian theatre. The performance shone like a glittering and brilliant diamond behind the footlights.'[29] Although Bloch—who served as stage director at the Danish Royal Theatre from 1881 to 1893 and again from 1899 to 1909—went on to stage an impressive succession of Ibsen's plays, including *Vildanden/The Wild Duck* (1885), *Fruen fra Havet/The Lady from the Sea* (1889), a miscarried *Hedda Gabler* (1891), a triumphant *Bygmester Solness/The Master Builder* (1893), and a somewhat belated *Gengangere/Ghosts* (1903), his *Enemy,* starring Emil Poulsen as a quietly ironical Doctor Stockmann, remains one of the earliest and most impressive examples of stage naturalism in Scandinavia. Stage direction had changed its character decisively since Ibsen's early days at Bergen: 'whereas before it only implied a logical arrangement of positions and settings, *mise-en-scène* has now developed into an art which requires an intensive study of the individual rôles, a minute working out of all details,' Bloch insisted.[30] His close attention to significant, tangible detail in his Ibsen productions was not an end in itself, but a means, later emulated by Stanislavski, of establishing an

---

[29] *Meninger om Teater* (Copenhagen, 1929), p. 246; see also Lise-Lone and Frederick J. Marker, 'William Bloch and Naturalism in the Scandinavian Theatre', *Theatre Survey*, XV, 2 (November 1974), pp. 85–104.

[30] Quoted in Neiiendam, *Det kgl. Teaters Historie*, IV, p. 60.

inner authenticity. 'The theatre should not be a mirror of life,' he maintained throughout his career, 'but a reflection of the hidden life of the soul, acting not a direct imitation, illustrating 'reality', but the indirect revelation of the ever-changing facets of the soul.'[31] Concurred his Swedish counterpart August Lindberg: 'Upon reading the play for the first time, the director must be inspired by the same fire as the author. He must feel and sympathize with all the figures in the play. He must see how they move, come and go, part and communicate. He must lead them toward one another, to struggle or be reconciled; he must penetrate their inner core and show the actors how they look inside. With an intensity that resembles that of a visionary, he must be able to transport himself and the actor to other times and other surroundings.'[32]

Ibsen's own concern with the credible fabric of *An Enemy of the People* is evident in his letter (dated 14 December 1882) to the Norwegian director of the play at Christiania Theatre, Hans Schrøder, in which the dramatist insists that the staging should reflect, above all, 'truthfulness to nature—the illusion that everything is real and that one is sitting and watching something that is actually taking place in real life. *An Enemy of the People*,' its author warns, 'is not easy to stage. It demands exceptionally well-drilled ensemble playing, *i.e.*, protracted and meticulously supervised rehearsals.' Bloch's direction represents the ideal realization of these instructions. From the eight or ten rehearsals common earlier, Bloch's usual rehearsal total had risen to twenty—an indispensable prerequisite for the precisely coordinated teamwork demanded by naturalism. During these rehearsals the director worked closely with each character and then, in Bloch's words, 'assembled the various individualities into a musical harmony of conversation within the inspired life of the ensemble'.[33] (Josephson's emphasis on a well-rounded ensemble is comparable: 'Through that alone is it possible to realize the full power and impact of a play. The ensemble, like each rôle depiction, must be a true mirror image of life . . . as it once has been or as our modern times have

---

[31] Henri Nathansen, *William Bloch*, p. 86.
[32] Per Lindberg, *August Lindberg* (1943), quoted in *Perspektiv på teater*, eds. Ulf Gran and Ulla-Britta Lagerroth, p. 28.
[33] Nathansen, p. 46.

shown it to be—in other words, as natural and true as possible.')[34]

Bloch's remarkably detailed promptbook for his *Enemy*, still in the Royal Theatre archives, contains not only set descriptions, ground plans and elaborate blocking patterns, but also instructions for line readings that convey his conception of the characters and their motivations. For the mass scene in the fourth act, a vivid demonstration of his naturalistic method requiring a separate booklet over a hundred pages in length, exclamations and snatches of dialogue were interpolated to concretize and individualize the attitudes and reactions of the crowd members.

Bloch's very faithful but adroitly amplified renderings of Ibsen's settings—Stockmann's 'neatly furnished and decorated' living-room in the first two acts, the 'gloomy and uncomfortable' office of the *People's Tribune* in the third act, the 'big, old-fashioned room' in Captain Horster's house that serves as the setting for the fourth-act public meeting, and, finally, Stockmann's disordered study with its broken window panes—became, with their solid walls and three-dimensional furnishings, strikingly lifelike comments on the life and situation of the characters. Critics admired Bloch's recourse to unpretentiously 'cozy and realistic interiors in the modestly furnished home of a doctor', starkly contrasted with the environment of 'broken windows and a view of a poor alleyway' in which the 'public enemy' finds himself in the final act. Here as always, Bloch exercised his incomparable ability to endow a stage environment with an atmosphere and life of its own. 'When I walk into the auditorium at night after the curtain has gone up,' he remarked, 'the atmosphere upon the stage should make me feel the same as any guest walking into a strange parlour; the kind of house it is, the kind of people there, and what goes on between them, before I even step inside.'[35]

The highpoint of the production was the raucous meeting in the fourth act in which Emil Poulsen's tendentious Doctor Stockmann came face to face with the 'compact majority', a gallery of types in which 'life, movement, and individuality ex-

---

[34] Ludvig Josephson, *Teater-Regie*, quoted in *Perspektiv på teater*, p. 14.

[35] Nathansen, p. 75. For his *Enemy*, Bloch held 32 rehearsals in all, 12 of which were devoted to the crowd scenes in Act IV.

tended to every group and every figure'. The printed text of the play is very sparing regarding the actual staging of the meeting: 'A large gathering of *citizens* of all classes. Here and there, women can be seen among the crowd, and there are a few schoolboys. More and more people gradually stream in from the back, filling the room.' Ibsen's letter (dated 12 December 1882) to Edvard Fallesen, head of the Royal Theatre, is remonstrative but offers few concrete suggestions: 'I would like to request that you will, as far as possible, give the minor parts in the fourth act to capable actors; the more figures you can have in the crowd that are really individualized and true to nature, the better. I beg your indulgence in making this request, which is probably a perfectly unnecessary one.' Bloch, a great believer that 'the task of the director is to elaborate creatively on the work of the dramatist', welcomed the challenge implied in Ibsen's letter. 'Where the author's functions end, those of the naturalistic director begin.'[36]

Although the field-marshal blocking of nineteenth-century mass scenes had usually been left to the balletmaster, for Bloch there were no mass scenes or general crowds. His *Enemy* added no fewer than seventy-five specific individuals to Ibsen's cast of characters, each one identified by his occupation and— by implication—his age, and assigned a number in Bloch's remarkable promptbook. One is a blacksmith, another a typographer, a third a wholesale merchant; others are shipmasters, masons, clerks, and so on. Each reacted individually and in character as the meeting progressed—not for gratuitous effect but in order to establish the specificity of the atmosphere and society in which Stockmann finds himself branded an enemy. In order to intensify the potential drama around the doctor's figure, Bloch brought his meeting to life slowly; long before any exchange of dialogue took place, a complex weave of impressionistic touches created the environment for the struggle. When the meeting proper began, following Stockmann's entrance, the small groups that had formed were dispersed and people were distributed evenly throughout the room facing the main contestants in the clash: the impetuous doctor on the speakers' platform, his brother the major (played with appropriate woodenness by Peter Jerndorff) at the opposite side

[36] *Politikens kronik*, 28 September 1922.

of the stage from him, and Aslaksen, Horster and the Stockmann family in front of the dais, downstage left. Bloch's direction emphasized the fickleness and irrascibility of the 'compact majority' assembled in Captain Horster's house, and the dialogue was continually punctuated by angry reactions, loud outcries, the noise of horns and lyres, whistling and imitations of barking dogs, crowing cocks and the like. Most of all, Edvard Brandes admired 'the excellent way in which the single interruptions are exclaimed, some sharply cutting, some resoundingly rude, some comically parodistic',[37] adding up to a complex, kaleidoscopic mosaic of responses that amplified—but never distorted—the thematic line of Ibsen's text. Bloch's directorial image of an accelerating, multi-faceted counterpoint that placed the basic ironic tone of the text in bold relief reached its culmination toward the end of the act, as Stockmann was pronounced an enemy of the people. Total pandemonium broke out. Everyone tried to fight his way toward the speakers' platform, shouting, screaming, whistling, and stamping their feet, while three continually disruptive schoolboys—who later engaged in a spirited fight with the Stockmann boys—threw orange peels at Doctor Stockmann. After the defeated doctor finally made his way slowly through the crowd with his family at the conclusion of the meeting, everything once again became dynamic movement and sound. Hooting and yelling, loud arguments and fighting again erupted as the meeting disbanded. The dramatic irony of the events was thrown into still bolder relief by Bloch when one group began to sing the word *folkefjende*—enemy of the people—over and over again to the tune of a popular song. The singing continued to be heard, fading gradually into the distance as the curtain fell.

The astonishing wealth of detail and nuance in William Bloch's production plan for *An Enemy of the People* testifies, perhaps more forcefully than any other example, to the character of the theatrical mode for which Ibsen's 'realistic' plays were intended. Fully aware that scenic truth is not to be equated with truth in life, Bloch set out to create a theatrical truth, an interpretation of the life of the drama, in terms that reduced to a minimum the barrier between art and reality. More important, his development of a particularized pattern of

[37] *Ude og Hjemme,* 11 November 1883.

concrete details and responses taken from daily life lent his theatre an added dimension of intensified dramatic mood and atmosphere. Every rôle, no matter how small, was meticulously characterized; every action and every movement on the stage was given a clear psychological motivation. Bloch, fully responsive to Ibsen's subtle subtextual dramaturgy, unswervingly maintained that the life of a dramatic character does not begin the moment he makes his entrance. Since the theatre reflects only a corner of the larger fabric of living reality, every line must, as in real life, refer back to the past. 'If the character depicted is to appear to the audience in the theatre not as an abstraction, living only a hollow life within the narrow circumference of the given conditions of the play, but as a living creature, possessing within himself infinite possibilities', Bloch insisted that 'the thoughts and feelings he reveals to us must be shown as they take root in his mind. Every utterance must be given a life of its own. It must be conceived, be born, live and die'.[38]

Less known, though no less significant than an Antoine or a Stanislavski or a Belasco, Bloch gained fleeting international recognition of a kind when Lugné-Poë, Antoine's renowned contemporary, staged *An Enemy of the People* at his Théâtre l'Oeuvre in 1893 and drew for guidance upon Bloch's remarkable Royal Theatre promptbook, secured for him in Paris by his resourceful adviser Herman Bang. In fact, however, the visit of the Théâtre l'Oeuvre to Scandinavia two years later inspired little critical enthusiasm for Lugné-Poë's ponderously 'symbolic' interpretations of *Rosmersholm* and *The Master Builder,* marked by an overwrought singsong style and a portentious 'sense of the mysterious'. 'No declamation. No theatricalities. No grand mannerisms!' Ibsen had advised Sophie Reimers, Laura Gundersen's replacement as Rebekka West in the Christiania production of *Rosmersholm* in 1887.[39] Watching Lugné-Poë's staging of this play eight years later, the laconic playwright complimented the visiting French troupe profusely and then added quietly: 'One would not think that I was a poet of passions and should be played passionately and not other-

---

[38] William Bloch, 'Nogle Bemærkninger om Skuespilkunst', *Tilskueren* (1896), p. 447.
[39] Letter dated 25 March 1887.

wise.'[40] In reality, it was not the Théâtre l'Oeuvre or the Théâtre Libre or the Moscow Art Theatre, but often William Bloch's own Royal Theatre that brought forward some of this period's most satisfying Ibsen productions. Writing of Bloch's staging of *Ghosts* in 1903, starring Betty Hennings in one of her greatest rôles as a forcefully determined Mrs. Alving, the critic for *Teatret* summed up the situation without undue exaggeration: 'The performance of this play proved once more that Ibsen is given his most outstanding interpretation here in Copenhagen. No stage in Europe performs the Norwegian poet as perfectly as the Danish national theatre. Every time a truly *great* evening occurs in this theatre, it is invariably with one of the Norwegian plays.'[41]

The naturalistic aesthetic promulgated and exemplified by Bloch in his pioneering production of *An Enemy of the People* constituted, of course, the core of a wider movement which shaped the Scandinavian premières of later Ibsen plays as well. Side by side with Bloch, the great Swedish and Norwegian actor-directors of this period—August Lindberg, Bjørn Bjørnson, Gunnar Heiberg—continued during the final two decades of the century to present a succession of significant productions of Ibsen's plays. Each was keenly aware of the implicit demand for a new approach raised by these dramas. 'With Dr. Ibsen's newest play we have entered virgin territory where we have to make our way with pick-axe and shovel,' Lindberg declared in a letter to the playwright prior to his presentation of *The Wild Duck* at Dramaten on 30 January 1885. 'The people in the play are completely new, and where would we get by relying on old theatrical clichés?'[42] In order to eliminate such stereotypes, Lindberg endeavoured, as had Bloch, to impart the texture and immediacy of real life to his performance. Stage environments were treated as real rooms with a transparent fourth wall, the actors moved in believable fashion among the furnishings and handled props which possessed the solidity and authenticity of life. The door frames were solid, the doors boasted real doorknobs and there was even a greatly discussed commode, com-

[40] A Lugné-Poë, *Ibsen* (Paris, 1936), p. 80.
[41] *Teatret,* II (February 1903), p. 65.
[42] Quoted in *Ibsen Letters and Speeches,* ed. Evert Sprinchorn (New York, 1964), p. 243.

plete with chamber-pot and wash-basin, which provided its own visually suggestive commentary on the home of the ruined Ekdal family. Above all, Lindberg strove in this controversial production to create an integrated, psychologically motivated ensemble tone unifying the complex character relationships of the play, and he sought to banish all mannerisms that might detract from the overall impression of verisimilitude. As a significant consequence, he cast the play with a number of new or comparatively unknown actors—a practice later followed by naturalistic directors from Antoine to Stanislavski, but one which at this time was a novelty that provoked lively critical controversy in the Stockholm papers even before the production opened.

As in the case of Lindberg's work, the Norwegian world premières of *The Wild Duck* (9 January 1885) and *Rosmersholm* (17 January 1887), directed by Gunnar Heiberg during his period as manager of Bergen's National Stage from 1884 to 1888, both derived their artistic vitality from their director's distinctive sensitivity to fine nuances, his ability to establish an intimate ensemble tone on the stage. 'He has the keen ability to see—with everything in its proper relationship—every detail as a link in the whole, every actor in his place, no one pushing himself in front of the others but each one fulfilling the precise task demanded by the rôle,' remarked a contemporary observer. 'All this . . . because he senses the mood of the play, the spirit in which it was created, and conceives of it as theatre—not as literature.'[43] Heiberg was profoundly responsive to Ibsen's repeated exhortations at this time requiring a style of performance cleansed of theatrical hollowness and pomposity, and capable of lending each mood in his plays 'credible, true-to-life expression'—a style that would take 'real life and exclusively that as the basis and point of departure'[44] for stage representation. The drama of Ibsen and Bjørnson was regarded by Heiberg as the foundation upon which a re-vitalized and distinctively Norwegian theatre culture should build. In his opinion, the all-important artistic agent facilitating the realization of this goal was the autocratic figure of the director. 'He must perceive the totality which constitutes the through-line,

[43] Quoted in Carla Rae Waal, *Johanne Dybwad, Norwegian Actress*, p. 147.
[44] Ibsen's letter to Sophie Reimers, 25 March 1887.

and he must perceive all the thousands of details that make up the volume and colour of life,' Gunnar Heiberg asserted. 'He must be the rock of righteousness upon which the actor's natural tendency to perform without regard for others strands. . . . He must be able to build up a milieu. He must be capable of moulding an ensemble.'[45]

The succession of Ibsen productions staged in Christiania during the first six years of Bjørn Bjørnson's directorial career there (1885–91) offered yet another reconfirmation of these naturalistic ideals. Beginning with his staging of *The Wild Duck* in 1885 and highlighted by the world première of *The Lady from the Sea* (12 February 1889), in which the young Johanne Dybwad was seen in her first Hilde Wangel rôle (her second Hilde, in *The Master Builder*, would later become the unparalleled triumph of her remarkable career), Bjørnson's contribution consisted in his ability to unify and synthesize the multiplicity of acutely observed realistic details seen on his stage. Clearly, then, the figure of the director, as delineated through the pioneering efforts of Bloch, Lindberg, Gunnar Heiberg and Bjørn Bjørnson, had become a dominant artistic force throughout Scandinavia by the closing decades of the century.

The turn of the century marked both a culmination and a new beginning in Scandinavian theatre. Animated by the tireless leadership and inspiration of Bjørn Bjørnson, the Norwegian stage arrived at its ambitious goal of a truly national theatre when the old Christiania Theatre was demolished and the present Nationaltheatret opened its doors on 1 September 1899. Henrik Ibsen and Bjørnstjerne Bjørnson, captured in bronze in the monumental statues flanking the theatre's entrance, were hailed by the audience and saluted by the stately King Oscar II as they took their seats on the momentous first night, which was dedicated to Holberg. The second evening was Ibsen's, and the choice of play—*An Enemy of the People*—seems characteristic. On the third and most festively patriotic evening of the three-day celebration, Bjørnson's expansive national saga drama *Sigurd Jorsalfar/Sigurd the Crusader* (published 1872), enhanced by a score composed and conducted by Edvard Grieg, was acted by Egill Eide as Sigurd, Johan Fahlström

[45] Gunnar Heiberg, *Ibsen og Bjørnson på Scenen*, p. 3.

as the noble King Eystein, and the celebrated Johanne Dybwad as Borghild. Nationaltheatret's auspicious inaugural season included yet another, more significant Bjørnson production, his lyrical masterpiece *Over Ævne I/Beyond Human Power* I, with Fahlström as the miracle-performing zealot Pastor Sang— reminiscent in so many ways of Ibsen's Brand and John Rosmer—and Johanne Dybwad as the bed-ridden wife Clara who gives her life to help accomplish her husband's greatest miracle. Finally, the beginning of the new century saw National- theatret's production of *Naar vi døde vaagner/When We Dead Awaken,* Ibsen's final judgment on the price paid by the artist and his last and deepest penetration into the 'new territories' he had set out to explore in *The Wild Duck.* The symbolic tone and associational technique of Ibsen's 'dramatic epilogue' had, however, already become forceful ingredients in the dramaturgy of his towering contemporary August Strindberg. If the pro- duction in 1900 of *When We Dead Awaken* signals an end, the epoch-making première of Strindberg's *To Damascus* I later that same year marks a new beginning, the gateway to the post- naturalistic modern theatre.

CHAPTER TEN

August Strindberg

The prodigious achievement of August Strindberg (1849–1912), not only Sweden's greatest dramatist but also the most versatile and creative innovator in the modern theatre, defies exploration in a brief chapter. Both as playwright and theorist Strindberg remained in close touch with the newest directions and developments in theatre and drama, ready not only to absorb them but to reshape and expand them more daringly than anyone else in his own time—or since. Of no one can it be said with greater justification that he gave more impulses than he received. The history of the modern theatre in Scandinavia has, as the following chapters will show, been to a very large extent synonymous with the advance toward a re-theatricalized stage form capable of articulating the imaginative dynamism of Strindberg's astonishing dramatic vision.

'It is impossible to set up rules for theatrical art, but it ought to be contemporary.' This statement, repeated by Strindberg in varying terms and contexts during the course of his forty-year writing career, reveals a central feature of his theatrical art—an art characterized by the restless search for new forms capable of meeting the changing demands of the consciousness of the times, as seen from his uniquely personal point of view. The truly amazing range and energy of his prolific genius are reflected in the sheer bulk and variety of his writings, which include not only drama but also fiction, poetry, autobiography, criticism, philosophy and scientific theory; his sixty-two plays comprise only a portion of the total literary production collected in the standard fifty-five volume edition of his works. His continual striving to re-interpret the spirit of the times made Strindberg not only the arch rebel and social iconoclast, the most modern of the moderns, but also the pioneer of a sweeping revitalization of the theatre, a total redefinition of the theatrical experience that would continue to exert its effect long after his death. The challenge posed by the theatre was, as Strindberg felt from the very beginning, a great one, and he prepared at twenty to meet it. His initial, unsuccessful encounter with the living theatre, during a brief, unhappy period as an aspiring actor in 1869, was highlighted by his stage début at Dramaten in Bjørnson's *Maria Stuart in Scotland*—as a messenger with a total of eleven words to speak. A prouder aspiration, his grand design to make his début as the titanic outlaw Karl Moor in Schiller's *The Robbers,* predictably came to nothing.

Although Strindberg first gained world recognition as a dramatist with his 'naturalistic' masterpieces, *Fadren/The Father* (1887), *Fröken Julie/Miss Julie* (1888), and *Fordringsägare/Creditors* (1888), it was the plays written during the second phase of his career, following a period of severe mental crisis, that came to exert the most seminal influence on the modern theatre. It has become almost a critical truism that with the 1900 production of *Till Damaskus I/To Damascus* I (1898), the first play to appear after the Inferno crisis (1893–7) during which Strindberg wrote nothing for the theatre, we stand at the entry to theatrical modernism—to a new kind of theatre representing a radical break with the accepted norms of dramatic construction and stage illusionism.

Hence between 1869, when Strindberg wrote his first (lost) play, and 1898, when he finished the first two parts of the *Damascus* trilogy, his approach to the theatre altered drastically. This change is not, however, a continuous, linear or consistent development. It is marked instead by an oscillating series of varied experiments, leading to a gradual rejection of the validity of nineteenth-century conventions of stage illusion as adequate means of expressing the mystic and visionary qualities that Strindberg, to an increasing extent, came to regard as the essential texture of reality. His practical efforts to transfer his

177

plays to the small stage of the experimental Intima Teatern in Stockholm, which he operated together with the young actor-director August Falck from 1907 to 1910, took the form of a series of experiments and suggestions aimed at dematerializing and simplifying theatrical expression. His remarkable efforts to lift the theatre out of its everyday atmosphere into a richer, more poetic world of grandeur and beauty place him in the very vanguard of those visionary theatre-men who were fighting their way out of the stranglehold of the illusionistic theatre at the beginning of the twentieth century.

Strindberg began his career as a playwright profoundly influenced by the romantic theatre's preoccupation with history and folklore, a tradition still in full bloom during the seventies in Sweden. His first produced play, a one-act verse drama called *I Rom/In Rome*, depicts the youthful struggles by the great Danish sculptor Thorvaldsen to follow his artistic calling; it was successfully acted at Dramaten on 13 September 1870 by an exceptional cast, headed by Axel Elmlund as an elegant, elegiac Thorvaldsen. The following October, Dramaten staged his next one-acter, *Den fredlöse/The Outlaw*, a saga play set in twelfth-century Iceland and based—with strong echoes of Oehlenschläger and the early Bjørnson and Ibsen—on the theme of the conflict of Christianity and heathenism. However, Alfred Hanson, a decorative but stilted actor with a soporific delivery, was no match for the viking Thorfinn, 'a titan, a Prometheus who struggles against the gods', in Strindberg's drama, and critical response to it was cool. Nine years passed before another Strindberg production was seen. Although the earliest prose version of his first truly major play, the much-revised historical drama of the Swedish reformation *Master Olof*, was completed in 1872, it was rejected by Dramaten and had to wait nearly a decade for its first production. Directed by the young August Lindberg at Josephson's Nya teatern on 30 December 1881, the play's loose form, multiple scene changes and incidental realistic details deliberately flaunted traditional dramatic rules. Taking an irreverent attitude toward the figures of Swedish history, it centres on the vacillating, hyper-reflective religious revolutionary Olaus Petri who, by becoming a tool for other men's purposes, ends as an unheroic figure and a traitor to his cause, branded a 'renegade' by the un-

178

compromising Anabaptist rebel Gert Bookprinter. A giant work in more than one sense, the première of *Master Olof* played for six hours in the theatre, in an electrifying production made memorable by William Engelbrecht as the weak-willed Olof and the impressively authoritative Emil Hillberg as the fanatic Gert. Subsequently one of Strindberg's most frequently performed full-length plays in the Swedish theatre, its portentous initial success marked the emergence of its author as a major dramatist in the early eighties.

Although he would later return with renewed energy to the specifically historical genre, Strindberg continued for a time to utilize medieval settings for the early plays that reflect his own initially happy but increasingly horrific emotional life with his first wife, the ambitious and strong-willed actress Siri von Essen. The Dramaten production of *Gillets hemlighet/The Secret of the Guild* in May 1880, featuring Fru Strindberg, marked a tentative prelude to his definitive breakthrough as a playwright. Indebted to Ibsen's *The Pretenders,* this four-act play dramatizes the opposing claims of two rival medieval master builders—the man who possesses the true strength of a great calling and the usurping 'pretender' who is ultimately thwarted in his ambition—for the honour of completing work on the cathedral at Uppsala. The Strindbergian theme of love and marriage as an emotional battleground first came strongly to the fore, however, in another medieval pastiche, *Herr Bengts hustru/Sir Bengt's Wife,* which again starred Siri von Essen when it was acted at Nya teatern in late 1883. Margit, Strindberg's Nora in a play which quite evidently contains his reply to *A Doll's House,* is here re-united with her husband at the end, as the warfare of the sexes is overcome by the bonds of a love stronger than either rational logic or individual will.

Continuing to employ a vaguely medieval setting in *Lycko-Pers resa/Lucky Per's Journey,* which became one of his most resounding popular successes when it was staged at Nya teatern in December 1883, Strindberg moved in this fairy-tale fantasy in a new and profoundly significant direction, embarking on a drama of pilgrimage that he was to continue in the bleakly pessimistic *Himmelrikets nycklar/The Keys of Heaven* (1892) and to carry to fruition in his revolutionary expressionistic masterpieces, the *Damascus* trilogy, *Ett drömspel/A Dream*

Play (1901), and his last play *Stora landsvägen/The Great High-way* (1909). The bitter-sweet, fairy-tale atmosphere of *Lucky Per's Journey* reverberates with echoes from the great works of Scandinavian romanticism—Oehlenschläger's *Aladdin,* Ibsen's *Peer Gynt,* and, above all, the tales and fairy-tale dramas of Hans Christian Andersen. Young Per leaves the belfry in which he has been brought up, to wander through the world in search of happiness, only to discover that nothing is what he had imagined it to be and that the realization of his dreams of gold and honour and power bring only bitter disillusionment. The fleeting, dream-like transitions in the play, its replacement of the logic of reality by the fairy tale's logic of fantasy, and its magical realism of the unreal are all signposts that point ahead toward the dramaturgy of the mature dream plays. Using a multiplicity of elaborate décors for its short, kaleidoscopic scenes and employing both transparencies and startling trans-formations, *Lucky Per's Journey* strained the sophisticated illusionistic resources of the romantic theatre to the limit. (Consider, for example, a literal approach to the second-act *changement* in which 'a snow-covered forest' at dawn, with 'an ice-covered brook' running across the stage in the fore-ground, is transformed 'from winter to summer: the ice melts on the brook and it rushes freely over the stones, while the sun shines over the entire scene'!) Eventually, Strindberg came to regard as 'wasted effort' the kind of concrete pictorial re-presentationalism used for the first production of *Lucky Per's Journey,* and to look upon the careful, detailed staging re-quired by this literal approach as something which detracted from, rather than reinforced, its mood effects. Before this re-orientation toward simplification, however, he had yet to pass through a phase coloured, as he himself later writes, by a 'naturalistic taste [which], adapted to the materialistic ob-jectives of the time, strove for realistic accuracy'[1]—a phase, in other words, during which he sought to concretize and crystal-lize scenic mood by intensifying the illusion of objective reality on the stage.

From the early 1880s Strindberg, always closely attuned to new theatrical developments (and, unlike Ibsen, always ready

---

[1]   *Open Letters to the Intimate Theatre,* trans. Walter Johnson (Seattle, 1967), pp. 289–90. Referred to in the following as *LIT.*

to acknowledge debts of literary or theatrical influence) was preoccupied with the naturalist's search for 'a new formula' for art. In *The Father* (1887), he felt that he had found the formula which 'the young Frenchmen' were still trying to discover. To Strindberg the dramatist, the term 'naturalism' was synonymous from the outset with what he calls, in *On Modern Drama and Modern Theatre* (1889), 'the great style, the deep probing of the human soul'. Never attracted by the mere photographic aspects of naturalism or by its sometimes exaggerated insistence on the reproduction of the surface of reality ('If a woman is seduced in a hothouse, it isn't necessary to relate the seduction to all the potted plants you can find there and list them all by name,' he commented dryly),[2] the 'great naturalism' was for Strindberg that 'which seeks out the points where the great battles are fought, which loves to see what you do not see every day, which delights in the struggle between natural forces—whether these forces are called love or hate, rebellious or social instincts —which finds the beautiful and ugly unimportant if only it is great'.[3] The elements of external illusion in this style became in his interpretation simply a means of intensifying dramatic mood and conflict. Hence, the unrelenting struggle for dominance and survival between those gigantic contestants, the Captain and his wife Laura, in *The Father*, is endowed with the additional horror of precise delineation by being solidly anchored in a recognizable nineteenth-century Swedish bourgeois milieu. Like the ineluctable warfare of the sexes in *Creditors* and the grim, passionate battle of wills between the married couples in *Bandet/The Bond* (1892) and *Dödsdansen/The Dance of Death* I–II (1900)—all of which exploit the naturalistic pattern of surface detail—the compressed conflict in *The Father* swiftly takes on an added dimension beyond mere realism, as it presents us with a macabre vision of hell. For the Captain, the suggestion that he is not the father of his only child festers and grows to an obsession that severs his ties with objective reality, undermines the reason and foundation for his entire existence, and culminates in a fatal stroke after he has been lured into a

2 In his autobiography *The Son of a Servant*, trans. Evert Sprinchorn (Garden City, N.Y., 1966), p. 6.
3 'On Modern Drama and Modern Theatre', trans. Børge Gedsø Madsen, in *Playwrights on Playwriting*, ed. Toby Cole (New York, 1961), p. 17.

straitjacket at the end of the play by the she-vultures surrounding him. The thrust in this and other of Strindberg's misogynist marriage plays is not directed primarily toward the conventional naturalistic interaction of character and a convincingly real environment. In their depiction of a grotesque, nightmarish atmosphere intensified by a painstaking and sharply focused realistic technique, the vision and attack of these dramas come closer to the mode of magic realism in painting.

Yet, despite Zola's comment to Strindberg that his 'Captain without a name [and] the others who are almost entirely abstract figures do not give me as powerful a sense of reality as I demand',[4] the response to the noteworthy world première of *The Father*, staged at Casino Theatre in Copenhagen on 14 November 1887 by the Strindberg enthusiast and minor actor Hans Riber Hunderup, was almost entirely coloured by the intense impact of the production's realistic immediacy. Vigorously championed by the Brandes brothers (Georg Brandes even took the unusual step of participating in the rehearsals) this controversial performance became in itself a battleground of opposing tastes and ideologies. 'From the very outset one could sense how numerous the Strindbergians, or those whose natures were more or less in sympathy with the Strindbergian tendency, were in attendance; the applause which was heard from beginning to end was actually enthusiastic,' wrote *Nationaltidende* the next morning, adding: 'Whether this success will last longer than a very few evenings remains quite another question. So far as we are concerned, we do not think so.' Despite their praise of the play's technique, most of its first reviewers took strong exception to the unrelenting despair of Strindberg's vision. At the eye of the critical hurricane was the shocking straitjacket scene. 'How far have we already drifted, when the grim instrument of the insane asylum, the straitjacket, has managed to become a means of gaining effect on the stage?' demanded the outraged reviewer for *Dagbladet* (16 November 1887). 'An uglier, more revolting scene has probably never been presented in a Danish theatre. Those who have merely read the play have no conception of how incredibly nerve-racking this sight is. . . . The mood of the real audience—those who had not attended a demonstration—was oppressed

[4] Letter dated 14 December 1887, published in *Politiken*, 18 December 1887.

and indignant.' This particular observer's logic is interesting: precisely because a play like *The Father* speaks to everyone in the theatre, he insists, modern drama 'has no right to use such unrefined and raw means to achieve effect'. Though *Aftenbladet* (16 November) might argue that 'in its scenic effectiveness it ranks on a level with the very best in modern dramatic literature', the terrifying straitjacket scene remained the chief source of conservative umbrage. 'The drama is black enough as it is, so crushing and depressing that this scene is the drop that makes the cup run over,' wrote the critic for *Nationaltidende*, whose like-minded counterpart at *Dags-Telegrafen* (15 November) added: 'We can well understand why individual spectators stood up this evening during the third act and left the auditorium.' *Berlingske Tidende* (15 November) summed up the reaction of a large conservative majority impervious to the Brandes brothers' fervent campaign for Strindberg and modernism: 'Despite the talent revealed in the technical construction of the play, it nevertheless remains a bitter, unpoetic fruit on the arid tree of realism.'

Although the Casino actors, accustomed to a light repertoire, lacked the requisite strength and technique for the demanding task, their performance, starring Hunderup and his future wife Johanne Krum in the leading rôles, won high praise. 'When one must daily hold an audience through the aid of exaggerated outward action with many gestures and grimaces,' wrote Edvard Brandes in *Politiken* (15 November), 'it is no small problem when, for once, one must return to the evenness and naturalness which are the devices of all good plays.' Nevertheless, he added, it was again proven 'that the good plays create good actors, who through artistic work come to an awareness of and a reliance upon their abilities'. He reserved special acclaim for Johanne Krum's outstanding portrayal of Laura, acted with 'a natural and heavy tone of voice that has an extremely intense effect'. Strindberg's own conception of the play's performance style was, at first, very similar and emphasized a realistically subdued approach. 'Play the drama as Lindberg plays Ibsen,' he advised its first Swedish cast shortly after the Copenhagen opening. 'In other words, not tragedy, not comedy, but something in between. Do not take the tempo too quickly, as we did here at Casino at first. Rather let it creep

183

forward slowly, evenly, until it accelerates by itself toward the last act. Except from this: the Captain's lines when his obsession has taken root. They are to be spoken quickly, abruptly, spat out, constantly interrupting the mood.' Remember, adds the playwright, that 'the Captain is not an uncultivated soldier, but a learned man who stands above his profession'.[5] This rôle should be acted 'tastefully, quietly, resignedly', Strindberg emphasized in another letter, 'with self-irony and the tone of the somewhat skeptical man of the world who . . . goes with relatively undaunted courage to meet his destiny, enveloping himself in the spider-web of death that, for reasons of natural law, he cannot tear apart'.[6]

Two decades later, when *The Father* was revived by the Intima Teatern in 1908 with August Falck in the title rôle, Strindberg's concept of the realistic fabric of the drama had changed. He now wanted it played in a simplified setting of drapes, so that 'the play will be lifted out of its heavy everyday atmosphere and become tragedy in the grand style; the characters will be sublimated, ennobled, and appear as from another world'. The acting was to develop this idea further: '*The Father* should be played as tragedy! Grand, broad gestures, loud voices . . . let loose the passions.'[7] The 1911 film of the Intima production, one of the oldest surviving Scandinavian films, indicates, however, that in fact the playwright's earlier vision of a very subdued, untheatricalized atmosphere came to shape this performance, one of the small experimental theatre's greatest successes.

'Perhaps you know that I have no sympathy for the abstract,' Zola had written to Strindberg in 1887 in connection with the French translation of *The Father*. 'I demand to know everything about the characters' positions in life so that one can touch and perceive them, sense them in their own atmosphere.'[8] With *Miss Julie*, Strindberg adhered more closely and deliberately to Zola's programme. He himself considered it 'the first naturalistic tragedy in Swedish drama'; 'ceci datera! = this play will go down in the annals of history,' he added, with characteristic

---

[5] Quoted in Gunnar Ollén, *Strindbergs dramatik*, p. 116.
[6] Martin Lamm, *August Strindberg*, p. 178.
[7] Letter to members of the Intimate Theatre, 23 April 1908.
[8] Letter dated 14 December 1887.

directness, in his letter offering the work to Bonniers for publication (10 August 1888). (Bonniers' rejection of the play lives
on in the history of the great publishing house as its most
monumental blunder!) In the famous Preface which Strindberg
added subsequently, he consciously set out to promulgate the
ideas of theatrical reform championed by Zola and Antoine; in
so doing, he formulated what has come to be considered to this
day one of the most succinct descriptions of the aims of
naturalism in the theatre. In performance, the story of the
Midsummer-Eve seduction and trance-like suicide of the aristocratic Miss Julie was meant to be perceived as an unbroken
slice of living reality. To enable the audience to experience the
stage events as though they were actually happening in
reality, no disruption was allowed to disturb the intense focus
on the dramatic confrontation between Julie and the valet
Jean, and hence the playwright eliminated the usual inter-
mission that could break the spell of the 'author-mesmerist's
suggestive influence'. To further strengthen the illusion that
this was a slice of the broad fabric of life, the large kitchen in
which the action is set was meant to be solidly three-dimensional, eliminating the strain of having 'to believe in painted
pots and pans', yet at the same time impressionistically and
evocatively asymmetrical, stimulating the imagination and
leading 'one's eyes off into an unknown perspective'. En-
visioning the elimination of footlights and heavy makeup and
the introduction of strong side-lighting to reinforce eye and
facial (*i.e.,* psychological) expressiveness, Strindberg advocated
a close-up drama of subtler reactions 'mirrored in the face
rather than in gesture and sound'. Following Antoine's lead, he
called for the actor to disregard the audience beyond the
fourth wall and to perform *within,* rather than in front of, the
set, each scene being played 'at whatever spot the situation
might demand'. 'I do not dream that I shall ever see the full
back of an actor throughout the whole of an important scene,'
he declared, 'but I do fervently wish that vital scenes should
not be played opposite the prompter's box as though they were
duets milking applause'.

Like his views on theatrical production, Strindberg's dramaturgical precepts in his celebrated Preface often combine
strong features of the naturalistic aesthetic with innovative

ideas that point in a new, distinctly 'modern' direction. A complexity of motives—psychological, biological, environmental, hereditary—underlies the behaviour of a naturalistically conceived character—yet Strindberg's 'split and vacillating' patchwork characters, 'agglomerations of past and present, scraps from books and newspapers, fragments of humanity, torn shreds of once fine clothing that has become rags', are potentially Pirandellian in their characterlessness. His advocacy of an asymmetrical, non-sequential, impressionistically arranged dialogue, mirroring the casual haphazardness of everyday conversation, foreshadows Chekhov's dialogue of free association. Finally, Strindberg's analogies to musical theme and structure in the Preface to this, his first chamber play, come fully into focus in his own later dream-play dramaturgy.

Miss Julie, representing not only innovations in form and technique but also, as it turned out, explosively daring subject matter, was originally written with a view to performance by an experimental theatre. The foundation of Antoine's Théâtre Libre in Paris in 1887 had triggered a widespread interest in the free, independent theatre as an instrument for introducing new plays and production methods. Strindberg, immediately attracted by this idea and having actually entertained the notion of his own theatre as early as 1876, approached the enlightened actor-director August Lindberg, who had been the first to stage Ibsen's *Ghosts,* with the suggestion that they jointly form an independent touring company. His dynamic sales' pitch was characteristic: 'Ibsen you cannot rely on any longer, since I am sure that he won't write much more, and his genre is his specialty and is on the wane. . . . He for himself and we for us!' Instead, this amazing and irrepressible man proposed a theatre dedicated to a repertory composed solely of his own plays, and only new ones at that. 'Holes in the repertory need not occur, as I write a one-acter in two days,' he reassured Lindberg, to whom all the leading parts were to be tailored. Strindberg's wife Siri von Essen was to have all the female leads—but, he adds, 'if you want your wife included, then I'll write every other rôle for her, every other for my wife, and all parts for you.' 'I will write the plays so that no costumes, sets, or properties have to be dragged along,' he suggested with practicality, but he entertained no illusions about fermenting a revolution:

186

'To transform the theatre or to reform it is something I wouldn't dream of, for that is impossible! It can only be modernized a bit!' (Letter dated 3 June 1887).

When Strindberg at last did succeed in establishing his own 'Scandinavian Experimental Theatre' in Copenhagen nearly two years later, however, the venture survived only a week. The initial response to the project had hardly been enthusiastic: 'A manager without sense—in theatre affairs, of course—a theatre without a location, a primadonna without lines, and the male parts without actors. That the auditorium will be without spectators seems quite certain, which then means a cashbox without cash,' sneered *Dagbladet*.[9] The day before the scheduled opening of *Miss Julie*, which was to have inaugurated the new enterprise at Copenhagen's Dagmar Theatre, the play was belatedly banned by the public censor. Undaunted, Strindberg's experimental theatre quickly changed its plans, opening a week later with a single performance at the Dagmar Theatre on 9 March 1889 that included the world premières of *Creditors* and two *quarts d'heure* written for the project, *Den starkare/The Stronger* and *Paria/Pariah*. All three plays are designed—for practical as much as for artistic reasons—to be performed by a small company with a minimum of technical and economic resources (Strindberg aptly characterized *Creditors* as a 'naturalistic tragedy, even better than *Miss Julie*, with three characters, a table and two chairs, and no sunrise!').[10] As the first Adolf in *Creditors*, the celebrated humourist and playwright Gustav Wied made a luckless acting début ('People laughed till they had tears in their eyes,' commented one critic unkindly)[11] but Siri Strindberg was effective as the loquacious Mrs. X in *The Stronger* while Hans Riber Hunderup scored a triumph as X in *Pariah*, which was retained in the Dagmar Theatre's normal repertory.

After the ban on a public performance, the world première of *Miss Julie* itself was forced to take place at a private showing before 150 spectators in a makeshift theatre in the University of Copenhagen's student union on 14 March 1889, featuring Strindberg's wife as a subdued Julie and Viggo Schiwe as a

9 Quoted in Ollén, p. 162.
10 In a letter to Bonniers dated 21 August 1888.
11 Quoted in Ollén, p. 162.

polite Jean. 'Too cold, much too cold, and one gets no impression at all of the kind of woman who would seduce a man like Jean,' was the critical verdict[12] on Siri von Essen's performance, while Schiwe, the same reviewer felt, 'hardly suggested a servant; his manner was much more that of a gentleman and *viveur*.' Despite the primitive production facilities, however, Strindberg's demands for a realistically three-dimensional stage environment seem to have been met. 'The décor . . . looked surprisingly like a real kitchen,' commented *Dagens Nyheter*. 'A plate rack, a kitchen table, the speaking tube to the floor above, a big stove, not omitting the rows of copper pots above it, in short: everything is there to convey a vivid impression of an actual kitchen.'

Without wishing to belabour further the much-overworked 'biographical' approach that seems to be a cherished facet of much Strindberg criticism, it is nonetheless indisputable that, in theatrical terms, the shattering Inferno crisis which the playwright lived through during the mid-1890s was followed by a radical change and renewal in his art. *To Damascus* I, the first play he wrote after this mental cataclysm, marks a striking shift in his aesthetic orientation and in his attitude toward theatrical illusion. He himself regarded the work as a drastic departure from accepted traditions, 'a new genre, fantastic and shining like *Lucky Per,* but playing in a contemporary setting and with a full reality behind it' (letter dated 24 May 1898)— though the 'full reality' underlying this dramatization of the agonizing pilgrimage of the Unknown through the stations on the road toward a distant salvation is now an inner reality, a spiritual, magic realism of the soul. In Emil Grandison the playwright found a director able and willing to seek new ways of interpreting his remarkable vision on the stage. 'Grandison,' Strindberg wrote later, 'went beyond [Harald] Molander's 'externals' and admitted I was right when I was right, seeing that the effect or the impact of the play depended on something other than what was piquant in the situation and the scenic effects' (*LIT*, p. 127). Grandison's refined but simplified taste for the internal values in the later plays permeated his Strindberg offensive at Dramaten, highlighted by his productions of

[12] Stockholm's *Dagens Nyheter,* 18 March 1889.

Påsk/Easter (1900), *Brott och brott/Crimes and Crimes* (1901), and *Karl XII* (1902). Above all, however, his celebrated production of *To Damascus* I at Dramaten on 19 November 1900 was, in Strindberg's words in the same letter, 'something new and a masterpiece by way of direction!'

Simplification achieved by using projections rather than solid scenery was the basis of Strindberg's original staging concept for the play. As early as half a decade before the Inferno period, Strindberg had begun to toy with new approaches to staging, in particular the idea of replacing conventional painted backdrops with projected pictures. In 1889, while an adaptation of his novel *Hemsöborna/The People of Hemsö* was being staged at Djurgårdsteatern in Stockholm, he wrote to August Lindberg about plans for a new play, 'a semi-fairy tale dealing with the French Revolution, and using mainly a large magic lantern'[13] as an evocative and economical means of transferring its pictures of historical scenes to the stage. This notion of projecting scenery in order to achieve a simplified, flexible and dematerialized stage atmosphere was again taken up by Strindberg in 1899, after a stay in Paris during which he, like Lugné-Poë and many other symbolist artists, had become wildly enthusiastic about the fleeting, dream-like effects produced in the shadow-plays shown at Henri Rivière's famous cabaret Chat Noir on Montmartre. 'I don't want to use ordinary theatre decorations for my new plays,' he declared shortly later in *Svenska Dagbladet* (21 January 1899). 'All these old-fashioned painted theatrical rags must go! I only want a painted background representing a room, a forest or whatever it may be, or perhaps a background could be produced by a shadow picture painted on glass and projected onto a white sheet.' His theory of simplification involved not merely the reduction of scenery, costumes, and props to the barest and most meaningful essentials: a neutral platform stage ('something in the style of Shakespeare's time') was meant to replace the photographically real parlours and kitchens of the naturalistic-environmentalist theatre. The 'Shakespearian' stage that impressed Strindberg as an ideal solution for the modern theatre was that introduced in Munich ten years before by Karl von Perfall; in Strindberg's *Open Letters to the Intimate Theatre* this stage would again be-

[13] See Gösta M. Bergman, *Den moderna teaterns genombrott*, p. 273.

189

come a favourite example in his continuing campaign for the dematerialization of the theatre. 'All this heavy theatre nonsense which absorbs the stage and makes a play heavy without increasing its value must be abolished,' he continued, in terms that are typical of the era of Craig, Poel, and Granville-Barker. 'It is the play itself, the dialogue, the plot which matters and which must capture the audience and produce illusions.'

In order to achieve these effects in Grandison's *Damascus* production, preliminary experiments with projected pictures that would eliminate the heaviness of conventional painted scenery were conducted. A large and effectively clear pictorial background was created by means of the sciopticon, but, because the area in front of the backdrop had to be kept dark to prevent the projection from being washed out by the stage lights, it proved impossible to see the actors clearly enough. Eventually the experiments were abandoned and conventional perspective backcloths, painted by the traditionalist designer Carl Grabow, had to be used to depict the shifting scenes, or stations, which the Unknown passes on his symbolic journey. However, this scenery was given a stylized character that differed strikingly from the three-dimensionality of naturalism by painting furniture and other requisite items directly on it, thereby also facilitating the quick scene changes that took place, according to Strindberg, by means of blackouts and 'a silent pulley' (*LIT*, pp. 282–3). Side wings were dispensed with and the ephemeral, dream-like quality upon which the play depends was created by giving Grabow's painted drops a stylized framework modelled on that utilized by von Perfall's Shakespeare stage in Munich. Divided into two parts, the stage became in effect two stages—an inner and an outer—joined by three communicating steps. Framing the inner stage was a second proscenium, mentioned by Strindberg in his *Open Letters* as 'an unusually attractive arch painted by Grabow' (p. 292). Hedvall describes this inner proscenium arch as resembling 'an ancient wall of antiquity with a large portal-shaped opening like the majestic vault in a triumphal arch. Above the wall one glimpsed the sky, in which during the nocturnal scenes a single star shone'.[14]

By concentrating the action on the raised inner stage and by

14 Quoted in Ollén, p. 234.

utilizing subdued, impressionistic lighting, Grandison succeeded in projecting a strong impression of unreality and distance.
'The figures that appear have thus become smaller,' wrote the
reviewer for *Aftonbladet*, (20 November 1900) 'and in the half
light, which eliminates the contours and which often leaves the
faces in shadow, it is easy to imagine oneself in a hallucinatory
state caused by fever.' This distancing effect was especially
pronounced in the pivotal scene in the Asylum, the turning
point in the weary pilgrimage, for which a second arch and a
yet smaller and more removed inner stage were introduced.
Through this arch, seated at a long table and bathed in a green-
ish light, Strindberg's ghostlike supper, vividly described in his
stage directions, was seen: 'At the table to the right are sitting
the Pallbearers in Brown from the first act; the Beggar; a
Woman in Mourning with two children; another Woman who
resembles the Lady but is not she, and is crocheting instead of
eating; a Man who resembles the Doctor but is not he; the Mad-
man's Double; doubles of the Father and the Mother; the
Brother's Double; the Parents of the 'prodigal son', and others.
All are dressed in white but over their white gowns they are
wearing gauze costumes in various colours. Their faces are
waxen and deathly white.' In this and other scenes, as the
actors appeared and disappeared from the sides 'as if by
magic', Grandison articulated the hallucinatory and mystical
qualities of Strindberg's mutational vision in a *mise-en-scène*
that foreshadowed, but did not immediately precipitate, the
sweeping theatrical advances that came after Strindberg's
death. A surviving rehearsal photograph (Plate 33), showing
the reunion of the Unknown and the Lady by the sea in Act IV,
illustrates the combination of a painted backdrop and a raised
inner stage in this unusual production.

Although August Palme's Unknown was rich in lyrical
warmth and profound but suppressed suffering, the focus of
the *Damascus* première was—not least for Strindberg himself—
the twenty-one-year-old Harriet Bosse's impressive interpretation of the Lady. Strindberg's encounter with the in-
triguing young actress, who had attracted attention earlier that
season as Puck in *A Midsummer Night's Dream*, is memorably
recaptured in his *Occult Diary* (15 November 1900). At the
dress rehearsal for *Damascus* on that day, the author came up to

offer advice about the kiss given to the Unknown by the Lady
at the end of the first scene. 'As we stood there on the stage
surrounded by many people, and I was speaking earnestly
about the kiss, Bosse's little face was suddenly transformed,
enlarged, and took on a preternatural beauty, seemed to press
in on mine, and her eyes surrounded me with black flashes of
lightning. . . . Afterwards, Bosse haunted me for three days, so
that I felt her in my room.' 'It was great and beautiful,' he
wrote to her after the opening (letter dated 19 November),

33. From the world première of Strindberg's *To Damascus* I,
1900: the Unknown (August Palme) and the Lady
(Harriet Bosse) are reunited by the sea in Act IV ('Put
your hand in mine and let's move on from here together').
Carl Grabow's painted backdrop is seen in the background

'even though I had imagined the character somewhat lighter, with small traces of roguishness and with more expansiveness. A little of Puck—those were my first words to you! and they remain my last! A laugh in the midst of suffering indicates hope, and the situation certainly does not prove to be hopeless!' Life, dream and drama were for Strindberg inextricably bound up: the Unknown's fateful encounter with the Lady and his encounter with Bosse on stage during the scene's rehearsal were interchangeable mirror images of each other. Six months later, Harriet Bosse became his third wife.

'Anything can happen; everything is possible and probable. Time and space do not exist; on a slight groundwork of reality, imagination spins and weaves new patterns made up of memories, experiences, unfettered fancies, absurdities and improvisations.' The renowned prefatory remarks to *A Dream Play*, a work which, more than any other Strindberg play, remained a fascinating source of challenge and renewal to the next generation of directors and designers, had little effect on the first production of Strindberg's expressionist masterpiece. Staged at the Swedish Theatre in Blasieholmen (formerly Josephson's Nya teatern) on 17 April 1907 and featuring Harriet Bosse, now divorced from Strindberg, as a darkly beautiful Indra's daughter, the world première paid heed neither to Grandison's prior example nor to the author's unequivocally anti-realistic stage directions, calling for 'stylized murals suggesting at the same time space, architecture, and landscape' which would remain unchanged at the sides throughout the action, and would be supplemented by changing backdrops. Director Victor Castegren, enjoined by Strindberg to 'transform the dream into visual representations without materializing it too much' (*LIT*, p. 293), experimented, again unsuccessfully, with a sciopticon, obtained in Dresden, and background projections. When the *Damascus* alternative of arches and backcloths was also rejected by theatre-owner Albert Ranft, 'the only thing left to do,' as Strindberg put it, 'was to "go to Grabow"' (*LIT*, p. 294). Carl Grabow's traditional pictorialized designs (Plates 34–6), palpable and solid but devoid of overtones, resulted, the playwright complained, in staging which 'was too material for the dream' and required endless intermissions. Inept lighting techniques failed to convey the

AUGUST STRINDBERG

Gouache designs by Carl Grabow for the world première of Strindberg's A Dream Play *(1907)*

34. The cloverleaf door (above)   35. Fairhaven (below)

play's visionary quality, and what symbolism there was seemed heavy-handed—the forestage represented a field of soporific poppies, and a frame behind it, within which the dream scenes appeared and disappeared, was also decorated with the same crimson emblems of sleep. 'The task is so incredibly difficult that one hardly even has a right to make comments,' wrote Tor Hedberg in *Svenska Dagblad*, but he went on to point out the lack of unity and coordination in the production.[15] Strindberg himself was less reserved in his disappointment: 'The whole performance became a "materialization phenomenon" instead of the intended dematerialization' (*LIT*, p. 294). He continued during the period which followed to grapple with a whole series of schemes and plans for mounting a simplified, dematerialized production of *A Dream Play* on the inappropriately tiny stage of the experimental Intima Teatern, which opened half a year after the première at the Swedish Theatre. Nearly thirty years would pass, however, before Olof Molander's legendary productions of this play would finally succeed in

[15] Cf. Vagn Børge, *Strindbergs mystiske teater*, p. 316.

36. *A Dream Play*: the Growing Castle

crystallizing the magic reality of Strindberg's vision.

Another major line of development leading out of the introspective Inferno crisis and running side by side with the dream-play dramaturgy is represented by the remarkable series of plays in which Strindberg returned to the pageant of Swedish history for his inspiration. Between 1899 and 1900 the explosively prolific playwright wrote, in quick succession, four full-length history plays, *Gustav Vasa, Folkungasagan/The Saga of the Folkungs, Erik XIV,* and *Gustav Adolf,* which were followed during the next decade by eight more, including *Engelbrekt, Karl XII,* and *Kristina/Queen Christina* (all 1901), *Gustav III* (1902), and, finally, *Bjälbo-Jarlen/Earl Birger of Bjälbo* (1908). Strindberg's original monumental scheme, which envisioned a cycle of plays covering seven hundred years of his country's heritage, was very much in the spirit of the nationalistic history cycle of fifty plays planned by Johannes Messenius three centuries before. The plays of the cycle which Strindberg did complete reaffirm the abiding fascination that history has continued to hold for the Swedish playwright of almost every era. Nevertheless, Strindberg's dramatic method in his history plays is unique and characteristic. Rather than endeavouring to provide a precise chronicle of the events of history, his plays in this genre interpret individual historical destinies by focusing on decisive moments, mood, and themes shaping the complex tissue of the past. 'Even in the historical drama,' he wrote, 'the purely human is of major interest, and history the background: the inner struggle of souls awakens more sympathy than the combat of soldiers or the storming of walls; love and hate, and torn family ties, more than treaties and speeches from the throne' (*LIT,* p. 256). Clearly, moreover, Strindberg applied to history the same perspective of sin and atonement that pervades his Damascus dramas. King Magnus in *The Saga of the Folkungs* is a Christian penitent groaning beneath the black cross of his ancestors' crimes. Erik XIV, Strindberg's Hamlet, was 'doomed to certain crimes' and his play was first thought of by its author as a Swedenborgian drama, calling to mind Swedenborg's idea that man suffered the punishments of hell already here on earth. On the character of Gustav Vasa, Strindberg remarked: 'Providence wanted to test him and temper its man, to whom the building of the kingdom was en-

trusted, and for that reason it struck him with all the mis-
fortunes of Job. That time of despair gives one the best
opportunity to depict the great human being Gustav Vasa with
all his human weaknesses (*LIT*, p. 256).

Indebted to his 'teacher' Shakespeare for the fluid, poly-
phonic structural pattern and the dramatic compression of
these history plays, as well as for their depiction of historical
figures 'both in their greatness and their triviality', Strindberg
also drew upon the inspiration of Walter Scott, whom he considered 'a great antiquarian', for his evocation of an effective
theatrical 'mood and atmosphere'. Like the artists of the
romantic theatre, Strindberg discovered in Scott's novels a
rich kaleidoscope of suitable 'ingredients, decorations and
stage properties' that could be incorporated into his own plays
in order to concretize the past (*LIT*, p. 303). These elements of
picturesqueness and vivid splendour played a vital rôle in the
first stage productions of his later histories, chief among which
was the triumphant première of *Gustav Vasa* at the Swedish
Theatre on 17 October 1899. Affording Albert Ranft one of his
greatest successes at this theatre, Strindberg's immensely demanding drama was staged with lavish opulence by Harald
Molander (feared by businessman Ranft because he 'requisi-
tioned as if he were a secretary of war levying forced contributions' [*LIT*, p. 292]) and featured outstanding performances
by Emil Hillberg as a majestic, Odin-like Gustav Vasa, Anders
de Wahl as a nervously lyrical and weak Prince Erik (XIV), and,
above all, Tore Svennberg in a richly detailed and provocative
interpretation of Göran Persson, Erik's iron-willed adviser and
the underling born to rule. 'The Hanseatic office and the Blue
Dove in *Gustav Vasa* were real museum sets,' remarked Strindberg of Carl Grabow's painstaking naturalistic décors for the
performance. 'They were beautiful, but they would not have
had to be so expensive to work' (*LIT*, p. 292).

By contrast, for the single history play staged at the Intima
Teatern, the small theatre's slender physical and financial resources obviously necessitated a very different and barer
mise-en-scène. Strindberg, who to an increasing degree had become opposed to illusionistic staging, was convinced that by
now public taste had also undergone a significant reversal: 'by
the end of the century . . . the imaginative became active, the

197

material gave way to the immaterial' (*LIT*, pp. 289–90). Simplification had now become a key word, and the setting devised by August Falck for *Queen Christina,* which became one of the Intima's great successes in 1908 with Manda Björling in the title rôle, came as a revelation to the dramatist. It made, he declared, the discovery that scenery can be dispensed with, without making the production either monotonous or shabby. The stylized décor which Falck introduced for the revolutionary première on 27 March 1908 consisted entirely of reddish-brown drapes of heavy velvet which served both as backdrop and side wings; on barriers positioned at either side near the footlights, emblematic attributes were placed to suggest a change of scene. In the first act, set in Ridderholm Church in the text, all references to the church were simply deleted and the action was presented merely as a gathering of people. The Treasury in the following act was symbolized by a pair of bookshelves in the Accountant's room—but even these were a superfluous distraction, insisted Strindberg, who also criticized the elaborate and expensive costumes obtained by Falck from Berlin. Stripped to essentials the drapery stage possessed, in Strindberg's view, distinct advantages for the actor, sustaining his art because it created 'a mood of calm and reverence on stage that is extremely important to the performer. . . . The open wings (three on each side) provided nuances of light and shadow, and made unnecessary all opening and closing of doors; entrances and exits were made without disturbance of any kind. With a soft carpet added, the artists at the Intima lived in a carefree, pleasant milieu, in which they felt at home and could create their rôles undisturbed by the noise and commotion of the theatre and the stagehands' bustle which otherwise is part of it' (*LIT*, p. 77). The momentous production of *Queen Christina* had far-reaching effects upon the speculations about simplification that were one product of Strindberg's association with the Intima. His letter to Falck six weeks after the opening (dated 9 May 1908) is a noteworthy summary of his theories in this respect: 'With simplicity one wins the solemn calm and quiet in which the artist can hear his own part. With simple décor the really important points become evident: the personality, the part itself, the speech, the action and the facial expression. . . . Yes, the spoken word is everything. You see this in *Christina* in the artistic weaving together of destinies and wills. But the play can be acted anywhere, even in front of a Smyrna mat hung up in a cellar in the country.'

The evolution of Strindberg's chamber plays, the last strand in the rich skein of his dramatic experimentation, is also directly related to the short-lived but famous experimental theatre which he and the young actor August Falck established in November 1907. While plans for the Intima were still in the formative stages and its organizers were hoping for a small theatre of 400–500 seats, along the lines of Reinhardt's Kleines Theater in Berlin or von Perfall's Shakespeare stage in Munich, Strindberg composed four 'chamber' plays in the style which he considered suitable for the new stage: 'intimate in form, a simple theme treated with thoroughness, few characters, vast perspectives, freely imaginative . . . simple but not too simple, no huge apparatus, no superfluous minor parts.'[16] In each, 'the significant and overriding theme' is orchestrated as in a piece of music: the atmospheric evocation of the twilight of summer and of life in *Oväder/Storm Weather,* the harrowing motif of vampirism in *Spöksonaten/The Ghost Sonata* and *Pelikanen/The Pelican,* the mordant view of the world as a weave of lies and counterfeits in which death comes as the settling of accounts in *Brända tomten/The Burnt House.*

In reality, the actual theatre on Norra Bantorget which Falck eventually acquired proved far more 'intimate' than either he or Strindberg had been prepared for: although an attractive carpeted auditorium in muted greens and yellows seated 161 spectators, the (often frustratingly) tiny stage measured only twenty feet in width and thirteen feet in depth! Appropriately, the proscenium was decorated with two free renderings of Böcklin's haunting painting 'Die Toteninsel' (Island of the Dead), which appears as a backdrop for the final symbolic tableau in *The Ghost Sonata,* Opus III and the best known of the chamber plays. During the three seasons of its existence, the Intima was almost exclusively a Strindberg theatre, performing twenty-four of his works for a total of 1,025 performances, ranging from his romantic dramas and naturalistic tragedies through *To Damascus* and *Queen Christina* to the chamber plays. (The latter, all four of which were staged during the two-

[16] Letter to Adolf Paul dated 6 January 1907.

month period from November 1907 to December 1908, proved to be among the theatre's least popular and most harshly criticized productions.) Atmosphere—'a synonym for poetry', adds Strindberg—pervaded the setting in *Art Nouveau* style which the playwright demanded for *The Pelican,* Opus IV of the chamber plays, which opened the Intima Teatern on 26 November 1907. A contemporary newspaper sketch shows a room in typical *Art Nouveau* taste, a light and airy interior with stylized trees, pine cones in vases, high white-painted bureaus and a rocking chair. But, Strindberg remarked, 'there was something else in that room; there was atmosphere, a white fragrance of sickroom and nursery, with something green on a bureau as if placed there by an invisible hand. "I'd like to live in that room," I said, though one sensed the tragedy that would play its last act with classic tragedy's most horrible motif: innocently suffering children and the sham mother Medea' (*LIT,* pp. 296–7). The young cast was no match for the challenge represented by this intensely emotional drama, however, and its first production failed: box-office receipts for the third day were $7.80!

In attempting *Storm Weather* the following month, the Intima ensemble was brought face to face with the inadequacies of its cramped stage, which proved incapable of projecting the heightened reality of the Östermalm street scene in the first and third acts. Nevertheless, the stylized and simplified second-act interior created by the gifted young designer Knut Ström delighted the author, who found it 'a room in which one could live and enjoy living; there was a home that was more comfortably homelike than any I had ever seen on stage before. . . . It was successful in its simple beauty, and with it we had left the Preface and *Miss Julie*' (*LIT,* p. 297). With the drapery-stage production of *Queen Christina* later that season, Strindberg took to the proselytizing of simplification with a vengeance, even at the expense of his own art in the naturalistic plays; both *The Father* and *Easter* were to be done in drapes, he insisted, because 'the characters will be sublimated, ennobled, and appear as from another world'. *Easter,* the Intima's last new production of the 1907–8 season, should, if its author had his way, be staged with 'curtains, door hangings and a Brussels carpet' (*LIT,* p. 291) and should appear 'as if played in the clouds: but should also be acted in the same way'[17] (!). Happily, Falck stood his ground, and the indispensable concreteness of this play's oppressive environment—the glass verandah of a middle-class house in a small Swedish town—was conveyed by a conventional closed interior. Strindberg's poignant family drama of atypical peace and consolation, always one of his most popular works, became the Intima's most performed production, as the shy intensity and poetry of Anna Flygare's gentle, clairvoyant Eleonore won her the greatest triumph of her career.

Although prolonged rehearsal periods were not uncommon at the Intima (Falck mentions eighty rehearsals for their production of *The Dance of Death* I-II) the eleven young members of the company seem—almost in eighteenth-century fashion—to have functioned without a director, relying instead upon mutual consultation and adjustment. At the end of the first season, however, Falck invited Strindberg to assume the position of director: 'Not that we now wanted to introduce a new style or transform our whole idea, but only that we should have access to a judge and leader in connection with our artistic work. I thought that a director would be of great help with regard to rhythm and adjustment.'[18] Although he agreed and took his new responsibility very seriously, Strindberg attended only a few rehearsals and never actually functioned as a director in the modern sense of the term: 'The actors found their own way during rehearsals,' he relates, 'adjusted themselves, with the help of the director, to each other's acting, and obtained good results with *The Father* [the first production of the 1908–9 season] and *Svanevit* [*Swanwhite*, opened 30 October 1908] without my help' (*LIT*, p. 143). Although he soon retired from this post, Strindberg's brief involvement as a director had one particularly remarkable result—his intensely human and revealing *Open Letters to the Intimate Theatre,* prefaced by his famous Memorandum to the cast, signed 'The Director', in which he formulates his new views on the art of the actor.[19] Widely republished and discussed in detail elsewhere, Strindberg's ideas on such matters as the sovereignty of the actor, the

17 See August Falck, *Fem år med Strindberg*, p. 163, and Bergman, p. 294.
18 Falck, p. 193.
19 See, *e.g.,* G. M. Bergman, 'Strindberg and the Intima Teatern', *Theatre Research* IX, 1 (1967), pp. 14–47.

superfluity of a director, the harmfulness of too many rehearsals and the necessity of keeping the audience in mind at all times are reminiscent in some respects of the older, pre-naturalistic aesthetic of acting. The decorum and restraint of Goethe's Weimar style ('a lady should never snap or be cross even if her part involves conflict, but she should always be pleasing in moments of anger. This is an example of the beauty which is truth' [*LIT*, p. 140]) are merged in Strindberg's theory with a Yeatsian concern with the subordination of the actor to the text and the spoken word.

Strindberg continued to bombard Falck with plans, suggestions, and sketches for new staging methods, but their association ended in 1910, when Falck decided to mount a subdued and highly successful production of Maeterlinck's *The Intruder*. 'You have *A Dream Play*, *Damascus* (both with parts for your wife) and you have *Svarta Handsken/The Black Glove*, which you have scornfully refused,' wrote the insulted and irascible Strindberg in September 1910.[20] The breach was decisive, and the final performances at the Intima on Norra Bantorget took place on 11 December 1910, with *Queen Christina* at one-thirty, *The Father* at four-thirty, and *Miss Julie* at eight o'clock in the evening.

Strindberg's desire for a larger chamber-theatre and an infinitely variable and flexible stage remained unfulfilled. As significant as the brief history of Intima Teatern is in the evolution of modern Swedish theatre, the resources of its miniature stage were severely limited. Many of Strindberg's plays, Pär Lagerkvist argued in his revolutionary essay *Modern Theatre: Points of View and Attack*, issued six years after Strindberg's death in 1912, 'could be played to advantage on such a stage. But many, and among them the most important ones, could only lose by it. The fact cannot be avoided that a small stage implies, first and foremost, reduced possibilities. Such a stage is confined within a small space from beginning to end. When an effect built upon contrasts is necessary it is hopeless and can do nothing. It has no possibility of expression through proportions, distance and antitheses'.[21] The full scenic articulation of

---

[20] Quoted in Bergman, *Den moderna teaterns genombrott,* p. 287.
[21] Thomas Buckman translation in *The Tulane Drama Review*, VI, 2, 1961 reprint, p. 25.

the dynamism and expansiveness of Strindberg's art was dependent upon the new stagecraft and new techniques introduced to Scandinavia's major theatres during the period of renewal that followed World War I. The entire range of Strindberg's immense production, from the earliest plays of the romantic period to the naturalistic dramas, the dream plays, the histories, and the chamber plays, would be eagerly re-explored by a new generation of theatre artists, dedicated to the re-theatricalization of the theatre and fired by Lagerkvist's seminal reassessment of the stature and significance of Strindberg's poetic achievement.

CHAPTER ELEVEN

The Modern Theatre

'The modern stage is a sorcerer's magical box full of a thousand possibilities, and we make a mistake if we do not use them.' Pär Lagerkvist's manifesto *Modern Theatre* (1918), with its ringing rejection of the constrained 'one-sidedness' of naturalism and 'the typical Ibsen drama with its silent tramping on carpets throughout five long acts of words, words, words',[1] marks a critical turning point in the development of the Scandinavian theatre in this century. The European revolt against stage naturalism mounted by such theorists as Appia, Craig, Yeats and Copeau was, despite Strindberg's sweeping renewal of modern drama, relatively late in reaching Scandinavia. The naturalistic style so forcefully enunciated in the meticulous productions of Bloch and August Lindberg was slow to disappear. As late as 1912, the Danish Royal Theatre production of *Indenfor Murene/Inside the Walls,* Henri Nathansen's genial, bitter-sweet slice of Jewish family life, was a triumphant reaffirmation of the naturalistic aesthetic; the roster of actors whose performances through the years have kept the traditions of this popular favourite alive to our own day is a list to conjure with: Karl Mantzius, Sigrid Neiiendam, Johannes Poulsen, Holger Gabrielsen, Clara Pontoppidan—and the unforgettable Poul Reumert.

[1] Thomas Buckman translation in *The Tulane Drama Review,* VI, 2, 1961 reprint, pp. 11, 10. Further references are to this edition.

Following Strindberg's death in 1912, however, a new generation of directors and designers began to emerge in Scandinavia, attuned to the anti-naturalistic demands for simplification, stylization and suggestion being voiced by Edward Gordon Craig and the adherents of the New Stagecraft. New staging and lighting techniques—particularly the introduction of the turntable stage, projections, and the cyclorama—opened the way for a new and more meaningful approach to Strindberg's mystic and visionary dream plays. The revitalization and 're-theatricalization' of the Scandinavian theatre which took place during the first third of this century has, in turn, had a deep and permanent effect on the theatrical climate, as a succession of gifted and imaginative directors, from Per Lindberg and Olof Molander to Alf Sjöberg and Ingmar Bergman in our own time, has sought to redefine the nature of the dramatic experience. Obviously, no more than a scant introduction to some of the major forces and figures behind theatrical advance in the modern period can be offered in the present chapter.

Theatrical activity broadened its base considerably in this century, as new theatres and companies sprang up and began to offer healthy competition to the established national theatres in Copenhagen, Oslo and Stockholm. Casino and Folketeatret, the first two private theatres in Denmark founded at mid-nineteenth century, were followed by Dagmar Theatre in 1883 and the New Theatre in 1908. Under Thorkild Roose's management in the early twenties, Dagmar Theatre quickly emerged as one of Scandinavia's most exciting theatres, as the Poul Reumert-Bodil Ipsen interpretation of *The Dance of Death,* under the richly detailed direction of Henri Nathansen, was hailed as the definitive performance of Strindberg's play. Stockholm acquired a whole fleet of new theatres around the turn of the century, most of them controlled by the formidable theatre king Albert Ranft. The Vasa (opened 1886) and the Swedish Theatre in Blasieholmen (famous as Nya teatern during Ludvig Josephson's management in the 1880s) became for a time in the late nineties important sources of fresh initiative under the artistic leadership of Harald Molander. Gustaf Collijn's new Intima on Engelbrektsplan, while it did not continue the traditions of the Strindberg-Falck era, nevertheless established its significance in the second decade of the century with an ensemble dominated by Sweden's Strindberg actor *par excellence*, Lars Hanson. The Royal Dramatic Theatre, housed since 1863 in Mindre teatern in Kungsträdgårdsgatan and reorganized in 1888 as a separate, privately-owned share company, renovated its fire-prone building when electricity was installed in 1898, the same year in which the Royal Opera moved to its present quarters. In 1908, Dramaten's own impressive new home on Nybroplan was completed (the incorrigible Bernard Shaw thought it resembled a bank when he saw it shortly after its completion). Oslo, too, acquired its share of new theatre companies around this time. The Central Theatre opened in 1902. In 1929, plans for a literary theatre dedicated to performing new Norwegian drama (whenever such could be found) were finally realized when Oslo's New Theatre, under the management of actor Ingolf Schanche, opened with an ambitious three-evening production of Knut Hamsun's trilogy, *Ved Rikets Port/ At the Kingdom's Gate, Livets Spil/Game of Life*, and *Aftenrøde/ Evening Glow*. A more remarkable type of theatrical experiment was represented, however, by the opening of Det Norske Teatret in 1913, an event which crowned the efforts of more than half a century to establish a separate theatre for 'Landsmaalet', the 'new Norwegian' language based on peasant dialects and programatically independent of Danish. For their première Det Norske Teatret chose Holberg's *Jeppe on the Hill* in a suitably *nynorsk* translation; fierce rioting soon ensued, but the dialect theatre has persisted and thrived.

Numerous privately run professional theatres, commercial as well as experimental, large as well as small, have continued to appear (and disappear) in Scandinavia throughout the modern period. Some, such as those just mentioned, have exerted considerable influence on the theatrical climate and taste of a particular period. A few—probably the most recent of which is Eugenio Barba's much-publicized Grotowski-oriented Odin Theatre in Holstebro—have laid claim to revolutionary status. It would, however, be a serious error to assume—as critics unfamiliar with the development of Scandinavian theatre might unwittingly be led to do—that any of these enterprises has, in the long run, seriously challenged the focal position occupied by the three national repertory theatres, the Royal Theatre, Dramaten, and Nationaltheatret, whose resources, equipment, and rich traditions have represented an unparalleled potential (not always exploited, to be sure) for bringing to fruition the ideas and experiments of the leading directors and designers of the modern period.

Scandinavia's first glimpse of the new ideas and techniques which were revolutionizing twentieth-century European theatre was provided by the visits of Max Reinhardt and his smoothly disciplined company. For Reinhardt, the theatre was neither a moral nor a literary institution. 'The theatre belongs to the theatre,' declared the 1911 Foreword to the *Blätter des Deutschen Theaters* issued by his office. 'It has always been our aim to give it back to itself. Its fantastic richness of colour, its limitless resources and variations, the blend of sound, words, colour, line and rhythm create the basis from which its profoundest effect stems.'[2] Swedish audiences first encountered Reinhardt's new stage forms and expressive groupings in the Circus Schumann production of *Oedipus Rex,* starring the renowned Alexander Moissi, which he brought to Stockholm's Circus in 1911. Four years later, Reinhardt's guest performances of Shakespeare at the Royal Opera stirred up lively controversy among the Stockholm critics. His staging of *A Midsummer Night's Dream,* which had established his reputation as a director, was called a 'symphony' of contrasting elements, 'a masquerade, scenically lyrical and scenically grotesque, theatre in the theatre' (*Dagens Nyheter,* 14 November 1915). In *Twelfth Night* his indispensable revolving stage caused some reviewers to lament the 'earthquake in Illyria: we saw ships and houses dancing by' (*Stockholms-Tidningen,* 11 November 1915).

Reinhardt's most powerful impact in Scandinavia was, understandably enough, created by his Strindberg productions, which, for the young reformer Per Lindberg, 'opened our eyes to the visionary, musical power in Strindberg's last dream plays'. Reinhardt's boldly expressionistic presentation of *The Ghost Sonata,* seen in Stockholm in 1917 and again in Copenhagen in 1920 with Paul Wegener as a ghastly and terrifying Hummel ('evil, cruelty and brutality in a deeply human and fantastically transfigured form,' marvelled playwright and

[2] Quoted in Gösta M. Bergman, *Den moderna teaterns genombrott,* p. 428.

critic Sven Lange in *Politiken*[3]), succeeded in blending the frightening, grotesque and confusing elements of the play into a 'nightmare of marionettes'. Reinhardt's skilled integration of theatrical effects in his Stockholm production of *The Pelican* in 1920 created, in the young Olof Molander's enthusiastic opinion, 'a scenic masterpiece which is not even suggested by a reading of this chamber play'.[4] The following October marked a controversial highpoint in Reinhardt's Strindberg offensive. As guest director at Dramaten, aided by the experimental designs of the Austrian artist Alfred Roller, he staged a provocative, 'dematerialized' production of *A Dream Play* which contrasted dramatically with the dry conventionality and literalism of the first production of Strindberg's play at the Swedish Theatre fourteen years before. Not all critics agreed with his interpretation: exercising directorial prerogative to alter the dramatist's conciliatory intentions, he allowed Indra's Daughter to sink into the flames rather than enter the growing castle, from which the flowering chrysanthemum was also eliminated. Critical disagreement notwithstanding, however, the seeds of theatrical revolt and advance had already been sown. The slow and gradual process by which Strindberg's mutational, dream-play dramaturgy achieved a scenic form that would fully project the intense visual dynamism of his remarkable vision took a quarter of a century, and constitutes a main line of development in modern Scandinavian theatre.

Productions of *Everyman* (in Hugo von Hofmannsthal's adaptation) on the Scandinavian stage provided an early source of inspiration in the struggle for a new stagecraft and an open stage. Johannes Poulsen, already at the height of his career as an actor, mounted a spectacular, Reinhardt-inspired *Everyman* at the Royal Theatre in Copenhagen in 1914 which established his position as one of this century's ablest Danish directors. (American audiences were treated to a grandiose revival of Poulsen's medieval spectacle in the Hollywood Bowl in 1936.) In 1916, Tor Hedberg's staging of *Everyman* in Stockholm became one of Dramaten's most important artistic successes. Having studied the Copenhagen production, Hedberg aimed for a *mise-en-scène* that was independent of the Reinhardt-Poulsen

---

[3] Quoted in Vagn Børge, *Strindbergs mystiske teater*, p. 354.

[4] *Scenen*, 1 January 1921.

pattern. An open stage was built out over the orchestra pit, while in the background an imposing construction of steps and levels led up to the heavenly gates. The Swedish director discarded conventional lighting techniques in favour of a 'decorative and symbolic' area illumination provided by powerful frontal spots, the use of which his production introduced at Dramaten. Far from perfectly realized, Hedberg's attempt at stylized theatre nevertheless struck immediate responsive chords with the new generation of reformers. Twenty-five-year-old Pär Lagerkvist, devoting a rare review to the performance, asserted that 'the new stylistic austerity which is most forcefully exemplified in modern art has not as yet to any degree inspired the art of the theatre'. Only partially satisfying his demands for simplicity, daring and formal purity, the *Everyman* production was, he felt, marred by elaborate realistic touches and by the highly embroidered, individualized acting of Anders de Wahl as Everyman—a part which requires a medievalized acting style, 'stiff, heavy, stringently stylized'.[5]

The spare structure and style of medieval drama would continue to have its impact on Lagerkvist's own dramatic writing. In 1917, the year after the *Everyman* production, he published his first expressionistic play, *Sista mänskan/Last Man,* a desolate picture of a frozen landscape, lit by a dying sun, in which the last desperate survivors of a ruined city carry on a shrill struggle for existence. Predictably enough, this bleak portrayal of existential *angst* was not acted. Nor were the two experimental 'marionette' plays by Hjalmar Bergman (1883–1931), Lagerkvist's great contemporary, that *were* performed by Dramaten in that year—*Dödens Arlequin/Death's Harlequin* and *En skugga/A Shadow*—even understood by their director or their audience. The impending breakthrough of modernism after World War I came, not through the work of new playwrights, but through the efforts of a group of young directors and designers.

In the vanguard of the new movement was Per Lindberg, who returned to Sweden in 1918 after an intensive study of Reinhardt's directorial techniques in Berlin. A conjuncture of ideal conditions blessed Lindberg's modernist offensive. The theatrical climate, crystallized in Lagerkvist's revolutionary manifesto

[5] *Forum,* 12 February 1916, p. 83f.

Modern Theatre: Points of View and Attack, was ripe for change, for the creation of 'a theatre which gives the imagination of both dramatist and actor greater freedom of movement and greater audacity, a simpler, more immediate and more expressive form' (p. 31). Lindberg, too, had seen Dramaten's *Everyman* production as a prelude to 'a subsequent classical repertoire staged in accordance with modern principles'.[6] The theatre to which Lindberg became attached in 1918, the Lorensberg Theatre in the west coast seaport city of Gothenburg, was a splendidly equipped modern facility that provided the young director with a perfect instrument for his art. Inaugurated two years before with the Danish director Svend Gade's production of *A Dream Play* (a symbolically strained

[6] *Acta Academica,* February 1916, p. 6.

37. Design by Svend Gade for his production of *A Dream Play* at the Lorensberg Theatre, Gothenburg, in 1916

interpretation that featured a black velvet-covered stage with individual, vaguely symbolic set-pieces), the 1000-seat Lorensberg Theatre was the first totally modern Swedish stage, incorporating a turn-table, a cyclorama and an advanced lighting board that permitted 'so-called horizon lighting from seventy projectors to produce a candle-power of no fewer than 250,000 ordinary lights'.[7] Finally, in addition to the auspicious theoretical climate and the Lorensberg's technical wonders, a third and decisive factor in Lindberg's success was his judicious choice of the talented scene painter and director Knut Ström, who had functioned for six years at the avant-garde Schauspielhaus in Düsseldorf, as his chief designer. Ström, justly called Sweden's first modern stage designer, continued to be a seminal influence in the theatre until the late 1950s; remaining in Gothenburg, he designed the stage and machinery for the ultra-modern Gothenburg City Theatre which replaced the Lorensberg in 1934 and which is still one of the most technically advanced playhouses in Europe. It was during the epoch-making years between 1919 and 1923, however, that Lindberg and Ström mounted a daring series of—mainly classical—productions which thrust the Lorensberg Theatre to the forefront of the modern movement, as the revolutionary force in Scandinavian theatre.

Well educated and articulate, Per Lindberg is an eloquent spokesman (first in 'Några ord om regi' 1919) for a theory of directing that relates clearly to the ideas of Reinhardt and Meyerhold. Directing, he asserts, is 'a scenic and personal amplification of the drama, so forceful that all the resources of the stage can be unified around the predominant directorial image for that particular play'. For the actor, decidedly the most important element on Lindberg's stage, the chief prerequisites are physical freedom, elimination of strain and vocal and muscular control—he casts an envious eye toward the 'purely circus-like training' given the actor in the modern Russian theatre. Plastic statuesqueness, an architectural rather than a painted stage, rhythmic, linear movement and a musical harmony of colours—these were for Lindberg, as they were for Meyerhold, basic ingredients of modern theatrical art. 'Modern stage décor should be decorative, rhythmic, an outgrowth of

---

[7] Quoted in Bergman, p. 527.

the play. . . . Why should it be enough for a stage picture to be imitated nature? Drama is rhythm. Why then should a setting be a dead copy?' he demands impatiently. His views on stage lighting reflect the theories of Appia and Craig. In addition to providing simple illumination and establishing an atmospheric rhythm, modern stage lighting must also become a means of creating accent, surrounding the characters with a plastic, sculptural lighting that will draw them closer to the audience. For herein, he insists, lies the key to the theatre's power: 'to establish, by every means permissible, contact between stage and auditorium, to bring the actors and audience closer to each other'. [8]

The remarkable series of classical productions staged by Lindberg at the Lorensberg Theatre quickly and effectively put his revolutionary ideas into practice. *As You Like It,* presented at the close of the first season, set the tone for the kind of adventurous experimentation that was to follow. Lindberg's directorial image was rooted in the play's original festive occasion as a wedding celebration: love shared the stage with melancholy in his buoyant conception, as the festivity of a stylized pastoral landscape contrasted with the darker, fresco-like court scenes. The audience was drawn into the action by every means available; a built-out forestage was equipped with broad steps down into the auditorium, where green-clad pages sounded a festive fanfare to introduce the spectacle. The iconographic style of Lindberg and Ström avoided the purely mechanical or the abstract; its aim was an imaginative orchestration of line, movement, rhythm, and grouping that would suggest the essential, prevailing mood of the production. Lindberg's *Hamlet* (1920), mounted in 'a fixed framework of blocks with strong vertical accentuation, blocks whose rhythm and colour can quickly and easily be transformed and change during the nineteen tableaux', [9] had more than a touch of Craig about it. The production became a symphony in red and black—'the streaming blood and the eternal darkness'—and each of the nineteen scenes was a variation on the theme. The sombre colour scheme of the structural surfaces, running from black

[8] 'Några moderna teaterproblem' in *Perspektiv på teater,* eds. Ulf Gran and Ulla-Britta Lagerroth, pp. 52–60.

[9] Per Lindberg, *Regiproblem* (Stockholm, 1927), p. 53.

through grey and dark brown into reddish brown, purple, and cerise, was carried through into the drapes and costumes, culminating in Gertrude's startlingly red dress. For *Othello* and *King Lear* (both 1921), similar principles were put to work. In the former, Knut Ström's décor was dominated by heavy, solid masses, including a drawbridge accentuated boldly against the sky for Othello's arrival on Cyprus. In the *Lear* towering walls with abstract patterns and textured surfaces conveyed a rough-hewn, pre-medieval impression. In *Romeo and Juliet* (1922), one of the period's most memorable productions, the stylized realism of Ström's graceful arches, low smooth walls and spiked cypresses created the subtle impression of Italian Renaissance art (Plate 39).

Newer drama played a relatively less central rôle in the Lindberg-Ström collaboration at the Lorensberg, though plays by such modern Scandinavian writers as Ibsen (*Peer Gynt*), Gunnar Heiberg (*King Midas*), Knut Hamsun (*Livet i vold/In the Throes of Life*), and Hjalmar Bergman (*Lodolezzi Sings* and the symbolic mood piece *Mr. Sleeman is Coming*) did receive a hearing. Of paramount significance, however, are Lindberg and Ström's seminal experiments with Strindberg's plays. Light was rapidly becoming, for a theatre pioneer like Lindberg, 'the theatre's palette. The deep stage with its dark perimeters, its bunched rays of light between rolling or gliding planes and levels, this was a whole new, independent, pathetic world. Where imagination and poetry belonged. Where new settings could be created with the slightest possible change of décor and without pauses'.[10] Only within such a theatrical context could Strindberg's imaginative genius come to its fullest realization. Far more than his productions of *Gustav Vasa* (1919) and *Creditors* (1920), Lindberg's staging of the poetic version of Strindberg's *Master Olof,* which included for the first time the dramatist's disillusioned epilogue depicting 'the creation of the world and its true meaning,' was a landmark in Swedish theatre. Performed in early 1920, the production's most revolutionary element was the bold simplicity of Knut Ström's impressive sets and costumes. Eliminating once and for all the history-play pattern, popularized by the Meininger, of naturalistically reproduced architecture, interiors and archeological

---

[10] Quoted in Gunnar Ollén, *Strindbergs dramatik*, p. 236.

accessories, Ström espoused new principles whose influence would continue to be felt for decades to come. 'What can and is to be included of the historical milieu', wrote Axel Romdahl in a perceptive review (*Svenska Dagbladet*, 21 January 1920), 'is decided solely according to the principle that nothing unnecessary must be stated, that nothing false must be stated, and

38. Design by Knut Ström for the Lindberg production of Strindberg's *The Saga of the Folkungs* (1920) at the Lorensberg Theatre

39. Design by Ström for Lindberg's production of
Shakespeare's *Romeo and Juliet* (1922) at the Lorensberg
Theatre

that, if anything beyond the unavoidable is stated, this must
have a suggestive weight capable of underscoring and em-
phasizing the dramatic action.' In the fall of the same year, the
sprawling historical masterpiece *The Saga of the Folkungs* was
directed by Lindberg in a similarly stylized Ström setting whose
raked, checkerboard stage and intentionally naïve, asymmetrical
rendering of a Serlio-type square suggested the atmosphere of a
sixteenth-century woodcut (Plate 38). 'The first great square
scene with the celebratory Te Deum [hailing King Magnus] is
quite simply a miracle,' commented August Brunius. 'We have
never seen anything as magnificent on a Swedish stage as this
immense altar-piece in which every figure stands in clear sculptural plasticity, completely enveloped in a dreamy mist and
etched against a storm-blue horizon. Its beauty culminates in the
possessed woman's pale silhouette against the sky—a Giotto
fantasy as fascinating for the eye as for the mind, a picture and

a dramatic revelation of equally striking power.'[11] Again challenging the barrier between stage and auditorium, Lindberg attempted to heighten the coming of the plague in the fourth act by surrounding the audience with cries of 'Pesten, Pesten!' A final Strindberg milestone at the Lorensberg Theatre is the world première of *To Damascus* III in November 1922, designed and directed by Knut Ström in a powerfully acted and judiciously shortened performance. An effectively simplified anti-illusionistic set, dependent for its impact on geometrical planes and bold contrasts, such as the silhouette of a signpost outlined against the sky, conveyed through its spareness a sense of immense height and space. Ström's apprentice Sandro

[11] Quoted in *ibid.*, p. 266.

40. Black chalk sketch by Ström for his production of Strindberg's *To Damascus* III (1922) at the Lorensberg Theatre

Malmquist, himself soon to become one of Sweden's most imaginative designer-directors, introduced into this production the use of images projected on the cyclorama as a substitute for constructed scenery.

Although the luminous Lindberg-Ström campaign in Gothenburg in the early twenties represents the most definitive and influential instance of the breakthrough of the new modernism, it was by no means an isolated phenomenon. The anti-naturalistic revolution predicted in Lagerkvist's *Modern Theatre* was rapidly taking shape throughout Scandinavia. 'Our time, in its lack of balance, its heterogeneity, and through the violent expansion of its conflicting forces, is baroque and fantastic, much more fantastic than naturalism is able to portray it,' Lagerkvist insisted (p. 16), and a bewildering variety of theatrical and dramatic experiments endeavoured—in Scandinavia as elsewhere in Europe and America at this time—to lend expression to the new postwar spirit of unrest and anguish. 'Dionysus, grant us again a feast! Give us again a temple for intensified life!' intoned the Danish critic and playwright Svend Borberg in 1919. 'We renounce science and all its deeds, the uniformity of time, place, and action, analysis, the logical construction, the false realism and the false psychology, "parts and points"—and we embrace instead only the unity of thought, the totality of atmosphere, the artistic composition. Grant us then the intoxication, the ecstacy, the great visions! Give us again a place of revelations.'[12] The road to the temple took many turns, but the rediscovery that theatre is, above all, theatre—not staged literature or imitated life—informed each new experiment.

At the Royal Theatre in 1919, as Lindberg assumed the management of the Lorensberg and Borberg was making his heady pronouncements, Johannes Poulsen, perhaps the most technically accomplished practitioner of the Reinhardt style of *mise-en-scène* in Scandinavia, accounted for one of the most extravagantly spectacular months in the Danish national theatre's history, dominated entirely by thirty evenings of his controversial revival of Oehlenschläger's *Aladdin*. 'Not anywhere else in the world,' wrote the production's designer Svend Gade, himself a stage and film director of wide international experience, 'have I seen a theatre production that on

12 *Teatret på Kongens Nytorv 1748–1948*, ed. H. Gabrielsen, p. 256.

217

the whole has been of greater magnificence and quality.[13] Enhanced by Carl Nielsen's music, Poulsen's 'Circus Schumann' *Aladdin* became a sweeping and colour-drenched oriental paraphrase of Oehlenschläger's classic that extended over two evenings, characteristically subtitled 'Thalia' and 'Melpomene'. At Dramaten later in the same year, Olof Molander, whose epoch-making Strindberg revivals in the 1930s marked the brilliant culmination of the search for a modern production style in Scandinavia, made his directional début with *The Merchant of Venice,* a festive and provocative fanfare to the succession of radically simplified and painstakingly orchestrated classical productions which he staged at Nybroplan during the twenties.

A far more explosive development than these, however, was marked by the Royal Swedish Opera's legendary presentation in early 1921 of Camille Saint-Saens' three-act opera *Samson and Delilah*, for which, perhaps inspired by the example of other European theatres, director Harald André engaged the well-known modernist painter Isaac Grünewald to design the sets and costumes. The step was a daring and, in some ways, a reactionary one, presenting as it did a demonstratively two-dimensional, pictorial alternative to the three-dimensional use of mass and space advocated by Appia and Craig and practised by Lindberg and Ström. Ushered in by intense controversy and an unprecedented box-office response, Grünewald's adventurous, collage-like design concept opened the way for a new attitude toward theatrical décor as 'decorative logic'. Production problems abounded: Grünewald's eleven scene designs involved complicated set changes and necessitated a partial re-working of Saint-Saens' opera; the orgiastically colourful, architectonically constructed costumes that in many cases could hardly be sewn, let alone worn, presented a dizzying contrast to the deliberate two-dimensionality of the settings. Not everyone understood the artist's intentions, and Grünewald barely prevented the planting of 'a photographically real moon' in his sky—'despite the velvet cactuses and shining silver trees, and despite the fact that my heavens were green'.[14] Nevertheless, as this remark suggests, the production provided an

[13] *Mit Livs Drejescene,* pp. 129–30.
[14] *Scenen* (1923), reprinted in *Isaac har ordet* (Stockholm, 1959), p. 48f.

incomparable visual feast. In the first act Samson confronted Delilah for the first time in a barbarically luxuriant garden whose fairy-tale vegetation included palms that sprouted sunflowers, mountain-high cactuses, and gleaming silver tree trunks (Plate 41). Somewhat more restrained in form but no less vivid was a second act grotto scene, held in a rich range of red tones, in which towering cliffs resembling multi-faceted basalt columns dwarfed the title figures, while brilliant suns exploded in reds and yellows against the violet cyclorama (Plate 42). Grünewald's most effective (and least exuberant) setting depicted the shorn Samson grinding at the mills in the prison at Gaza. In the water colour and gouache design, the chained and blinded Samson drives a monumental mill wheel whose towering dimensions are accentuated by the dim, focused lighting and the shadowy green-black background (Plate 43). It is no exaggeration to state that stage design took on a totally new dimension with Grünewald's *Samson and Delilah*; the sensational lawsuit occasioned by the artist's formidable bill for services rendered in the production drew renewed public attention to the figure of the theatre artist, whose work during this period now began to occupy a separate section in the reviews of some drama critics.

Another related manifestation of the new theatrical climate is found in the first productions of the expressionistic plays of Nobel Prize winner Pär Lagerkvist (1891–1974), the prophet of the New Theatre and Strindberg's most significant heir. In describing the technique of Strindberg's plays in *Modern Theatre,* Lagerkvist characterizes his own dramatic method as well: 'Here, everything is directed to one purpose—the liberation of a single mood, a single feeling whose intensity unceasingly grows and grows. Everything irrelevant is excluded even if rather important to the continuity or to the faithfulness of representation. Everything which occurs is meaningful and of equal weight. . . . And actually no "persons" in the usual, accepted meaning, no analysis, no psychological apparatus, no drawing of "characters." And yet, no abstractions' (p. 21). Even more central to their kinship is the shared intense awareness of suffering—given a meaning and viewed in a broader metaphysical context of fate and redemption by Strindberg, but seen as a meaningless correlative of a fundamentally absurd and evil universe by the uncompromisingly pessimistic Lagerkvist. Inevitably, both the form and the themes of Lagerkvist's dark dramatic vision would strike a responsive note with the theatrical innovators of the twenties. Knut Ström had first staged *The Tunnel,* an expressionistic nightmare which explores the difficult passage from life to death after a fatal crash and which is the first in the cycle of three brief plays about the moment of death called *Den svåra stunden/The Difficult Hour,* at the Schauspielhaus in Düsseldorf in 1918. It was not until 1921, however, that Lagerkvist received his first public performance in Sweden with the Intima ensemble's pioneering production of the one-act *Himlens hemlighet/The Secret of Heaven,* a grim and highly theatrical view of a group of grotesque and helpless creatures living out a meaningless existence on 'a huge blue-black sphere, partly illuminated by a lightbeam'. Seen in the same year as both Grünewald's *Samson* at the Royal Opera and Reinhardt's *A Dream Play* at Dramaten, the Intima's *Secret of*

41. Isaac Grünewald's revolutionary designs for Saint-Saens'
Samson and Delilah at the Royal Swedish Opera, 1921:
Act I. Watercolour and gouache

42. *Samson and Delilah*, Act II

43. Act III

221

Heaven was a diametrically opposite but no less revolutionary type of theatre experience. A boldly stripped and concentrated design concept by the artist Yngve Berg utilized a spherical elevation over the stage floor to create a nightmare vision of the globe, surrounded by black space and glaringly illuminated by a ghastly violet spotlight, upon which the isolated figures in the drama live out their splintered lives.

Although Lagerkvist's next play *Den osynlige/The Invisible One,* a loose and rather overstated poetic allegory about the miserableness of man's enforced existence on earth, reached the Dramaten stage under Olof Molander's firm direction and in Bertil Damm's imaginative décor in 1924, it remained for Per Lindberg to evolve a distinct style of theatrical presentation for Lagerkvist's dramas. The twenty-year association of Lindberg and Lagerkvist is one of the best examples of a rewarding collaboration between a dramatist and a director in the modern theatre. Lindberg's richly inventive visual imagination was given ample opportunity for expression in *The Tunnel,* which he directed at the Club Theatre, an experimental stage sponsored by Dramaten, in 1927. Lagerkvist's own minutely detailed description of the stage setting is in itself a startling cubist vision that corresponds perfectly to the new principles at work in the visual theatre:

In the darkness on the stage, transparent forms are discernible: farthest to the right the blue gable of a house leans sharply in toward the audience; up to the left a barrier which cuts obliquely across the entire stage opening; in the background the fragment of an arch, illuminated from below by light, billowing smoke which whirls in under the arch and disappears; above this, in the darkness a red dog rushing wildly forward; to the right of the dog two great hands stretched out as if in terror; to the left a large pale head without hair, and still higher up the number S 8007, in large print. All the forms are in different depths and in planes that cross each other, all in confusion. The colours fantastic, but dull. The stage in a blue-violet half-darkness.

In Düsseldorf, Ström had used a diagonal scrim separating the play's two 'characters', the dead Man in Tails and his dark antagonist the Hunchback, to suggest something of Lagerkvist's remarkable expressionistic visualization of death. In Lindberg's production the Man in Tails and the Hunchback, emerging out of the darkness of the tunnel, appeared in a light of different colours from a stationmaster's swinging lantern. A sudden flash of light revealed 'a setting of expressionistic torment and chaos', after which the stage was plunged into darkness 'intersected by beams of white light'.[15]

Of far greater significance was Lindberg's production at Dramaten in 1928 of *Han som fick leva om sitt liv/The Man Who Lived his Life Over,* one of Lagerkvist's best plays and a turning point in his dramatic technique. Abandoning much of the visionary and abstractly symbolic method of the earlier plays, Lagerkvist here provides a far more concrete framework for the internal conflict between good and evil that takes place within the title figure, a shoemaker named Daniel, who struggles without success to make his second life more meaningful than his first. A recurrent motif in all of Lagerkvist's work is forcefully stated in Daniel's anguished, existential cry for a chance to live his 'real life,' his 'own life' in the face of a hostile and indifferent universe. A moving response is provided by the old man Boman, a minor figure who is nonetheless one of Lagerkvist's most brilliantly drawn characters, sensitively interpreted in the original production by the talented character actor Ivan Hedqvist:

I'm Boman, the man with one leg. Perfectly correct, yes. He who goes from place to place selling shoelaces. Because my life is to sell shoelaces. My soul was elected for that. . . . But we live as best we can, we do our best. Yes, we ought to do that. . . You should too! And then no one can ask more of you. . . Yes, we live the best we can. . . this hard, hard life. . . we put up with it. . . drag ourselves through it. . . day by day, year by year. . . as well as we are able. . . And we have our dreams, we have our dreams! Have you thought of that? And there is kindness, there *is* kindness. . . And we have our dreams.

Sandro Malmquist's response in his stage design to the blend of symbolism and heightened realism in Lagerkvist's drama was a realistic shoemaker's workshop located in a dimly lit void accentuated by the silhouette of a cross.

'Pär Lagerkvist continued toward the goal which he had set himself: "The struggle for a new form must also be the struggle for a deeper personal vision"',' wrote Per Lindberg in an essay on Lagerkvist's dramaturgy. 'His drama is what drama was originally: a cultic action, a hypnotic festival for the moral

---

[15] Erik Lindorm, quoted in Thomas R. Buckman, 'Pär Lagerkvist and the Swedish Theatre', *TDR* VI reprint, p. 85.

edification of mankind.'[16] A highpoint among Lindberg's later
productions of Lagerkvist was his staging of *Bödeln/The Hangman* in 1934, first at the National Stage in Bergen, where
audience enthusiasm, he states 'almost grew to the proportions
of a folk movement', and then at Stockholm's Vasa Theatre.
The Hangman is an intense statement of personal moral re-
vulsion at the growing barbarity of Hitler's Nazi Germany.
Written to be performed without interruption and utilizing
striking cinematic techniques and tableaux, the play consists of
two scenes: a dimly lit medieval tavern filled with beer-
drinking workmen is suddenly transformed into a garish,
glaringly lighted night-club patronized by hysterical and frenzied Nazis. Dominating both environments is the sinister figure
of the Hangman, acted with incredible force in Stockholm by
the fascinating and brooding Gösta Ekman, regarded by many
as the greatest actor of his generation. Looked upon by the
superstitious medieval workmen with a mixture of fascination
and aversion—a recognizable scapegoat for the accumulated
guilt of the people—the Hangman becomes in the second section
an object of frenzied admiration by an already blood-crazed and
brutalized world. 'They call me still, and I come,' says the grim
figure, breaking his ominous silence:

I look out over the lands—the earth is febrile and hot, and the cries of
sick birds are heard in the empty air. Then the rutting-time of evil is at
hand! That is the hangman's hour!

The point of Lagerkvist's frightening indictment is not merely
that his contemporaries are as blindly superstitious and savage
as their medieval forebears, but that they are far more murder-
ously destructive than even the office of the weary and blood-
stained Hangman ('your Christ, with the hangman's mark on
my forehead! Sent down to you!') can suggest.

During the decade between this production and Per Lindberg's early death in 1944, the versatile director staged three
other Lagerkvist plays, two of them in nation-wide touring
productions that were an integral part of his energetic campaign
to create a 'folk theatre' and to establish Lagerkvist as 'a son
and a poet of the people'. Lindberg's brother-in-law Hjalmar

---

[16] 'Några synspunkter på Pär Lagerkvists dramatik' (1940), reprinted in
Lindberg's *Bakom masker*, pp. 15–17.

Bergman, whose brilliant career ended abruptly with his tragic death in a Berlin hotel room on New Year's Day 1931, had of course already achieved this kind of wide popularity by exchanging the mordant disillusionment of his early plays for the more congenial humour of his later comedy successes, *Swedenhielms* (1925), *Patrasket/Rabble* (1928), and his adaptation of his successful novel *The Markurells of Wadköping* (1929). On the other hand, the ethical seriousness and thematic density of Lagerkvist's art could hardly be expected to carry the same broad popular appeal in the theatre. *Mannen utan själ/The Man Without a Soul,* in which Lagerkvist returns to a framework of heightened, suggestive realism as a background for the inner drama of a terrorist (The Man) who renounces violence when he meets and falls in love with the wife of the man he has just killed (The Woman), began its tour of regional theatres in Lindberg's *mise-en-scène* in early 1937. In a production which (unlike Alf Sjöberg's much starker staging of the play at Dramaten the following year) emphasized a concrete and importunate environment, Lindberg created a crescendo of sound, lighting and even smoke effects to suggest the war which rages during the play. The Damascus-like stations through which The Man passes in his quest for redemption—the coffee-bar, the Woman's room, the hospital, the cemetery, and the prison where he ends his life—were designed with vivid, fundamental simplicity by the gifted Danish artist Helge Refn, who here scored one of his first important successes. In particular, Refn's atmospherically realistic coffee-bar, bathed in green dusk and lit by red lamps, presented a dramatic contrast to his startlingly naked cubistic design for the hospital room, consisting only of glaring white walls, a glass centre door and the iron bed on which The Woman dies in childbirth. Suspicious (and justly so) of the spurious, melodramatic religious note sounded by the 'floods of radiance' through which The Man walks to his execution in the text, Lindberg carefully maintained a sober open-mindedness that eliminated all Christian symbolism from his stage version.

Lindberg's cycle of Lagerkvist productions came to an end with *Seger i mörker/Victory in the Dark* and *Midsommardröm i fattighuset/Midsummer Dream in the Poorhouse. Victory,* another analysis of individuals caught in the clash of Nazism and democracy, was directed by him at Oslo Nationaltheatret and on tour with the Swedish National Touring Theatre in 1939. *Midsummer Dream*, a muted fantasy in which the young girl Cecilia is lifted out of the poverty and squalor around her by the story of an old man's unhappy love, was staged at the Blanche Theatre in Stockholm in 1941. Clearly, the twenty-year friendship and unique collaboration between these two artists has left an important mark on the evolution of Lagerkvist's dramaturgy and accounted in no small measure for the impact which performances of his plays often had in the Swedish theatre during the twenties and thirties. As central as Lagerkvist's plays are to the development of modern Scandinavian drama, however, it would be misleading to ascribe to them an exaggerated causal influence in the history of modern theatre in Scandinavia. They reflected, rather than accounted for, the sweeping stylistic upheaval heralded in Lagerkvist's *Modern Theatre*; the chief impetus for change came, however, from the new *mise-en-scène*, with its demand for a more creative and theatrically imaginative approach to the great classics of Shakespeare and Strindberg, launched by Lindberg and Ström at the Lorensberg Theatre and mastered during the decade that followed by Olof Molander.

The second wave of the ineluctable advance toward modernism in Scandinavian theatre had been prepared for not only by the eye-opening guest performances of Max Reinhardt and the Lindberg-Ström era in Gothenburg but also by such revolutionary experiments as the Intima's *Secret of Heaven* and Grünewald's *Samson and Delilah*. The decisive turning point came when Lindberg, having left Gothenburg in 1924, mounted his ambitious stylistic assault on the capital during the 1926–7 season—not at one of the established theatres, but in an unlikely partnership with Ernst Eklund, whose specialty was sophisticated drawing-room comedy, at Stockholm's newly built Concert Hall. This formal, curtainless platform stage accorded well with Lindberg's democratic view of theatre as a totally sensory experience that involves everyone in the area of activity. Such an open stage, he insisted, 'is a part of that space common to both the actors and the audience in which a performance is experienced, and experienced not only through illusion, but chiefly through the rhythm and the intensity of the drama and the acting'.[17] His extraordinary season is unique in the history of Scandinavian theatre. For his opening production he chose *Antony and Cleopatra,* with Harriet Bosse and Carl Ström in the leading rôles. Interestingly enough, he turned to Isaac Grünewald, whose work might seem the antithesis of the sculptural three-dimensionality required by Lindberg's open stage, for the design concept. The result was one of Grünewald's brightest achievements: a relatively neutral framework, light and airy in tone, within which a general's tent or a hoisted sail served to evoke a change of scene. The Egyptian-Roman dichotomy central to Lindberg's directorial image was skilfully visualized in Grünewald's rich and connotative costume scheme, which utilized predominantly orange and red tones for the Egyptians and blues and whites for the Romans. In his staging of *The Bonds of Interest,* Lindberg exploited to the fullest Benavente's conception of his *commedia dell'arte* characters as puppets 'moved by plain and obvious strings, like men and women in the farces of our lives'; transforming the play to a festively choreographed, Grünewald-designed marionette comedy, he punctuated each clever line with a gay pirouette. In a darker mood, Ingolf Schanche was an elegant and subtle Hamlet. The other productions of this remarkable season—Sophocles' *Oedipus Rex,* Romain Rolland's historical play *The Wolves,* and Swedish playwright Tor Hedberg's political drama *Johan Ulvestjerna*—were eclipsed, however, by Lindberg's revival of *To Damascus* III. A striking expressionistic setting by John Jon-And featured a drastically stylized mountain landscape made up entirely of angular, abstract planes and contours and dominated by a weirdly deformed cross. Although Harriet Bosse played the rôle of the Lady which Strindberg had written for her, Ingolf Schanche stole the spotlight as the Tempter with his 'mocking and expressive countenance'. (Schanche, whose ability to combine irony and dread in his interpretations made him the ideal Strindberg actor, collaborated once again with Lindberg seven years later when the latter mounted his adventurous one-evening version of all three parts of *To Damascus* at Nationaltheatret in Oslo. Here, Schanche touched the peak of his career with his gripping Faustian portrayal of the Unknown, 'the defier, the stormer, the exile, a disharmonious being who,

[17] Quoted in Buckman, p. 78.

227

with the shifty and evasive glance of a slave, rouses himself to one single defiant no to heaven, only to retreat in immediate terror into the ingrained dread of his earthly mask'.[18])

Obviously, Lindberg's artistically aggressive and demanding Concert Hall season could hardly be expected to prove a viable financial venture—his partnership with Eklund was dissolved before the season was out—but its reverberations were soon felt. Responding with alacrity to the implied challenge, Olof Molander staged *A Midsummer Night's Dream* at Dramaten in April for which he, too, drew upon Grünewald's unique gifts to create a sparkling framework for Shakespeare's comedy. Grünewald, making his début at the national theatre, created a setting more modestly subordinated to the intentions of the dramatist and director, consisting of a recognizable Athenian palace whose white columns and moss-green and red-violet walls were counterbalanced by the soft blues and greens of his seductive romantic wood. Early in the following season Molander's restless experimentation with form and style took a bolder turn with his controversial constructivist production of Racine's *Phèdre*—reminiscent in some ways of the famous Tairov performance of the play in Moscow five years before. Transposed to a barbaric pre-historic era, Molander's interpretation utilized a defiantly non-representational set by Jon-And, the focal point of which was a gigantic, megaphone-shaped column, much smaller at the base than at the top and surrounded by a graceful spiral of steps, pillars and inclines (Plate 44). Racine survived the assault, however, due principally to Tora Teje's majestic Phèdre, the rôle in which she first emerged as one of this century's foremost tragic actresses.

Ironically, one of the new modernism's most resounding failures during this period of ferment and experiment in Scandinavia was accounted for by Edward Gordon Craig, the foremost spokesman for a New Theatre, in connection with his ill-starred production of Ibsen's *The Pretenders* at the Danish Royal Theatre in November 1926. Although this well-known event is usually seen by scholars in the relatively rosy light shed upon it by Craig's own descriptions in *The Mask* and in his sumptuous portfolio entitled *A Production* (Oxford, 1930), a glance into the Royal Theatre archives tends to modify this

[18] Herbert Grevenius, quoted in Ollén, p. 380.

view and places the outraged comments of the contemporary
reviewers of the performance in their proper perspective. The
play was chosen specifically as a festive commemoration of the
twenty-fifth anniversary of the acting débuts of Johannes and
Adam Poulsen: Johannes, following in the footsteps of his
father Emil, was a compelling Bishop Nikolas, a frightening,
toothless old schemer; his brother Adam was a villainous, red-
bearded Skule who lacked the full tragic force of Ibsen's

44. Design by John Jon-And for Molander's constructivist
production of Racine's *Phèdre* at Dramaten in 1927

character. As the director of the production, Johannes Poulsen had invited Craig's assistance—and, to everyone's surprise, the legendary figure arrived in Copenhagen to engage in what was to be his last venture in the practical theatre.

The results of the Craig-Poulsen 'collaboration' (subsequently, each was anxious that the 'honour' of the achievement should befall the other) were not as positive as Craig's comments and sketches would suggest. As might be expected, the production set out to alter completely the more traditional approach to the play taken by its previous director, Julius Lehmann, when it was last acted in Denmark in 1899. A comparison of the stage manager's copious records of these two productions is extremely instructive. One very obvious change was, of course, the development from painted scenery in 1899 to plastic, three-dimensional forms in 1926. Another—less obvious and less advantageous—change was the abandonment of the older scheme of a relatively open and neutral playing area *surrounded* by scenery in favour of the cluttered, layer-cake profusion of platforms and abstract shapes that crammed Craig's stage space. By far his best scene was his often-reproduced design for the splendid opening in the churchyard of Christ Church in Bergen, as the crowd outside the church awaits the outcome of Inga's ordeal by fire. 'The curtain rises and we see a forest of lances grow toward the sky,' wrote Svend Borberg, 'while behind them, projected on a cyclorama: a dream in yellow light and bluish shadow, a half de-materialized cathedral.'[19] 'We were at once removed from the usual theatre gothicism,' agreed Christian Gulmann. 'No painted church as a background for Meininger processions, but a beautifully effaced impression of high columns of light, and a forest of lances above the richly colourful warriors—a square in Florence rather than a picture of medieval Norway.' In the ground plan for this scene, '22 new gravestones' and a number of the ubiquitous 'new grey set-pieces used in all acts and scenes' filled the entire stage.[20] For the more intimate interior scenes in Ibsen's drama, however, Craig's ponderous background of non-representational shapes and platforms seemed obtrusive and inappropriate to

[19] Reviews of this production, dated 15 November 1926, are from the Royal Theatre Library press clipping collection.

[20] *Maskinmesterjournal*, Royal Theatre Library.

most observers. The opening scene of the third act, a room in the Bishop's Palace in Oslo, drew the severest criticism. Treated in Ibsen's stage directions and in the 1899 ground plan as a simple, closed interior which opens into a lighted chapel in the background, this scene was staged by Craig in a very different manner, by placing an armchair and an ornate divan with 'new bolster' among twenty-odd of his grey forms. 'The Bishop's moving death scene was acted in something resembling a churchyard, in which he breathes his last on a divan,' reported one critic. 'The Bishop's room, resembling a warehouse cellar in the dockyards, filled with packing cases, robbed [Johannes Poulsen's art] of all its mystique, in spite of a violet spotlight on one of the packing cases,' grumbled another. 'The strange blocks among which the Bishop dies' were, Valdemar Vedel stated categorically, among the most unfortunate elements in the production.

An inexplicable penchant for over-elaboration led to the substitution of an ornate, tent-like 'Ladies Pavilion' for the simple palace interior from which the women watch the royal election (I, ii). Similarly, the plain palace room which, both in Ibsen's text and in the 1899 ground plan, contains a bench, chairs, and 'a cradle in which the royal child sleeps' (III, ii) became in Craig's hands 'Haakon's Bedchamber', dominated by a large, canopied four-poster bed downstage centre. 'When Skule visits King Haakon in order to negotiate a compromise, we are shown the royal bedchamber, which more than anything else resembles a Parisian variety star's boudoir,' wrote one observer sarcastically. One way or another, every reviewer emphasized the stylistic inconsistency and the consequent failure on Craig's part to respond creatively to the specific Nordic tone and atmosphere of Ibsen's drama. Disappointment, rather than reactionary outrage, was the Scandinavian theatre's response to its unique encounter with the great English theoretician. 'We have nothing against the simplification and stylization which Mr. Craig advocates,' wrote Viggo Cavling, 'and we agree with him completely that all the old-fashioned theatre art is often offensively glossy. But if one wants to stylize, one cannot stylize in general, but only within the framework and tone and milieu in which the play takes place—as Max Reinhardt and Jessner have done time and time again, with sublime results.

And the Craigian method could undoubtedly have been applied with success here, if only the coldness of the North, the harshness of the Middle Ages, the darkness of Catholicism had been allowed to come through.'

Precisely in the terms which Cavling prescribes, Olof Molander mounted a series of Strindberg productions during the thirties—imaginative in their application of the principles of the new stagecraft yet firmly anchored in the concrete milieu and tone of Strindberg's Stockholm—which mark the final culmination of the striving toward a modern directorial style in Scandinavia. 'Lindberg agitated, Molander built'—and an impressive cycle of productions during his tenure as Dramaten's chief from 1934 to 1938 gradually established a fluid and responsive scenic form that was perfectly attuned to Strindberg's associational, mutational dramaturgy. The director's responsibility reached, in Molander's artistic canon, far beyond such matters as décor, blocking and rôle interpretation. 'He bears the responsibility for the whole development, character and integrity of the play. It is he who must assemble the resources, put them into action, distinguish what is important from what is less so, fill the cracks, tone the colours, and assemble the lives of the separate characters into one unified life—that of the drama.'[21] Unmistakably Harald Molander's son in his sense for concrete, characteristic detail, Olof Molander combined painstaking directorial analysis with a fine sensibility that restored to Strindberg's plays a relevance and a Swedishness that displaced the Germanic Strindberg of Reinhardt and his followers.

Molander's first production of *A Dream Play* in October 1935 remains a legendary and focal event in Scandinavian theatre and culture, singled out, for instance, by Ingmar Bergman in the introduction to his *Four Screenplays* as a 'fundamental dramatic experience' in his own career. In striking contrast to Reinhardt's production fourteen years before, Molander's *Dream Play* maintained a lucid undertone of resignation and consolation, a recognition of the humanity so often absent in the German *Schrei*-versions of Strindberg's plays. The spine of his conception was his identification of the Dreamer, in all three of his voices, with Strindberg himself—a

[21] *Perspektiv på teater*, p. 89

presence felt in the young, eternally expectant Officer, in the mature Lawyer whose hideous face reflects the tawdry and vicious affairs in which he deals, and, above all, in the aging Poet who, made up in Molander's production to resemble Strindberg, learns at the feet of Indra's Daughter that poetry, reality and waking dreams are all inextricably bound up together. As the Lawyer, Gabriel Alw projected a furrowed, agonized Christ-image bent beneath the cross of the world's woes—'and to Christ bearing his cross he was transformed before our very eyes,' wrote Herbert Grevenius, 'when during the ghost-like doctoral promotion beneath the church's mighty vault a crown of thorns, rather than the laurel wreath, was pressed down upon his head.'[22] The vibrant centre of the production, balancing Tora Teje's majestically sonorous and melancholy Indra's Daughter, was Lars Hanson's irresistibly buoyant and hopeful Officer—'in walk and carriage a marionette of dreams, sorrow, and unhappiness, his face frozen in an unforgettable mixture of eagerness and pained surprise', wrote Frederik Schyberg when the production came to the Danish Royal Theatre later in the same season. 'The scene in which the officer is suddenly seated on the school-bench again and must grind out the old forgotten lessons and tables' was 'a tangible, inescapable nightmare—a dream we all know and now suddenly recognize in an actor's brilliant portrayal of it.'[23]

Of far greater impact than any of the individual performances, however, was the imaginative *mise-en-scène* into which they were integrated. Its basic style can be called surrealistic: a fluid progression of suggestive, dream-like settings, tastefully designed by Sven Erik Skawonius and built up of fragmented bits of sharply etched reality, was supplemented by the muted dematerialized visions of Strindberg's Stockholm projected by Isaac Grünewald on the cyclorama (Plate 45). Each of Skawonius' dream-pictures had its strongly lighted focus—a table at which the invalid Mother sits, the announcement-board with hymn numbers in the church, a diagonal fragment of wall—beyond which one saw dark recesses of space intersected only be spotlights. Grünewald's projections, sometimes dominating the stage

---

[22] *Ibid.*, p. 95.
[23] *Berlingske Tidende,* 2 May 1936, reprinted in Schyberg's *Ti Aars Teater,* p. 141.

and sometimes serving as a background, anchored the action to specific, recognizable views of *fin de siècle* Stockholm. The audience glimpsed the old Dramaten with Jacob's Church in the background; the Horse Guard barracks became the growing castle; outside a fragment of the old Royal Opera the Officer 'waits, waits, as the years pass, his roses wither, and he himself becomes an old man, though still with his cap cocked at the same jaunty angle and his moustache curled up in the same jaunty way'.[24]

In 1937, the twenty-fifth anniversary of the dramatist's death, the Strindberg renaissance created by Molander was at its height. In February, armed with the astute critical advice of Martin Lamm and the unpretentiously discreet, half-realistic,

[24] *Perspektiv på teater,* pp. 94–5.

45. Grünewald's design for a projection (Fairhaven) in the famous Molander production of *A Dream Play* at Dramaten in 1935

half-fantastic designs of Skawonius, Molander staged his epoch-making production of *To Damascus* I at Dramaten. The heart of the performance was once again Lars Hanson, whose sympathetic and unhysterical Unknown captured the strange mixture of tragic anguish and irony in the play. 'With an intuition which is quite unique,' wrote one reviewer, 'Lars Hanson has grasped and has allowed his infinitely revealing face to express what in some ways lies hidden at the very core of the rôle—a little, frightened and helpless young man with a bad conscience, unable even to comprehend why he is buffeted so hard by fate.'[25] In October of the same year came the Molander-Skawonius production of *The Saga of the Folkungs*, a sweeping medieval spectacle conceived on a staggering scale. For the great scenes on the square and for the coming of the plague, Molander choreographed an almost overwhelming pictorial display that offers an interesting foretaste of Bergman's cinematic art. Critic Herbert Grevenius wrote:

A gallows stands like a grim pointer toward eternity, and an immense
iron chain stretches a meaningful greeting from a distant heaven to a
desperate earth. Grotesque tumult and ceremonies, royal splendour and rags,
drunken torchlight processions, Dominicans and Franciscans with
flaming candles, the fever-red Plague Girl whirling about with her broom
and chalking her crosses [on the doors of the doomed], the flaggelants'
frenzied monotone dance with blood streaming down their naked backs,
King Magnus groaning beneath his black penitential cross, the Possessed
Woman on the roof shouting out her 'You have blood in your crown,
King Magnus.' One is caught in the grip of these intense visual
pictures.[26]

As if this were not enough, *The Dance of Death* was also to be seen at Dramaten during this astonishing Strindberg year, guest starring Poul Reumert opposite Tora Teje. 'In the round, empty room, as in a cage, the two antagonists prowl cautiously round each other like a pair of tigers, hissing and growling,' commented one observer.[27] Captain Edgar was throughout Reumert's career one of his most compelling and most completely observed characters. His shattering performances with Bodil

---

[25] Sten Selander, quoted in Ollén, p. 238.
[26] *Ibid.,* p. 268.
[27] Carl G. Laurin, quoted in *ibid.,* p. 340.

Ipsen at the Dagmar Theatre in 1920 have never been equalled; his appearance in the rôle at the Odéon in 1928 fired the imagination of Paris audiences who still recalled his triumphant Tartuffe (in French!) at the Comédie-Française three years earlier. Opposite Teje at Dramaten, Reumert usurped the audience's sympathy for his Captain in a performance that reminded some critics of Lars Hanson's amiable and unreflecting Officer in *A Dream Play*. 'Without sparing us a single detail in the gradual process of his degradation,' wrote Agne Beijer, 'Reumert forced us in some strange way to identify and to sympathize with this monstrous man. As deeply as this man suffered, as gripping and as persuasive as these expressions— genuinely masculine in all their helplessness—of his vengefulness as well as his suffering were, it would have seemed an absurdity to ask whether his torment was self-inflicted or not. The Captain became more than an individual, Reumert's art transformed him into an image of the torment which our own helpless inability to understand and to live in harmony with our fellow man constantly brings down upon ourselves and others.'[28]

Although the unique 'fantastic realism' introduced by Olof Molander in his revolutionary Strindberg productions of the mid-thirties remained the hallmark of many of his later Strindberg revivals as well, its form varied considerably, as seen in the *six* other interpretations of *A Dream Play* which this restlessly inventive artist staged throughout Scandinavia. At the Danish Royal Theatre in 1940 and again at the enormous new Malmö Civic Theatre in 1947, Molander discarded the too obviously localized Stockholm projections. In Malmö they were replaced by evocative photographic images of neutral street scenes and summer villas in dream-like greys and whites. In his controversial closing scene, as each of the characters places his offering upon the altar the gigantic silhouette of a heavy wooden cross rose slowly in the background, bearing the familiar inscription 'Ave o crux spes unica' (Hail, O Cross, our last recourse): an enormous reproduction of the cross that marks Strindberg's grave. In Gothenburg later the same year, Molander's fourth distinct approach to *A Dream Play* suddenly

[28] *Göteborgs Handels- og Sjöfartstidning*, 3 May 1937, reprinted in Beijer's *Teaterrecensioner 1925–1949*, p. 256.

assumed a different, darker tone permeated by defiance and despair. The bearing force in this production was no longer a buoyant and hopeful Officer but the intense and embittered Lawyer created by Anders Ek, whose crowning with thorns and symbolic crucifixion in the doctoral promotion scene became a harrowing experience. Projections were eliminated altogether, and Molander now experimented with solid, naturalistic elements. The growing castle was a three-dimensional miniature of the Horse Guard barracks, resting on piles of straw and flanked by immense, multi-coloured hollyhocks. In the closing scene, flames licked at its roof but no faces appeared in the empty windows; as it sank noiselessly into the ground, a Molander cross once again rose in the background—this time, however, not the marker from Strindberg's grave but a high, stark silhouette etched against a fiery horizon and towering above the black ruins of a bombed-out city. In the foreground stood the lonely figure of the Poet, with his sombre Strindberg countenance.

For Molander, no interpretation of this play would ever be the final one. 'I will never get the chance to mount *A Dream Play* in the way I would like,' he told an interviewer in 1965, the year before his death, when he staged the work's Norwegian première in Oslo. Dissatisfied that only forty-three rehearsals had been held for this, his seventh and last, production of the play, the demanding seventy-three-year-old director added: 'The resources, not least on the acting level, which this Strindbergian masterpiece requires in order to, in my opinion, come even close to doing it justice are so colossal that no theatre has them at its disposal.'[29] The remarkable history of his voyage through *A Dream Play* is in itself characteristic. For Molander and for the directors who came after him, Strindberg's plays, like Shakespeare's, have continued to afford a rich and multifarious source of theatrical inspiration, stimulating new interpretations and new technical advances. The Shakespearian productions of Alf Sjöberg or the original approaches to Ibsen and Strindberg by Ingmar Bergman during the second half of the century, fully independent in their own right, nevertheless owe the favourable context in which they thrive to the strong spirit of modernism and experiment

[29] *Perspektiv på teater*, pp. 88–9.

fostered in Scandinavia by such pioneers as Per Lindberg and Johannes Poulsen, and built into a viable tradition by Olof Molander.

Just as modern principles of directing and design reached their full articulation in Molander's productions of the mid-thirties, these fervent years also saw the emergence of a vigorous wave of new dramatists, inspired in large measure by the new theatricality and deeply concerned, each in his own way, with a social and political situation that was becoming more ominous every month. Although Kaj Munk (1898–1944), the outspoken Danish poet-priest whose name took on virtually symbolic proportions during the Second World War, made his début as a dramatist in 1928 with an aborted production of his masterpiece *En Idealist/Herod the King,* it was not until three years later that he won a name as a playwright with the Royal Theatre performance of *Cant,* a free-verse denunciation of self-righteous hypocrisy and sham piety brought vividly to life by Johannes Poulsen's splendidly gross Henry the Eighth. A vastly different environment, the primitive society of a small Danish village, was explored by Munk in *Ordet/The Word,* first staged at the Betty Nansen Theatre in 1932 and later popularized by Carl Dreyer's 1954 film. In its controversial conclusion, in which Johannes, who imagines himself to be Christ, 'raises' his brother's wife from the dead, Munk's 'legend of today' is an unmistakable rejoinder to Pastor Sang's miscarried 'miracle' in Bjørnson's *Beyond Human Power* I. With *De Udvalgte/The Elect,* Munk returned to his predominant mode, the theatrically ambitious and grandiose historical genre, rich in Shakespearian and Oehlenschlägerean borrowings. In this biblical drama in 'four chapters', King David, like Johannes in *The Word,* is one of God's elect, who may sin and err and fall but yet remain invulnerable because they retain something of 'God' within. The Royal Theatre production in November 1933 married the monumentality of Johannes Poulsen's *mise-en-scène* with the fiery hebraic splendour of Isaac Grünewald's décor, but Poul Reumert's fascinating and diabolical portrait of the homosexual minister Achitophel made the inadequately drawn character of David seem all the more unconvincing. In striking contrast, the memorable revival of *Herod the King* in January 1938, with Reumert as the pathological, power-mad dictator who defies God and Clara Pontoppidan as his venemous, hunchbacked sister Salomé, became the most convincing affirmation of Munk's unusual ability to depict a gaudy and brutal world of history in which 'necessity knew no law and good and evil no longer existed, because everyone thought only of himself and was his own God; while heads toppled, brains burst and limbs were shattered, and peace when it came brought workers' feuds and frauds and callousness and poverty and pestilence'.[30] Kierkegaard's phrase, 'purity of heart is to will one thing', is an apt epigraph not only for *Herod* but for Munk's dramaturgy in general; its intoxication with the notion of the single-minded historical strongman beyond good and evil, which for a time led the playwright to the brink of fascism, remains the chief source of dramatic interest in his plays.

Ideologically and theatrically, Munk's antithesis was Kjeld Abell (1901–1961), whose eighteen plays, extending from the sensational international success *Melodien der blev væk/The Melody that Got Lost* to *Skriget/The Scream*, completed just before his death, comprise—in the opinion of many critics—the most significant body of work produced by a Danish dramatist in this century. Abell's ceaseless and imaginative experimentation continually challenged the realistic bias of the post-Ibsen theatre. 'Why is there anything in the theatre called realism?' he demanded in a seminal essay from the thirties. 'Can theatre ever be realistic? Has "the human comedy" anything in common with every-day reality? Where should the sofa stand? Must the actors always stand facing the audience? . . . Who has decided how reality should look? Does it always look like that?'[31] Questions multiplied. Theatre, in Abell's view, had congealed into 'a picture which with its wealth of correct details left nothing to the audience—the audience was not allowed to be an active part of the endeavour'. With his distinctive style and his astute sense of the potentialities of the stage, he set about changing the shape of Scandinavian drama as he found it. *The Melody that Got Lost*, first staged by the avant-garde director Per Knutzon at his tiny Riddersalen on

---

[30] Quoted in *Five Plays by Kaj Munk*, trans. R. P. Keigwin (New York, 1953), p. 16.

[31] 'Realisme—?' *Forum*, October 1935, reprinted in Kjeld Abell, *Synskhedens Gave*, ed. Elias Bredsdorff (Copenhagen, 1962), p. 189.

6 September 1935, combined the techniques of expressionism, film, and political cabaret in a fresh and original manner. Acted throughout Scandinavia and in London, Abell's first play mounted a trenchant satirical attack on contemporary society, as Larsen, a proletarian everyman, loses life's 'melody' when he succumbs to the bourgeois quest for career and conventionality. A year later, the Royal Theatre production of *Eva aftjener sin Barneplight/Eve Serves her Childhood* won, in the gracefully ironic *mise-en-scène* of the gifted actor-director Holger Gabrielsen, a decisive victory for Abell's radically anti-naturalistic techniques, utilized in this case to depict the plight of Eve, mother of us all, who leaves her museum to experience the childhood years she never knew, only to find herself enmeshed in the prejudices and stereotypes of the respectable middle-class family into which she is born.

Earlier in 1936, Royal Theatre audiences were introduced to the third outstanding dramatist of the prewar era, the richly endowed Norwegian writer Nordahl Grieg (1902-1943), whose social goals were no less revolutionary than Abell's but whose harsh tone differs markedly from the Giraudoux-like irony of his Danish contemporary. *Vår ære og vår makt/Our Power and Our Glory,* Grieg's first stage success, was completed and first acted in Bergen in May 1935; the effective Copenhagen première less than a year later marked the débuts of Bodil Ipsen as a director and Helge Refn as a designer. Grieg's drama is an uncompromising attack on the ruthless profiteering of some Norwegian merchant-ship owners during World War I, and its highly effective use of sound and lighting effects, cinematic structure and presentational techniques—indebted both to Grieg's exposure to Russian experimental theatre and to Noël Coward's film *Cavalcade*—places it in the mainstream of theatrical development during the thirties. Grieg's theatre was a theatre of instructive fact: 'Since real life, in all its grotesque brutality, is so much more powerful than anything a person can think up, one would have to be very stupid not to use archives and old newspapers,' he told an interviewer.[32] In *Nederlaget/ The Defeat,* among the most impressive Scandinavian plays written during the modern period, he turned to a more distanced actuality, focusing on the last heroic stand of the Paris

[32] Quoted in *Five Modern Scandinavian Plays* (New York, 1971), p. 294.

Commune against the government troops in 1871. Balancing the cynicism and bitterness present in Grieg's grim vision of a brutalized world are, however, the ringing last words of the fanatical believer Delescluze: 'But we can go from here calmly, because we know that our hope will come again. Hope will come again on earth. Those out there may scorch the grass off with their grenades, but they can never kill the earth's ability to become green.' *The Defeat* was performed throughout Scandinavia in 1937, but its Copenhagen production, only partially successful in Svend Gade's overly naturalistic staging, is particularly memorable for another reason: in the small rôle of Schulze the eighteen-year-old Mogens Wieth, whose brilliant talent shone like a sun that warmed us all during his cruelly brief career, made his début.

If plays like Lagerkvist's *The Hangman* and Grieg's *The Defeat* echoed with the reverberations of a collapsing world, Kjeld Abell's *Anna Sophie Hedvig,* produced on New Year's Day 1939, sounded the defiant call to stand and fight the brutality and inhumanity of Nazi aggression. Deftly directed by Holger Gabrielsen and starring Clara Pontoppidan in the title rôle that Abell had created for her, this ringing indictment of the passive tolerance of evil was couched in the story of a quiet spinster schoolteacher who kills to defend her small world against the destructive tyranny of a vicious school principal. 'Must we not defend our small worlds? Do they not together make up the great world?' asks Anna Sophie Hedvig, and when the German invasion of Denmark and Norway came during the dark days of April 1940, the theatre's artists were among the first to answer gallantly. Nordahl Grieg, who immediately joined the Norwegian government in exile and enlisted in the armed forces, ended his life at forty-one in a bombing raid over Berlin in December 1943. Kaj Munk was forty-five when he was shot to death by Gestapo thugs and left in a wayside ditch near Silkeborg in January 1944. In *Dronning går igen/The Queen on Tour,* produced during the Occupation in 1943 and depicting an aging actress's determination to tour with *Hamlet* at this very time, Abell paid a veiled tribute to the theatre as the sanctuary of free speech—while with far more outspoken and dangerous directness he dashed onto the stage of the Royal Theatre on the January evening in 1944 when it had become known that the

241

Germans had murdered Munk, risking arrest by the Gestapo in order to exhort the audience to resist and remember. In occupied Norway, intolerable interference by the Nazis quickly crippled theatrical activity, but the Royal Theatre in Copenhagen, under the courageous leadership of Cai Hegermann-Lindencrone, continued—in the face of curfews that sometimes forced performances to start at 4 p.m., anonymous bomb threats, and warnings of demolition by the Germans (not least because the playhouse served as a Resistance arsenal of weapons and explosives)—to function, more obviously than ever before in its two-hundred-year history, as a symbol of national identity and unity. During the years 1941–5 an average of 72 per cent of all Royal Theatre performances played to sold-out houses.

The Scandinavian theatre emerged from the five bitterest years in Danish and Norwegian history—not unchanged, but with a renewed sense of the exuberance that has always been one of its hallmarks. New directors, designers, actors and playwrights have continued to appear and to enrich or defy or modify its strong traditions during the second half of this century. However, the redefinition of the modern theatre set in motion during the formative years between the two world wars—the implementation of Lagerkvist's Strindberg-inspired vision of the stage as a 'sorcerer's magical box' brimming with a thousand possibilities—has remained an on-going process that has continued to impart its spirit and excitement to the Scandinavian theatre of our own day.

CHAPTER TWELVE

Since 1945

Though they are obviously essential to a balanced survey of the history of Scandinavian theatre, the trends and developments of more recent years are, in many ways, the most difficult of all to chart concisely. In part, we are still too close to the picture to perceive its pattern. Partly, too, the experimental eclecticism of the postwar theatre, in Scandinavia as elsewhere, resists the convenience of categories. A welter of styles and innovations, born of spiritual or political restlessness or artistic dissatisfaction with the status quo, has prevailed during the fifties and sixties. During this time the traditional ascendancy of Scandinavia's three national stages has been challenged by large rival commercial theatres and tiny experimental groups alike. Both the advent of television and the dramatic expansion of regional theatres and national touring companies have profoundly affected the place of theatre in the general cultural environment. New playwrights of note have been slow to emerge during the postwar period. On the other hand, a new generation of gifted directors has brought renewed excitement and, particularly in the case of Ingmar Bergman, international recognition to the productions of the last decades.

By mid-century each of the three Scandinavian countries could, and did, look back with satisfaction upon a considerable tradition, and commemorative jubilees became the order of the day as the established theatre paid homage to a proud past.

Outshining all such postwar celebrations was the ambitious cavalcade of productions presented to mark the bicentenary of the Danish Royal Theatre in 1948—an astonishing repertory programme that in itself testifies forcefully to the range, resources and national consciousness of Scandinavia's oldest state theatre. During the sixteen days from Holberg's birthday (December 3) to the anniversary itself (December 18), four ballets and *twenty* plays—including three Holberg comedies, revivals of Gustav Wied, Ewald, Wessel, Oehlenschläger, Heiberg, Hertz, Hostrup, and Nathansen, five modern plays (including Kjeld Abell's *Ejendommen Matr. Nr. 267. Østre Kvarter/Lot No. 267 East District,* a sparkling tribute to the theatre of illusion commissioned for the occasion), and four works from the international repertory (*Tartuffe, Othello, The Wild Duck,* and *The Ghost Sonata*)—were offered. The adjacent 'New Stage,' which by 1957 had become the regular second stage of the Royal Theatre, was also pressed into use to accommodate the bicentennial festival.

This impressive bicentennial was followed in 1949 by a 'younger' national theatre's jubilee, the fiftieth anniversary of the opening of Norway's Nationaltheatret. Before long, however, some of the more established and increasingly influential rivals of these state theatres began to boast jubilees of their own. In 1963, for example, fifty years of vigorous activity was commemorated by Det Norske Teatret, the pioneering 'new Norwegian' language theatre responsible for such landmark productions as Hans Jacob Nilsen's revolutionary anti-romantic reinterpretation of *Peer Gynt* in 1948, in which Grieg's splendid but inappropriate romanticism was replaced by the stark and disturbing tones of Harald Sæverud's new score for the play. One of Scandinavia's oldest functioning private theatres, Copenhagen's venerable Folketeatret, celebrated its triumphant centennial in September 1957, signalled by an unprecedented series of congratulatory guest performances by the national theatres of Finland, Sweden, Norway, and Iceland. Under the indomitable Thorvald Larsen's long and palmy reign, Folketeatret extended the popular 'folk theatre' concept to embrace first-rate productions of the classics as well as of contemporary works by dramatists like Munk and Soya. The determined efforts of Thorvald Larsen to break the Royal Theatre's (now virtually defunct) monopoly on the Danish classics are reflected in the choice of the play which marked the one-hundredth anniversary of his theatre: *The Political Tinker,* the comedy with which Holberg had launched Denmark's first vernacular theatre in 1722, inventively cast with the popular revue comedian Osvald Helmuth in the title rôle. Across town, meanwhile, the New Theatre, the Royal Theatre's strongest rival during the fifties and early sixties and the best example of the shift of power that was taking place in this respect, celebrated its own golden anniversary in September 1958. The festival production was an opulent revival of Sheridan's *The School for Scandal,* ably directed by Sam Besekow and designed with taste and brilliance by Oliver Messel. Messel's rococo costumes and sets, created in the spirit of an elegant and subtly stylized period pastiche, wittily recaptured the essence of the comedy's tone and atmosphere by viewing it, so to speak, through the prism of the age in which it was written. The riot of colour and ornament in the décors—which incorporated such pictorial strokes as the combination of deliberately artificial, flat cut-out vases and real, three-dimensional flowers —endowed the production as a whole with rare artistic finesse as well as genuine theatricality.

Relying upon a fashionable international repertoire, supported by talented directors like Besekow and Edvin Tiemroth, and armed with a responsive ensemble headed by the period's ideal couple, Mogens Wieth and Bodil Kjer, manager Peer Gregaard proceeded to mould his New Theatre into one of the most successful and critically acclaimed theatre companies of the postwar years, 'the national theatre's guilty conscience'.[1] A production such as the New Theatre's staging of Anouilh's *La valse de toréadors* in 1957 virtually embodied its period's predominant standard of 'poetic realism'. Sam Besekow's imaginative and wittily baroque direction, Bodil Kjer's overwhelming caricature of the sentimental heroine in Ghislaine de Ste.-Euverte, and, above all, Mogens Wieth's pathetic, grotesque, and moving reinterpretation of General Saint-Pé combined to create a memorable and long-running performance that epitomized the New Theatre's confident and urbane challenge to the national stage on Kongens Nytorv. (The

[1] Henrik Holm-Hansen, *Skuespil, opera og ballet in Danmark,* p. 26.

competitive balance shifted once again in 1966 when Peer Gregaard assumed the post of manager-in-chief of the Danish Royal Theatre.) In general, at various times and under widely differing circumstances, the years since 1945 have seen several major companies such as the New Theatre, Oslo's New Theatre (which merged in 1959 with Oslo's Folketeatret), or, more recently, the Stockholm City Theatre which have presented stimulating and provocative—if not always enduring—alternatives to the three national repertory theatres, Dramaten, Nationaltheatret and the Danish Royal Theatre.

Other developments underlying the diversification of theatrical endeavour in the three Scandinavian countries have had their parallels throughout the Western world: the growth of small experimental theatres, the increasing significance of regional and touring theatres, and the rise of the new medium of television. Of utmost importance during recent decades has been the gradual recognition of the need for experimental stages—small theatres in which young directors can have an opportunity to test new methods, where young actors are free to develop a style, where unestablished dramatists can hazard new techniques and ideas without the daunting prospect of having to mount a large-scale production inappropriate to the work being tried. A first crucial step in this direction was taken by Oslo's Studio Theatre, formally opened in October 1945 by a group of young theatre enthusiasts (the majority were under thirty) who had banded together and trained during the war years and whose aim was nothing less than the renewal of Norwegian acting. Their avowed model was Stanislavski, their adopted symbol the seagull of the Moscow Art Theatre, and in many respects their goals and methods resembled those of the off-Broadway theatres that were springing up in New York around this time. Consisting of nineteen actors, many of whom would later become leading personalities in the Norwegian theatre, the Studio Theatre was constituted as an actors' theatre, dedicated to the concept of ensemble and convinced that 'the actor is the creative artist and must not, as happened in certain modern developments between the wars, become a pawn in the director's hand.'[2] During its five-year existence

[2] Jens Bolling in Studioteatret's first programme, quoted in Øyvind Anker, *Scenekunsten i Norge*, p. 55.

the Studio Theatre produced thirty-four plays with such a consistently high standard that its example has had a lasting effect on the philosophy of actor training in Norway. Its repertoire, aimed not at an intellectual élite but at a broad—and particularly a young—audience, drew heavily upon the plays of established modern dramatists of this period—Wilder, Saroyan, Brecht, O'Neill, Chekhov, Sartre, Miller, Maxwell Anderson, Anouilh, Williams. In 1946 this actor-oriented collective carried its celebrated production of Thornton Wilder's *Our Town,* with its rejection of the trappings of conventional realism, to Finmarken and other war-devastated regions of the far north of Norway, playing under primitive conditions to audiences that had never before witnessed a theatre performance. Early in 1948 the world première of the young Ingmar Bergman's stage version of his film script *Hets* (called *Torment* in the United States and *Frenzy* in England), a startling study of young anger that marked the start of Bergman's career in the cinema, became one of the Studio Theatre's most debated successes. Ultimately, however, bleak economic conditions prevailed, and the world première of Sean O'Casey's *Cock-a-Doodle-Dandy* in October 1950 signalled the abrupt end of one of the contemporary Scandinavian theatre's most notable experimental groups.

The need for small experimental theatres remained apparent, however, and during the sixties the number of autonomous mini-theatres grew substantially. (By the end of the decade, moreover, all three national theatres were operating active experimental stages of their own.) Denmark's first and most influential chamber theatre of this kind, Fiolteatret (literally, the Fiddle Theatre), opened in 1962 and quickly established itself as the champion of the new *avant-garde* drama—Beckett, Ionesco, Pinter, early Albee—that was so well adapted to its postage-stamp stage. Its productions often incorporated the ingredients of revue and cabaret: as early as 1962 Bodil Udsen, an accomplished revue comedienne, delivered a rich rendering of Winnie in Beckett's *Happy Days* that gave Fiolteatret one of its longest-running successes. In a comparable vein, the Danish satirical poet Klaus Rifbjerg emerged as the Fiddle's first new dramatist of note with his plotless cabaret-style work entitled *Udviklinger/Developments,* 'a play for four jazz musicians, four

247

actors, and a small theatre', staged with fine rhythmic sense by the talented radio director Carlo M. Petersen in 1965. In Sweden, meanwhile, the 1960s saw a bewildering proliferation of small experimental stages, theatre collectives, and workshops dedicated to a heady mixture of political radicalism and theatrical revolt. Such Stockholm-based groups as the Free Pro Theatre, the Jester's Theatre, the Arena Theatre, the Pocket Theatre, the Pistol Theatre, and the Free Theatre have specialized—with considerably varying degrees of artistic achievement —in an eclectic programme of destruction happenings, street theatre, improvisations, houseboat theatre, Café La Mama-style cabaret, guerrilla theatre, and the performance of more conventionally structured agit-prop revues and plays. The now defunct Pocket Theatre, performing in a style imitative of the improvised *commedia dell'arte*, often took to the streets with its plays of social satire and criticism. The Jester's Theatre has toured city schools, the Swedish countryside, and has even reached Cuba itself with its collectively composed agit-prop drama of life in Cuba-before-Castro, called *The Girl of Havana*. No less radical in its ideology, the Free Pro Theatre regularly takes to the road with *lehrstücke* encouraging revolutionary socialism and castigating capitalists and reformist trade unions. Particular notice has been attracted by actor-director Lennart Hjulström's 'group theatre' productions at the Gothenburg City Theatre, team-generated improvisational collages such as *Flotten/The Raft* (1967), *Hemmet/The Home* (1967), and *Sandlåden/The Sand Box* (1968) which expose such social concerns as the welfare state, old people's homes, and mental institutions to scrutiny and criticism.

These activities, part of a much broader movement that has coloured theatre throughout the world during recent years, raise fundamental issues that cannot be dealt with here. The traditional rôles of director and playwright and even accepted definitions of what constitutes a theatrical event have been drawn into question and have stimulated acrimonious debate. However, if we return to the firmer ground of the Studio Theatre's belief in the efficacy of a small ensemble to train better actors, the latest and most widely discussed example of this viewpoint is Eugenio Barba's inter-Scandinavian Odin Teatret (in almost every respect the diametrical opposite of the

248

Studio Theatre). An Italian director-theorist and the first to champion and publicize the work of Jerzy Grotowski's Polish Laboratory Theatre in his book *Alla Ricerca del Teatro Perduto* (1965), Barba founded his own Grotowski-inspired troupe in 1964 and, after beginning his activities in Norway, was invited in 1966 to settle in the municipally owned and subsidized theatre in the small Danish community of Holstebro. Like Grotowski, Barba has attempted to create not a performing company but a laboratory for experimentation with theatrical techniques, specifically Grotowski's now famous philosophy of theatre as a ritualistic communal rite, dependent exclusively upon the psycho-spiritual confrontation and interaction of actor and spectator in a completely flexible space and unfettered by the 'rich theatre's' conventional notions of illusionistic scenery, costumes, lighting effects, plot-accompanying music, and literary text. The key to such 'collective introspection' in the theatre is, Barba makes clear in his seminal Grotowski interview 'The Theatre's New Testament', no less than the total psychic and physical redisciplining of the 'parochial' actor.[3] Needless to say, such an aesthetic has aroused its share of controversy and confusion in and beyond the small Jutland town of Holstebro, but its tangible effects, if any, upon the future direction and development of the Scandinavian theatre remain to be discerned.

Our Town in Finmarken, *The Raft* and other collages in Gothenburg, and Grotowski in Holstebro are merely isolated instances of the continued vitality and growth of regional theatre activity throughout Scandinavia. Permanent, subsidized regional theatres significantly broaden and enrich the theatrical culture of all three countries: Norway's National Stage in Bergen, Trøndelag Teater in Trondheim, and Rogaland Teater in Stavanger and Denmark's three municipal theatres in Aarhus, Odense, and Aalborg are all flourishing regional stages whose long traditions extend back to the nineteenth century. Sweden's impressive chain of eight fully supported municipal theatres is headed by the influential Gothenburg City Theatre and includes playhouses in Malmö, Hälsingborg, Borås, Linköping, Norrköping, Uppsala, and, since 1967, the northern outpost of Luleå. ('Shamefully, only about one-third of Sweden has so far had access to a permanent theatre', write the authors

[3] Jerzy Grotowski, *Towards a Poor Theatre* (New York, n.d.), p. 27f.

of a recent booklet from the Swedish Institute for Cultural Relations. 'It is not enough to have eight municipal theatres—we must have them in all our towns.'[4] This idealistic determination is characteristic.) A further consequence of the conception of theatre as a cultural good to which the entire population has a right has been the operation of a National Touring Theatre (Rigsteater), active in Sweden since the early 1930s and initiated in Norway, one of the largest but most thinly populated countries in Europe, in 1948. Journeying to hundreds of small communities throughout the year and often facing formidable practical obstacles, these travelling companies tour with a remarkable variety of professional productions which—like the Norwegian Rigsteater's marvellously simplified nine-actor *Peer Gynt* in 1960—have created and encouraged a wider popular involvement in the theatrical experience.

With the advent of television, an even broader base of theatrical activity was established in Scandinavia. From the very outset, theatre has occupied a central place in Scandinavian TV—typically, each of the three countries began its transmissions in the fifties with a dramatic sequence—and, far from posing a threat to the living theatre, a succession of first-rate television productions, often featuring Scandinavia's foremost actors and directors, has contributed positively and consistently to the quality of the theatrical environment. Danish television, born in 1951, has evolved a serious repertory that has combined such notable artistic achievements as its productions of Racine's *Britannicus,* Holberg's *The Eleventh of June,* Ibsen's *Ghosts,* and Strindberg's grim one-act comedy *Leka med elden/Playing with Fire* with an ambitious and often controversial pioneering of the works of Ionesco, Beckett, and Pinter. Swedish television, launched three years later, quickly proved attractive to the country's two leading directors, Alf Sjöberg and Ingmar Bergman. Such early broadcasts as Sjöberg's *Hamlet* and Bergman's exploration of Hjalmar Bergman's *Mr. Sleeman is Coming* lent from the outset strong support to the cause of televised theatre. Norway's TV theatre, started in 1959, not only boasts splendid revivals of such modern classics as Chekhov's *Uncle Vanya,* Nordahl Grieg's *The Defeat,* and Ibsen's *Rosmersholm,* but has also placed itself in

[4] Niklas Brunius *et al., Swedish Theatre* (Stockholm, n.d.), pp. 16, 55.

the vanguard of contemporary experimentation with its many premières of Ionesco, Beckett, Albee, Mrozek, and Pinter. Moving gradually from direct transmissions under primitive conditions to the more sophisticated technology of videotape, from adaptations of stage drama to a greater encouragement of original teleplays, and from photographed theatre to a style more responsive to the demands and potentialities of the medium, Scandinavian television, free of much of the mindless triviality that besets commercial TV elsewhere, has continued throughout the last decade to grow as a distinctive and viable part of the changing theatrical scene.

In the midst of this dynamic ambience of postwar change and experiment, however, a consistently high standard of acting and directing at the three national theatres has provided a stable and reliable constant. Especially during the fifties and early sixties, a number of towering performances and performers delineated and exemplified the dominant naturalistic mainstream of psychologically focused, minutely observed, and persuasively motivated acting. Luminous among these performances stands the historic world première of Eugene O'Neill's *Long Day's Journey into Night,* secured from O'Neill's widow through the help of Dag Hammarskjöld and staged by Bengt Ekerot at the Royal Dramatic Theatre in Stockholm on 10 February 1956. Certainly the most remarkable of Dramaten's celebrated premières of O'Neill's last plays (followed by the Molander production of *A Touch of the Poet* in March 1957, *Hughie* in September 1958, and the Karl Ragnar Gierow condensation of *More Stately Mansions* in November 1962), *Long Day's Journey* brought together Lars Hanson, Sweden's unsurpassed interpreter of Strindberg and of O'Neill, in one of the major achievements of his career as the sodden and disillusioned James Tyrone, Inga Tidblad as an unforgettably moving Mary Tyrone, Ulf Palme at the height of his powers as the alcoholic son Jamie, and Jarl Kulle in the O'Neillian self-portrait of Edmund. 'If it was not the most outstanding performance ever presented by this theatre, it was very close to it', commented Sten Selander in *Svenska Dagbladet.* One would have to look to Olivier's recent revival of the play at the National Theatre in London to find a match for Dramaten's

251

harrowing, shattering interpretation. '*Ghosts* appears like an idyll in comparison', declared *Dagens Nyheter* in its review of the 1956 production; 'Strindberg's uninhibited self-exposure suddenly seems like a contrived arrangement in comparison to the long, naked, unbearable, increasing cry of distress.'

Of all the modern Scandinavian theatre's many notable actors, however, one figure in particular seems to stand out above the rest as the virtual embodiment of the predominant 'psychological' style: Poul Reumert. Reumert, whose illustrious sixty-year career in Danish theatre culminated in a starburst of jubilees, must unquestionably be numbered among this century's foremost European actors. Not often has the astonishing versatility of his nearly four hundred parts been equalled: Molière's Tartuffe, Argan, Arnolphe, and Mascarille, Rostand's Cyrano, Shakespeare's Macbeth, Caesar, Polonius, and Jacques, Shaw's Caesar, Oehlenschläger's Hakon Jarl, Munk's Herod, Strindberg's Jean, Edgar, Gustav Vasa, and the Father, and Ibsen's Peer Gynt, Daniel Hejre, Manders, and Solness all took on new and fascinating contours under the spell of his metamorphic art. For his seventy-fifth birthday on 26 March 1958 this resilient performer delighted Royal Theatre audiences with his almost legendary portrayal of the sprightly Lieutenant von Buddinge in Hostrup's comedy vaudeville *The Neighbours,* a complex and incorrigibly witty caricature upon which Reumert embroidered for over three decades. As a deeply moving Ill in Dürrenmatt's *The Visit* the following year, Reumert nearly succeeded in stealing the entire show from his former co-star Bodil Ipsen who, to celebrate her own fiftieth anniversary as an actress, had hoped to have the last word as the relentless Claire Zachanassian. All former celebrations paled, however, before the resounding sixtieth jubilee of Reumert's début on 16 February 1962: his choice was again one of his most popular successes, the genially eccentric Nobel laureate Rolf Swedenhielm in Hjalmar Bergman's domestic comedy *Swedenhielms,* and when the final curtain had fallen the gala audience responded by escorting the laurel-crowned actor in triumphal procession to Christiansborg Palace. Although Reumert allowed no repetition of this homage on his eightieth birthday in 1963, the octogenarian remained active on the stage almost until his death in 1968. It would be difficult to exaggerate the influence of this extraordinary talent on the style and technique of his contemporaries; his discussions of the fundamental principles underlying his art rival those of Stanislavski in their persuasive clarity:

Everything, every single feature in the character we watch and hear on the stage, carries the actor's own stamp, and there is nothing about it which is not his personal possession. Every emotion, thought, and all the qualities from the best to the worst have been discovered by the actor within himself—some only in embryo, others as possibilities—and all of them, artistically transformed, are used by him for his both imaginary and true human creation. He gives of himself without reservation—not, in an immodest manner, his private person—but all the potentialities of his being, always in new selections and combinations. . . . Acting is in its profoundest sense self-confession. So little is there in it of 'make believe'.[5]

Even Brecht, who had spent an enforced exile in Denmark from 1933 to 1939, would willingly have parted with all his theories in return for seeing Reumert play Galileo—even on the actor's (and Stanislavski's) own terms. Ruth Berlau states unequivocally that the part was written specifically for Reumert,[6] and there are indications that an early version of *Leben des Galilei* may have been submitted to the Danish star as early as 1937. Sixteen years later Brecht asked again, but too much in the character, in the dramatist, and in his epic theories ran counter to Reumert's convictions. Far from being narrowly 'naturalistic' in its attack, however, Reumert's art represented an ideal conflation of the poetic and the concrete:

In the art of acting it is in no sense, as it is claimed, any realistic reproduction or verisimilitude that is the primary objective. It is a passionate, individualized search for naturalistic expression but also for that which is called poetic style, and which some years ago was referred to as romanticism, as opposed to realism.[7]

'All of which.' Reumert adds dryly, 'is only so many words and diagrams'. Above all, his distrust of delimiting theories of acting, Brechtian or otherwise, remained profound:

Some wise men have argued that we must be so affected by the rôle, that we must become involved in it to such a degree that we identify with it and hence do not act a part but live it. Other sages have stated just the

[5] Poul Reumert, *Om teater*, ed. Carl Bergstrøm-Nielsen (Copenhagen, 1971), p. 11.
[6] Interview in *Information*, 20 January 1959.
[7] *Om teater*, p. 100.

opposite: that we must be cold and detached, never allowing ourselves to be affected but simply portraying or rather presenting the character for our own and the audience's contemplation, consideration and criticism. All theory is grey, only the tree of life is green. . . . For it is, in fact, impossible to choose one or the other of these two proposed procedures. Whether we like it or not, we need to employ both of them—in conjunction. Of this we have no doubt whatsoever. At times we notice that the one has taken over, at times the other, and occasionally they are united in a strange, complementary harmony, different from one individual to another. Secretly conditioned by the intellect's richness and the body's elasticity.[8]

As the sixties passed, the ranks of Scandinavia's foremost actors were drastically thinned by the deaths of such older stars as Bodil Ipsen (1964), Lars Hanson (1965), Poul Reumert (1968), and Tora Teje (1970). Shockingly unexpected, on the other hand, was the heavy loss sustained through the sudden death of Mogens Wieth in London in September 1962, only a few days before his forty-third birthday and his eagerly awaited appearance as Antonio in the Old Vic production of *The Merchant of Venice*—the beginning of a four-rôle guest season at the Old Vic that was to have culminated in his performance of Othello. The short career that had led to such unusual international recognition had been one filled with the brightest promise as well as the harshest physical suffering. Still in his twenties during the years just before World War II, Mogens Wieth appeared, Aladdin-like, as the period's finest young talent, a superbly lyrical actor who was equally at home in character parts and comic rôles as well—in short, a robust, commanding, if somewhat overly idealized Peer Gynt. After the war, during which he had trained as a paratrooper in the RAF, Wieth returned to the Royal Theatre to become Denmark's—and Scandinavia's—most exciting new star. During the theatre's jubilee year, 1948, a succession of triumphs left no further doubt about his commanding position: his Hickey in *The Iceman Cometh*, a balding, jovial, but deeply and explosively tragic figure, and his Gregers Werle in *The Wild Duck*, an ice-cold psychopath brimming with fanaticism, were overshadowed only by his splendidly plastic and controlled Othello, a monumental study of unsentimental simplicity in which an innocent heart is led into the darkness of suspicion by the evil hypocrisy of his

[8] *Ibid.,* pp. 99–100.

surroundings. Like Reumert, his great model, Mogens Wieth drew the energy and spontaneity which galvanized his performances—even in the grip of the acute pain inflicted by a chronic lung illness—from uncompromisingly concentrated and methodical work. 'Intuition and inspiration were wrung from weeks of study at his desk and on the stage,' wrote director Sam Besekow in his memorial tribute. 'Artistic intention piled details upon details.'[9] Wieth's death left a gap which, notwithstanding the impressive depth of acting talent and training in Scandinavia, has been difficult to fill. An 'older' generation of actors—perhaps even an entire tradition—has now passed. Although new personalities, new tastes, and new approaches to the actor's art continue to emerge, only the passage of time will reveal their permanence.

In a comparable sense, although new plays and playwrights have continued to appear each season, no Scandinavian dramatist has laid convincing claim to the place left vacant by the death of Kjeld Abell, regarded by many critics as this century's foremost Danish playwright, in 1961. After 1945, Abell's art deepened and flourished. *Silkeborg*, written towards the end of the war while Abell was still 'underground' because of his Resistance activities, enjoyed a resounding reception when staged by Sam Besekow at the New Theatre in March 1946. This play, a searching examination of the attitudes and mentality of Abell's countrymen during the Occupation, functions both as a symbolic fantasy and, within its symbolic framework, as a realistic domestic drama of the wartime conflicts and complications which face a typical provincial family. Skilfully, Abell reveals and probes not only the shortsighted indifference and hypocrisy but also the courage of his characters and, by implication, of the society for which they stand. No simple Resistance panegyric, *Silkeborg* sounds its author's urgent call for a continued struggle for the spiritual liberation of mankind.

In December of the following year, the Royal Theatre produced Abell's *Dage på en Sky/Days on a Cloud*, probably the most unusual play in modern Danish theatre. Written in response to the new ethical problems posed by the discovery of the atomic bomb, this work, another Abellian indictment of

[9] 'Exeunt' in *Mogens Wieth,* ed. Knud Poulsen, p. 62.

escapist humanism and intellectual apathy, takes the form of an expressionistic fable. The action takes place in the mind of the central character, a disillusioned atomic scientist called He, during the split seconds between his suicidal plunge from an aircraft and his existential decision to release his parachute instead. The scene is a cloud in the heavenly regions through which he falls, populated by goddesses living a disconsolate existence among ruined temples and toppled pillars. Caught in the conflict between their realm—representing the constructive forces of love (Aphrodite), marriage (Hera), fertility (Demeter)— and the masculine world of Zeus and the gods, which is ruled

46. Design by Helge Refn for Kjeld Abell's *Days on a Cloud*, produced at the Danish Royal Theatre in 1947

47. Refn's award-winning design for Abell's *Vetsera Does Not Bloom for Everyone*, staged at Frederiksberg Theatre in 1950

by the destructive forces of power, egotism, and death, 'He' is brought to realize his responsibility toward the former values and elects to live. The Sartrean theme of engaged commitment rings clearly in Aphrodite's statement: 'The law says that he who steals the holy fire pays with his life. But the penalty should be heavier still if the fire dies in law-abiding hands. The choice is free.' A finely acted production, highlighted by Holger Gabrielsen's minutely coordinated *mise-en-scène* and Helge Refn's extraordinary surrealistic design (Plate 46), quickened and concretized Abell's somewhat enigmatic visionary fantasy.

Each year during the late forties saw the appearance of a new Abell play. After the dark, muted mood piece *Vetsera blomster*

257

ikke for enhver/Vetsera Does Not Bloom for Everyone (1950), a Chekhovian study of the loneliness and despair of a doomed era, four years elapsed before the playwright again returned, in *Den blå Pekingeser/The Blue Pekinese*, to the recurrent theme of inspiring a suicide with the renewed will to live. In his last plays, however, Abell turns from questions of political or social responsibility to the broader problem of individual human isolation and alienation. In *The Blue Pekinese,* a complex fantasy that draws together living, dead, and as yet unborn characters in an expressionistic concurrency of past, present, and future time, the struggle again stands between the forces of death (the isolation and threatened suicide of Tordis Eck) and life's unspoken and unrealized demands and potentialities, suggested by the strange controlling image of an invisible, bell-tinkling, horizon-blue pekinese called Dicky. The action un-

48. Design by Erik Nordgreen for Abell's *The Blue Pekinese,* produced at the Danish Royal Theatre in 1954

folds within the imagination of the central character, a detached spectator of life called André who is ultimately enabled to infuse both the suicidal Tordis and an unborn, life-denied child with the determination 'to live, to be part of life'. Once again, a stunning Royal Theatre production in December 1954 imparted clarity and persuasive emotional focus to Abell's difficult poetic experiment. John Price's direction established his position as one of the postwar theatre's most capable practitioners. Erik Nordgreen's designs for the old Victorian café that dissolves before our eyes into the unearthly dreamscape of the Villa Gullcry (Plate 48) provided a perfect visual framework for the moving performances of Bodil Kjer as the dying Tordis and Mogens Wieth, returning in triumph to the Royal Theatre stage after five years' absence, as André.

As Abell's career closed, three further works added substantially to the measure of his achievement. A spectacular Royal Theatre production of his commemorative tribute to Hans Christian Andersen in 1955 was followed by the New Theatre's polished Mogens Wieth-Bodil Kjer performance of *Kameliadamen* (1959), a reinterpretation of Dumas' novel *La dame aux camélias* that begins after Marguerite's death and unfolds in Dumas' shadowy study. Abell's last and most difficult play, *Skriget/The Scream*, was staged at the Royal Theatre a few months after the playwright's death in 1961. Set in the belfry of a village church inhabited by an Aristophanic gallery of bird-characters, this kaleidoscopic fantasy moves on several interrelated levels at once—biblical, contemporary, anthropomorphic. The scream of the title, a piercing cry that interrupts the Sunday morning service in progress in the church, symbolizes not only the scream of the doomed sacrificial victim but also a mystical sense of exultation in life felt by those still sensitive enough to be affected by the sound. To many theatregoers of the early sixties, Abell's posthumous tour-de-force seemed murky and inaccessible in performance. Subsequently, however, Abell's plays have begun to reach a wider audience than ever before through radio, television and stage revivals of his work.

Although new plays by other dramatists have been reasonably plentiful and occasionally remarkable, Abell's postwar contemporaries have somehow failed to create any sense of

259

consistent development in modern Scandinavian drama. Two of Scandinavia's outstanding novelist-dramatists, Sweden's Stig Dagerman (1923–54) and Denmark's H. C. Branner (1903–66), have contributed individual plays of distinction, notably Dagerman's formidably successful and evocative study of injustice and human callousness *Den Dödsdömde/The Condemned* (1947) and Branner's highly effective psychological character dramas, *Søskende* (produced in New York as *The Judge*, 1952) and *Thermopylæ* (translated as *Gates of Courage*, 1958). Prolific older writers such as Carl Erik Soya (b. 1896) and Vilhelm Moberg (b. 1898) have continued to be heard from, while a number of 'younger' dramatists (all of them in their late forties or fifties) have attracted attention during the past decade with a mixed handful of successful accomplishments: Jens Bjørneboe's Brechtian dissection of German tourism, *Fugleelskerne/The Bird Lovers* (1966), Finn Carling's symbolic zoo story *Gitrene/ The Bars* (1966), Werner Aspenström's absurdist sci-fi experiments *Det eviga/The Apes* (1959) and *Spindlarna/The Spiders* (1966), the lyric poet Lars Forssell's various visionary dramatizations of Swedish history. On rare occasions, a work of great promise like Ernst Bruun Olsen's murderous musical satire of the pop generation, *Teenagerlove,* which took audiences throughout Scandinavia and other European countries by storm following its promising author-directed première at the Danish Royal Theatre in 1962, seemed—at the time—to define a new and viable style of its own. On the whole, however, the modern Scandinavian theatre has not been rich in original plays and playwrights of lasting significance—a fact which some critics are ready at once to ascribe to the deleterious effect of this or that physical or organizational condition in the theatre. There is, so runs this sort of reasoning, always some condition that prevents, or fails to nurture, an uninterrupted flow of dramatic masterpieces. As the American designer Lee Simonson remarked, however:

The truth is that nothing prevents the creation of dramatic masterpieces except the extreme rarity at any time of geniuses capable of writing them. If the theatre had ever depended even for a single century on a steady output of dramatic literature it could never have existed continuously enough to have a history worth being recorded.[10]

[10] *The Stage is Set,* rev. ed. (New York, 1963), p. 215.

Perhaps the most powerful source of vitality and renewal in the twentieth-century Scandinavian theatre has been provided by the succession of unusually able and influential directors and stage designers who have left their stamp upon it. During the twenties and thirties, as we have seen, truly innovative directors—Per Lindberg, Johannes Poulsen, Olof Molander, Per Knutzon, Holger Gabrielsen—and a roster of talented new designers such as Knut Ström, Bertil Damm, Isaac Grünewald, Yngve Berg, Sandro Malmquist, John Jon-And, Sven-Erik Skawonius, Per Schwab, and Helge Refn reshaped and re-theatricalized the theatre of their time. During the second half of the century, this atmosphere of creative renewal and exploration continued to prevail. A number of the artists who had come to prominence before the war remained active (though Knutzon and Gabrielsen died in the fifties, the incomparable Olof Molander directed until his death in 1966), while important new contributions continued to be made by other directors like Sam Besekow, Edvin Tiemroth, John Price, and Hans Jacob Nilsen and designers such as Arne Walentin, Erik Nordgreen, Sven Erixson, Stellan Mörner, and Lennart Mörk—to name only a very few. Above all, however, the prodigious figures of Alf Sjöberg and Ingmar Bergman predominate among their accomplished contemporaries as the two best-known exponents of modern Scandinavian theatre art in our day.

Alf Sjöberg (b. 1903) has throughout his long and varied career been affiliated with the Royal Dramatic Theatre in Stockholm, first as an actor and for more than forty years as one of Dramaten's most exciting directors. During the mid-forties Sjöberg, drawing upon the talents of the country's prominent pictorial artists, dramatically altered the face of Swedish theatre with a succession of productions that represented some of the most visually exciting theatre in Europe. Lorca's *Blood Wedding* (1944), designed with utmost simplicity and great under-standing by Sven Erixson in a stark, atmospheric colour scheme of whites, blacks, reds and yellows, was characterized by a startling treatment of stage space as a dynamic and intrinsic component of the tragic action. For his politically intense production of *The Flies* the following year, Sjöberg called upon the sculptor Eric Grate for a plastic, textured design concept

49. Design by Sven Erixson for the Alf Sjöberg production of
Richard III (1947) at Dramaten

that embodied a surrealistic amalgamation of the archaic, antique, and modern associations which the director found
blended in Sartre's play. For *Twelfth Night* (1946) Sjöberg
turned to yet another gifted artist, Stellan Mörner, for an ex-
quisitely ethereal, suggestive décor comprised of impressionistic architectural screens and floating veils. Informing each of
these productions was Sjöberg's adamant rejection of the
'elevators, turntables, buttons, and cues' of the Germanic
Reinhardt style: 'We want to create productions with no other
resources than the simplest, the poorest. . . . The only technical
device which we cannot dispense with is light, with which we
build rhythms and forms, dissolve and transform the thing.'[11]

[11] *Prisma* (1950), quoted in Per Bjurström, *Teaterdekoration i Sverige*, p. 127.

Sjöberg's *Richard III,* mounted in collaboration with Erixson in 1947, established both a production aesthetic and an interpretational stance that were to remain typical of his epoch-making Shakespearian productions of the fifties and sixties. Shakespeare is often supplied with a political ambience by Sjöberg ('Shakespeare represents at the same time a poetic theatre and a theatre fighting for a political breakthrough, the breakthrough of democracy'),[12] and his directorial image for *Richard III* was heavily influenced by the recent war. 'In the play Richard definitely rises up out of a war, on its ruins there arises this ridiculous being who with cold calculation seduces an entire people,' he asserted in 1968. 'He was not at all hard to identify while Europe was still living in the rubble of the world war, and while we continually watched great ideological con-men rise up and try to seize power.'[13] Hence Lars Hanson's Richard became 'the fool crowned', dancing his grotesque mummery among the stern, baleful shapes of Erixson's set. This simultaneous décor, which divided the stage space into large neutral planes and levels, was transformed by means of changing light and groupings and was coloured by a wealth of banners, ensigns, tents, tapestries, shields, and costumes in clear patterns and brilliant hues (Plate 49). 'The ideal stage is and has always been a bare platform, cleansed of every technical finesse,' Sjöberg insists. 'The magic of a production is that, despite the stage, everything becomes transformed into a poem, into a song about something else.'[14]

With Sjöberg's production of *Romeo and Juliet* in 1953, his ideal of a 'bare', non-representational setting for Shakespeare that would preserve, in modernized terms, the spatial-dramaturgical relationships of the Elizabethan stage was fully realized. Sven Erixson's design—dictated by Sjöberg's intentions—incorporated a marvellously soaring, free-standing spiral staircase as the unifying centrifugal force in the production. It thus provided a stylistically neutral conglomerate to which the director's beautifully balanced and dynamic groupings added the relevant associations of time and place. Here as always, human interaction and the expressiveness of the human

[12] *Perspektiv på teater,* eds. Ulf Gran and Ulla-Britta Lagerroth, p. 110.
[13] *Ibid.,* p. 111.
[14] Bjurström, p. 127.

body constituted the primary concerns in Sjöberg's stage picture. Continuing to develop these ideas and methods in his subsequent productions of Shakespeare's plays (including a remarkable *King John* (1961) set in a rough-hewn and barbarously splendid milieu designed by Lennart Mörk, and an equally 'politicized' *Troilus and Cressida* staged in 1967), Sjöberg has succeeded in evolving a tradition of Shakespearian production unique in the Scandinavian theatre.

Not, however, that Sjöberg's versatile and inquisitive imagination has limited itself to traditional works. In one of his most famous experiments, he has presented provocative revivals of two plays by the hitherto unnoticed nineteenth-century dramatist Carl Johan Love Almqvist (1793–1866). Both *Amorina*, produced on Dramaten's studio stage in 1951, and *Drottningens juvelsmycke/The Queen's Jewel*, which followed in 1956, are grotesque, scurrilous fantasies whose staggering technical complexity presented a fruitful challenge to Sjöberg's directorial imagination. Yngve Larson's set for *Amorina*, consisting simply of two benches on trestles, a dais, a tree and a white surface for projections, and Lennart Mörk's effective use in *The Queen's Jewel* of an open stage whose bareness was counterpointed with strongly atmospheric accessories provided appropriate physical environments for Sjöberg's 'epic' staging of Almqvist's romantic plays. 'The Almqvist productions were thus extremely important for those of us who had Brecht in mind',[15] Sjöberg later remarked, and these experiments are particularly interesting as preludes to his highly original and successful Brecht productions of the mid-sixties (*Schweik in the Second World War, Puntila and his Servant Matti, Mother Courage*). During this same period, under Ingmar Bergman's brief but dynamic leadership of Dramaten, Sjöberg placed himself in the very vanguard of experimental theatre with his performances of the Polish playwright Witold Gombrowicz's long-forgotten absurdist dramas. *Yvonne, Princess of Burgundy*, a four-act tragifarce written in 1935 and demonstrating the Pirandellian proposition that 'each person deforms other persons while being at the same time deformed by them', was transferred to the stage by Sjöberg in 1965. The Dramaten production of Gombrowicz's multi-levelled nightmare fantasy *The Marriage*

[15] *Perspektiv på teater*, p. 115.

in 1966, close on the heels of the Paris première of this re-discovered twenty-year-old play, once again affirmed Sjöberg's consummate ability to concretize the abstract and to imbue even the most baffling material with bold theatrical lucidity.

Ingmar Bergman (b. 1918), Sjöberg's younger contemporary and one of the most highly respected of modern film directors, is relatively less well-known outside Scandinavia for his work in the living theatre. Nevertheless his nearly seventy stage productions have established him as one of the most influential and sought-after directors in Scandinavia today, and his theatrical career and working methods have a crucial bearing on his overall artistic physiognomy. Simultaneously with Alf Sjöberg's momentous Stockholm productions of the mid-forties, the twenty-six-year-old Bergman first attracted public notice as the manager of the Hälsingborg City Theatre; here he directed nine productions during the period 1944–6, including an intensely gothic and pictorially expressive *Macbeth* filled with brooding shadows and disembodied voices, in which Macbeth was shown torn between a grotesquely blurred vision of the witches and the image of an immense crucifix. In 1946 (the year after his first feature film, *Crisis*) Bergman was called to the prestigious and more demanding Gothenburg City Theatre, where he directed ten plays in four seasons and learned to master one of the most technically advanced stage facilities in Europe. From the very outset, in his notable production of Camus' *Caligula* (November 1946) starring Anders Ek in the title rôle, the young director displayed an expansive and pictorially striking approach that was effectively reinforced by Carl Johan Ström's carefully controlled design for a Roman atrium, dominated by the silhouette of a quadrangular roof pattern projected against a bright horizon. While always exploiting the potentialities of the physical theatre to the fullest, however, Bergman has at the same time never ceased to work for organically integrated, simplified effects: 'Superimposed trappings always hang loosely and rattle', he remarks dryly. 'One hears and sees from them that they hang on the outside and are dead, no matter how unusual or tasteful they may otherwise be.'[16] His Gothenburg period taught Bergman restraint, method and a formal control that imparted impressive

[16] Henrik Sjögren, *Ingmar Bergman på teatern*, p. 314.

265

coherence and clarity even to so sprawling and chaotic a work as Valle-Inclan's 'savage comedy' *Divine Words,* with which the adventurous young director concluded his assignment there in 1950.

Three elements only are essential, in Bergman's view, 'in order for theatre to take place': a subject, actors, and audience. An increasingly more direct, uncluttered, actor-oriented style characterized the fifteen or so major productions which Bergman staged during his epoch-making six-year stay at the Malmö City Theatre between 1952 and 1958. Interestingly but not unexpectedly, he became the first director to succeed in conquering the sprawling immensity of the main stage at Malmö. His first effort there was a controversial production of Strindberg's darkly lyrical folk drama *Kronbruden/The Bridal Crown* (November 1952), much of which, including the play's fateful bridal scene, was acted on an almost bare stage sparingly illuminated by selective atmospheric lighting (the magnificently conceived bridal scene was 'lit only by the moon's gigantic, flame-coloured stratospheric balloon in the background',[17] noted one observer). Recalling the radical dematerialization that inspired him in this production, Bergman later remarked: 'It struck me that absolutely no more was needed, no lighting was needed, nothing was needed—nothing more than the artist. It is that simple.'[18] In no sense restricted to a monotonous sameness of style, however, Bergman tackled an astonishingly versatile repertoire during his Malmö years, presented both on the main stage and in the intimate studio theatre and ranging from Strindberg, Ibsen, Pirandello, and Molière to full-scale popular renditions of *The Merry Widow* (1954) and *The Teahouse of the August Moon* (1955). It would be beyond the limits of the present context to deal in depth with his many notable achievements of this period. An intimately conceived and meticulously orchestrated production of *The Ghost Sonata* in May 1954, starring Benkt-Åke Benktsson in a monumental performance as a cynically overpowering but tragic Hummel, changed perceptibly in tone and atmosphere from act to act in order to emphasize the director's structural image of the play as a progression towards

[17] Per Erik Wahlund, quoted in Gunnar Ollén, *Strindbergs dramatik,* p. 358.
[18] Sjögren, p. 312.

purification and atonement. The result was a remarkable conflation of the Molander tradition's heightened concreteness and the stark, unadorned expressionism of the Reinhardt-style *Gespenstersonate*. Bergman's widely discussed *Ur-Faust,* staged in October 1958 with Max von Sydow, fresh from his triumph in *The Seventh Seal,* in the title rôle, depended upon an even bolder directional image. Faust and Mephistopheles were costumed and made up as identical twins, and the diabolical, controlling shadow of the latter was omnipresent—a struggle of merging identities reflected in the principal elements of Kerstin Hedeby's simple unit setting, a pair of gothic arches from atop which the figures of a madonna and a devil followed the action. Molière, a dramatist for whom Bergman has a particular affinity, enjoyed special prominence at Malmö. A highly stylized and broadly comic *Don Juan* (January 1955), acted on an uncluttered platform of rough-hewn boards against a naïvely painted backdrop, is a good illustration of Bergman's preoccupation with the active, participatory 'spiritual communication' which he insists must prevail between actor and spectator. From the very first sequence, in which a bleary-eyed, yawning, and ludicrously bald Don Juan in nightshirt is fitted out in his seducer costume and virile black wig by an illusionless Sganarel, the audience became an initiated partner in the comic intrigue. Again in *The Misanthrope* (November 1957), regarded by many as Bergman's best stage production, the director strove to establish a strong audience rapport with Max von Sydow's passionate, stubborn Alceste. To this end, further strengthening the bond between stage and auditorium, Kerstin Hedeby's glittering pastiche of a baroque interior seemed in the dim, atmospheric lighting to extend beyond the checkerboard forestage to include the audience in the same continuous space. (Bergman has, of course, tried various techniques aimed at involving his audience as a 'collaborator' in a production. Perhaps the most unusual of these has been his custom, first adopted for his production of *Woyzeck* at Dramaten in 1969, of holding open public rehearsals—a popular practice which aroused considerable interest among press and public during his most recent revival of *The Misanthrope* at the Danish Royal Theatre in September 1973.)

A pivotal highpoint in Bergman's directing career, occurring between his Malmö period and his years at the helm of Dramat-en, is his renowned staging of the Stravinsky-Auden opera *The Rake's Progress* at the Royal Opera in Stockholm in April 1961. In this enormously successful production Bergman captured and concretized the opera's essential tone of eighteenth-century pastiche. His sloping stage built out over the orchestra pit created an emphatic sense of perspective depth and lent to the playing area imposing baroque proportions, while Birger Bergling's black-and-white décor, with its stylized wings upon which mirrors, chairs, and tables were painted, completed the ironic theatrical comment on the period. Bergman has, as many of his films and stage productions suggest, a marked predilec-tion for the kind of medieval morality motif that underlies this opera, and Tom Rakewell's dire progress, from his faithful Ann Trulove, through the mephistophelian Nick Shadow's tempta-tions and the fearful kingdoms of the Devil and Death, to the final innocence of the madhouse, found its ideal expression in the rhythmic groupings and Hogarth-like tableaux of his *mise-en-scène*. The artistic harmony existing in this production (and heartily acknowledged by the aging Stravinsky) between the composer's original conception and Bergman's scenic realization of it calls to mind one of the latter's fundamental precepts re-garding his art: 'I cannot and will not direct a play contrary to an author's intentions. And I have never done so. Consciously. I have always considered myself as an interpreter, a re-creator.'[19]

Although Bergman himself seems to consider his three-year management of Dramaten (1963–6) a failure, his liberal, ex-pansionist administration was marked by both a healthy broadening of the theatre's artistic range (exemplified, for example, in Alf Sjöberg's productions of Brecht and Gom-browicz) and a dramatic increase in state subsidies and the size of the theatre's acting company. For reasons that seem obvious, Bergman's own productions became fewer during his managerial régime. However, these included a scathingly intense version of Albee's *Who's Afraid of Virginia Woolf?* (1963), a probing theatre-of-fact presentation of Peter Weiss's *The Investigation* (1966), and, first and foremost, the celebrated *Hedda Gabler* which he staged at Dramaten in October 1964 and later re-

[19] *Ibid.*, p. 293.

created for an international public in the London production of 1970. In this boldly untraditional interpretation, an uncluttered red room furnished with the utmost simplicity—a mirror, a sofa, chairs, a black piano, and a movable screen vertically dividing the stage—displaced Ibsen's detailed naturalistic interior with its portentous portrait of General Gabler. From the psychologically revealing opening tableau, in which Gertrud Fridh's vain, restless, lonely Hedda prowls the flaming red room and tries desperately to squeeze out her unborn child with her bare hands, to the final moment when she removes her elegant, high-heeled shoes before her fastidious suicide the audience was made an active participant in her drama. Deprived by the director of the comfortable fiction of an invisible fourth wall, the spectator felt himself to be in the same Tesman drawing room, face to face with its inhabitants. The curtain rose several minutes before the play actually began, the house lights remained up for some minutes after it started, later a glaring spotlight raked the auditorium. Bergman's customary preoccupation with frontal, closeup acting resulted in an immediacy and subtlety of facial expression very reminiscent of his films. Cinematic, too, was the juxtaposing of actual scenes with simultaneous peripheral action implied by but not described in Ibsen's text, thereby allowing the silent presence or eavesdropping of an 'off-stage' character, visible to the audience on the other side of the dividing screen, to provide a forceful commentary on the action. (Bergman's propensity for utilizing peripheral or off-stage action in this manner found perhaps its boldest manifestation to date in his 1972 production of *The Wild Duck*, in which Ibsen's fateful, unseen attic was placed squarely before the audience's view and virtually in its lap!) Bergman's *Hedda Gabler* is, then, an informative example of the interplay of the chief aims and techniques of his scenic art: radical simplification of milieu, conceptual clarity, a primary concern with the actor's art and a related attention to facial and pantomimic expressiveness, and an insistence on intense audience involvement predicated by Bergman's conviction that the drama must always be played in two locations at once, on the stage among the actors and in the consciousness of every spectator. Unifying all these concerns is a camera-like sharpness of focus provided by Bergman's famous concept of a

269

single magnetic 'focal point of energy' which the director must locate in every stage space, and in accordance with which he must calculate every move. 'In relation to this point one creates approach and withdrawal effects,' he explains. 'And it is always from the audience's point of view that it is determined.'[20]

Still in his fifties, Ingmar Bergman continues to enrich the contemporary Scandinavian theatre with some of its liveliest and most expressive moments—many of them provided by Strindberg's plays. Bergman and Strindberg are, in many respects, kindred spirits—the consanguinity is clearly in evidence both in Bergman's films and in the dozen or so Strindberg productions which he has directed, often more than once, for radio (*Playing with Fire, The Dutchman, Crimes and Crimes, Easter, The First Warning*), television (*Storm Weather*), and the stage (*The Pelican, The Bridal Crown, The Ghost Sonata, Erik XIV, A Dream Play*). In particular, Bergman's widely discussed and boldly personal reinterpretation of *A Dream Play*, first performed at Dramaten's 350-seat Lilla Scenen on 14 March 1970 and later transferred to the main stage, has already taken its rightful place within the wider, ongoing tradition of vigorous, imaginative creativity that characterizes modern Scandinavian theatre at its best. As we have seen, the challenge of *A Dream Play* has in a very special sense defined and spurred the advance towards modernism in Scandinavia. The 'materialization phenomenon' of the unsatisfactory 1907 première at the Swedish Theatre in Blasieholmen, Svend Gade's rather strained symbolic staging of the play at the new Lorensberg Theatre in 1916, Pär Lagerkvist's ringing call two years later for a new stagecraft capable of adequately expressing Strindberg's mutational dream-play dramaturgy, Reinhardt's innovative but controversial revival of the work in 1921, Olof Molander's epoch-making surrealistic production, with its recognizable views of Strindberg's Stockholm, in 1935, and this brilliant director's *six* subsequent approaches to the elusive masterpiece, comprise, as it were, a miniature history of the evolution of modern theatre in Scandinavia. Bergman's rendering of *A Dream Play* marks yet another important turning point in that history, a remarkable departure not only from the spectacular

[20] *Ibid.*, p. 292.

50. Two scenes from Ingmar Bergman's production of
A Dream Play at Dramaten's Lilla Scenen in 1970. Stage
design by Lennart Mörk, photos by Beata Bergström

Molander style but also from his own 1963 television version, and is a fitting example with which to conclude this survey of five centuries of Scandinavian stage production.

Stripped down to fifteen compact scenes, with a total playing time of one hour and forty-five minutes, this radically simplified stage version assumed the shape and style of a chamber play—Bergman's favourite Strindberg genre. Studying the published text, one senses the gifted film maker at work in the incisive cuts and effective transpositions of this fast-paced redaction. Much of the philosophical framework of Eastern mysticism has been excised. Indra's Daughter and Agnes are split into separate characters played by different actresses, and the Daughter, now deprived of all but her most 'divine' lines and no longer used to open the play, could almost as well have been (as Bergman apparently first intended) eliminated altogether. Photographs of the production (Plate 50) convey a strong sense of the roughness and starkness of the conception. The traditional identification of the Dreamer, in all three of his voices, with Strindberg himself was abandoned. Instead, the Poet, seated at his desk surrounded by the other characters who, dream-like, await his call, opened and closed the play with speeches originally given by the dramatist to Indra's Daughter. 'No castle burns on the stage, no rhetoric flames in the dialogue,' commented critic Bo Strömstedt. 'Nor is it a biographical Strindberg Show in Molander fashion. Some wear masks in this production—but no one wears a Strindberg mask.'[21] Lennart Mörk's austere design dispensed entirely with the visual effects usually associated with *A Dream Play*. Instead, utilizing only a black (or, for the Fairhaven sequence, a white) backdrop and a minimum of properties, Bergman relied on striking figure compositions, such as a grotesque Crucifixion tableau placing the Lawyer's humiliation in bold relief in the grandiose, organ-resounding Degree Ceremony scene, to animate his stage.

Bergman's compelling treatment of *A Dream Play* will, it seems certain, continue to stimulate discussion and constructive controversy for a long time to come. Its mingling of a vigorous experimental spirit with a sensitive loyalty to the integrity of the playwright's original conception offers, moreover, yet one

[21] Gunnar Ollén, 'Strindbergspremiärer 1969–70', *Meddelanden från Strind-bergssällskapet*, 45 (May, 1970), p. 2.

more instance of the viability of the ideal—championed by Lagerkvist over half a century ago—of a theatrical art which affords 'the imagination of both dramatist and actor greater freedom of movement and greater audacity . . . a theatre which stimulates the dramatist and the actor to *seek* instead of being satisfied, and which opens perspectives forward instead of enclosing us in the present and the past' (p. 31). Above all, one fundamental characteristic of the Scandinavian theatre has worked to foster this ideal of an audaciously imaginative theatre—an audience which goes to the theatre, one for whom the theatre has remained meaningful, and which therefore has preserved a remarkable responsiveness to the theatrical event. For without the response of such an imaginatively engaged audience, the theatre, as Ingmar Berman insists, 'lives with surface roots, and becomes an uncertain, staggering colossus, without any foundation in reality. A theatre's basis in reality is its audience.'

Chapter References

Full bibliographical citations are given here only for those items (mainly articles and chapters) *not* listed in the Bibliography.

ONE THE MIDDLE AGES
See: F. J. Billeskov Jansen, *Danmarks Digtekunst* I (1964); S. Birket Smith, *Studier på det gamle danske Skuespils Område*, 2 vols.; Hans Brix, *Analyser og Problemer* I; G. E. Klemming, *Sveriges dramatiska litteratur til och med 1875;* Torben Krogh, *Ældre dansk Teater;* Gustaf Ljunggren, *Svenska dramat intill slutet af sjuttonde århundradet;* Bert Möller, 'Stjärngossar och Trettondagsspel', *Folkminnen och Folktankar,* IV (Malmö, 1917); Thomas Overskou, *Den danske Skueplads* I (1854); H. Wiers Jensen, 'De liturgiske Skuespil og deres sidste Udløbere i Norden i Stjernespillet', *Norvegia sacra,* I (Christiania, 1921).

TWO THE HUMANIST STAGE
Principal references include: Billeskov Jansen, *Danmarks Digtekunst* I; Birket Smith, *Studier på det gamle danske Skuespils Område;* Brix, *Analyser og Problemer* III; Oluf Friis, *Den danske Litteraturs Historie* I (1945); Krogh, *Ældre dansk Teater;* Ljunggren, *Svenska dramat;* Nils Personne, *Svenska teatern* I (1913); August Petersson, *Studier i svenska skoldramat;* Oscar Wieselgren, *Bidrag til kännedomen om 1600-talsdramat i Sverige.*

THREE RENAISSANCE FESTIVITIES
See: Otto Andrup's 'Hoffet og dets Fester' in *Danmark i Fest og Glæde*, eds. J. Clausen and T. Krogh, I (1935); Torben Krogh's 'Optogsbilleder fra Christian IV's Kroningsfest' in his *Musik og Teater* and his *Hofballetten under Christian IV og Frederik III;* Ljunggren, *Svenska dramat;* R. Nyerup, *Efterretninger om Kong Frederik den Tredie;* and Personne, *Svenska teatern* I. Sources of information about the wedding festivities of 1634 include: J. J. Holst, *Triumphus nuptialis* (1648), published in Danish as *Regiæ nuptiæ* (1637), and Charles Ogier, *Ephemerides sive iter danicum svecicum polonicum* (Paris, 1656).

FOUR ROYAL TROUPES
See: Agne Beijer, 'Le théâtre en Suède jusqu'à la mort de Gustave III' and 'Le théâtre de Charles XII', *Revue de la société d'histoire du théâtre;* F. A. Dahlgren, *Förteckningen öfver svenska skådespel;* Anne E. Jensen, *Studier over europæisk drama i Danmark 1722–1770*, 2 vols.; Krogh, *Musik og Teater;* Ljunggren, *Svenska dramat;* Robert Neiiendam, *Mennesker bag Masker* and *Gennem mange Aar;* Eiler Nystrøm, *Den danske Komedies Oprindelse;* Personne, *Svenska teatern* I.

FIVE HOLBERG AND THE DANISH COMEDY
Additional references include: Jensen, *Studier over europæisk drama;* Krogh, 'Omkring Grønnegadeteatret' in *Musik og Teater* and *Studier over Harlekinaden paa den danske Skueplads;* and, above all, Nystrøm, *Den danske Komedies Oprindelse.* The standard critical edition of Holberg is his *Comoedierne*, ed. Carl Roos, 3 vols. The 250th anniversary of Grønnegadeteatret in 1972 elicited several commemorative volumes, including Anne E. Jensen's *Teatret i Lille Grønnegade 1722–1728* and Alfred Jeppesen's *Den danske skueplads på Holbergs tid.*

SIX ROCOCO PLAYHOUSES
Sources include: Beijer, *Slottsteatrarna på Drottningholm och Gripsholm;* Dahlgren, *Förteckningen öfver svenska skådespel;* Nils Erdman, *Ur rokokoens liv;* Jensen, *Studier over europæisk drama;* Krogh, *Christian VII's franske Hofaktører, Studier over de sceniske Opførelser of Holbergs Komedier,* and *Studier over Harlekinaden;* A. M. Nagler, *Sources of Theatrical History* (New

York, 1952), with information about the acting and costume reforms of Lekain and Clairon; Neiiendam, 'Hvordan det gik til' and Krogh, 'Dekorationer, Costumer, og Iscenesættelse' in *Komediehuset paa Kongens Nytorv 1748;* Neiiendam, *Det kgl. Hofteater* and *Scenen drager;* J. C. Normann, *Holberg paa Teatret;* Thomas Overskou, *Den danske Skueplads,* II (1856); J. C. Tode, *Dramatiske Tillæg til Museum og Hertha.* Margarete Baur-Heinhold's *Baroque Theatre* (London, 1967) also contains lavish reproductions of the playhouses at Gripsholm and Drottningholm.

SEVEN THE GUSTAVIAN AGE

See: Beijer, 'Ett regihistoriskt dokument' (on the *Gustaf Wasa* production) and *Slottsteatrarna;* G. M. Bergman and N. Brunius, eds. *Dramaten 175 År;* Per Bjurström, *Teaterdekoration i Sverige;* Johan Flodmark, *Bollhusen och Lejonkulan; Gustaviansk teater skildrad af Pehr Hilleström,* eds. A. Beijer and G. Hilleström (containing reproductions of Hilleström's scene pictures); Claes Hoogland and Gösta Kjellin, eds. *Bilder ur svensk teaterhistoria;* Oscar Levertin, *Gustaf III som dramatisk författare* and *Teater och drama under Gustaf III;* Personne, *Svenska teatern,* I.

EIGHT DENMARK'S GOLDEN AGE

Considerable material is available in English about this period. On Heiberg and Fru Heiberg, see Henning Fenger, *The Heibergs,* ed. and trans. by F. J. Marker; Søren Kierkegaard, *Crisis in the Life of an Actress,* trans. S. Crites (London, 1967); and Lise-Lone Marker, 'Fru Heiberg: A Study of the Art of the Romantic Actor', *Theatre Research,* XIII, 1 (1973). An extensive discussion of stage practices during this period is available in F. J. Marker's *Hans Christian Andersen and the Romantic Theatre.* Readers of Swedish are also referred to Gösta M. Bergman's in-depth studies, *Regihistoriska studier* and *Regi och spelstil under Gustaf Lagerbjelkes tid.* Other principal references include: Göran Avén, 'Hamlet på Kungl. Teatern 1819' in *Nya teaterhistoriska studier* (Stockholm, 1957); Billeskov Jansen, *Danmarks Digtekunst* III; August Bournonville, *Mit Theaterliv;* Johanne Luise Heiberg, *Et Liv gjenoplevet i Erindringen;* Hoogland and Kjellin, *Bilder ur svensk teaterhistoria;* Krogh, *Danske Teater-*

billeder, Oehlenschlägers Indførelse på den danske Skueplads (a reconstruction of the first production of *Hakon Jarl*), and 'Guldalderen' in *Teatret på Kongens Nytorv 1748–1948*, ed. H. Gabrielsen; Overskou, *Den danske Skueplads* IV (1862).

NINE IBSEN TAKES THE STAGE
Selected chapter references include: Øyvind Anker, *Den danske teatermaleren Troels Lund og Christiania Theater* and *Scene-kunsten i Norge fra fortid til nutid;* E. Ansteinsson, *Teater i Norge;* Herman Bang, *'Et Dukkehjem' paa Nationaltheatret* (Copenhagen, 1880) and *Kritiske Studier* (Copenhagen, 1880); T. Blanc, *Christiania Theaters historie 1827–77* and *Henrik Ibsen og Christiania Theater;* Edvard Brandes, *Dansk Skue-spilkunst;* Georg Brandes, *Henrik Ibsen;* Gunnar Heiberg, *Ibsen og Bjørnson paa Scenen;* Ludvig Josephson, *Err och annat om Henrik Ibsen och Christiania Teater* and *Teater-Regie;* Halvdan Koht, *Henrik Ibsen. Ett diktarliv;* Bernt Lorentzen, *Det første norske teater;* Per Lindberg, *August Lindberg, Skådespelaren och människan* (Stockholm, 1943); Audhild Lund, *Henrik Ibsen og det norske teater;* Frederick and Lise-Lone Marker, 'The First Nora: Notes on the World Première of *A Doll's House*', *Contemporary Approaches to Ibsen,* II, ed. Daniel Haakonsen (Oslo, 1971); F. J. Marker, *Hans Christian Andersen and the Romantic Theatre* and 'Negation in the Blond Kingdom: The Theatre Criticism of Edvard Brandes', *Educational Theatre Journal,* XX (December 1968); Michael Meyer, *Henrik Ibsen: The Making of a Dramatist 1828–1864* (1967); H. Nathansen, *William Bloch; The Oxford Ibsen,* ed. James Walter McFarlane, esp. Vol. I (1970) and Vol. II (1962) with Appendices; Evert Sprinchorn, ed. *Ibsen Letters and Speeches* (New York, 1964); P. F. D. Tennant, *Ibsen's Dramatic Technique;* H. Wiers-Jensen, *Nationaltheatret gjennem 25 aar* and (with J. Nordahl-Olsen) *Den Nationale Scene. De første 25 aar;* A. M. Wiesener, *Henrik Ibsen og 'Det norske Teater' i Bergen;* J. Wiingaard, *William Bloch og Holberg.* No reference is made in this list to the large body of critical writing on Ibsen. The standard critical edition of Ibsen's plays is his *Samlede Værker* (Hundreårsutgave), eds. Francis Bull, Halvdan Koht and D. A. Seip, 21 vols., in which the Introductions are particularly valuable. Bjørnson's plays are collected in his *Samlede Værker* VII-XI (1901–2).

TEN AUGUST STRINDBERG
Selected sources include: Agne Beijer, *Dramatik och teater;*
G. M. Bergman, *Den moderna teaterns genombrott;* Bjurström,
Teaterdekoration i Sverige; Vagn Børge, *Strindbergs mystiske
teater;* August Falck, *Fem år med Strindberg;* Alfred Hedvall,
Strindberg på Stockholmsscenen 1870–1922; Ingrid Hollinger,
'Urpremiären på Till Damaskus' in Bergman and Brunius, eds.
Dramaten 175 År; Martin Lamm, *August Strindberg;* Gunnar
Ollén, *Strindbergs dramatik.* Strindberg's *Open Letters to the
Intimate Theatre* has been published in translation by Walter
Johnson (Seattle, n.d.). As with Ibsen, no attempt is made here
to list critical and literary studies of Strindberg's plays. The
standard edition of the plays is Strindberg's *Samlade skrifter,*
ed. John Landquist, 55 vols. More recently, an important new
edition of the plays, *August Strindbergs Dramer* (Stockholm,
1962—), 4 vols. to date, has begun to appear, edited and ex-
cellently commented by Karl Reinhold Smedmark. A summary
of Strindberg's theories of acting and staging is found in
G. M. Bergman's 'Strindberg and the Intima Teatern', *Theatre
Research* IX, 1 (1967).

ELEVEN THE MODERN THEATRE
Principal references include: Anker, *Scenekunsten i Norge fra
fortid til nutid;* Beijer, *Dramatik och teater* and *Teaterrecensioner 1925–1949;* Bergman, *Den moderna teaterns genombrott;*
Bjurström, *Teaterdekoration i Sverige; Bogen om Johannes,
skrevet af hans venner,* ed. Michael Neiiendam (Copenhagen,
1945); Børge, *Strindbergs mystiske teater;* Edward Gordon
Craig, *A Production, Being Thirty-two Collotype Plates of Designs
projected or realized for The Pretenders of Henrik Ibsen and produced at the Royal Theatre, Copenhagen 1926* (Oxford, 1930);
H. Gabrielsen, ed. *Teatre på Kongens Nytorv 1748–1948;* Svend
Gade, *Mit Livs Drejescene;* Hoogland and Kjellin, *Bilder ur
svensk teaterhistoria;* Per Lindberg, *Bakom masker; The Modern
Theatre in Sweden,* Tulane Drama Review VI, 1961; Ollén,
Strindbergs dramatik; Perspektiv på teater, eds. Ulf Gran and
Ulla-Britta Lagerroth; F. Schyberg, *Ti Aars Teater; Teater-
historiska studier* (Stockholm, 1940). Ulla Poulsen Skou's
Genier er som Tordenvejr: Gordon Craig på Det Kgl. Teater 1926
(Copenhagen, 1973) includes a translation of the (quite limited)

exchange of letters between Craig and Johannes Poulsen. For English readers, the booklet *Swedish Theatre,* by Niklas Brunius, Göran O. Eriksson, and Rolf Rembe (Swedish Institute for Cultural Relations, n.d.) will also prove useful. For translations of Pär Lagerkvist, see his *Modern Theatre: Seven Plays and an Essay,* trans. Thomas R. Buckman (University of Nebraska Press, 1966). English translations and criticism of the plays of ,Munk, Abell, and Grieg are readily available: see, for example, R. P. Keigwin's introduction to *Five Plays by Kaj Munk* (New York, 1953), Elias Bredsdorff's 'Abell' in *The Genius of the Scandinavian Theatre,* ed. Evert Sprinchorn (New York, 1964), and Harald S. Naess's introduction to Grieg in *Five Modern Scandinavian Plays* (New York, 1971).

TWELVE SINCE 1945

In addition to the more ephemeral records of two decades of theatregoing (theatre programmes and reviews), the following items have proved relevant: Anker, *Scenekunsten i Norge;* Bjurström, *Teaterdekoration i Sverige;* Brunius, et. al. *Swedish Theatre;* Harald Engberg, *Brecht på Fyn,* 2 vols. (Odense, 1966) and *Teatret 1945–52; Et teater blev til,* Det Ny Teaterforlag [1958]; Gran and Lagerroth, *Perspektiv på teater;* Alf Henriques, *Det Kongelige Teater før og nu* (Copenhagen, 1967); Henrik Holm-Hansen, *et al. Skuespil, opera og ballet i Danmark;* R. Josephson and C. Hoogland, *Från Johanna till Amorina. Bilder och repliker från Dramatens spelår 1948–1951* (Stockholm, 1951); Jens Kistrup, 'Det moderne drama', *Politikens Dansk Litteraturhistorie,* IV (Copenhagen, 1966); Svend Kragh-Jacobsen, *Teterårbogen,* 1955f.; Thorvald Larsen, *Fra mindernes dragkiste* (Copenhagen, 1972); Hans Jacob Nilsen, *Peer Gynt, Ett antiromantisk verk* (Oslo, 1948); Knud Poulsen, ed. *Mogens Wieth;* Poul Reumert, *Masker og Mennesker* and *Teatrets Kunst* (1963) [selections anthologized in his *Om teater,* ed. Carl Bergstrøm-Nielsen (Copenhagen, 1971)]; Per Schwanbom, 'New Directions in the Swedish Theatre', *American-Scandinavian Review,* LXI, 3 (Autumn, 1973); F. Schyberg, *Teatret i Krig;* Einer Skavlan, *Norsk teater: 1930–1953.* Jerzy Grotowski's *Towards a Poor Theatre* was, of course, first published by Odin Teatrets Forlag in 1968. Henrik Sjögren has studied Bergman's theatrical art in depth in *Ingmar Bergman på teatern* and *Regi: Ingmar*

Bergman, the latter being a working diary from the Bergman production of *Woyzeck* at Dramaten in 1969. Also of interest to English readers are Michael Meyer's translation of the Bergman adaptation of *A Dream Play* (New York and London, 1973), unfortunately containing very little of the actual stage business, and Egil Törnqvist's 'Ingmar Bergman Directs Strindberg's *Ghost Sonata,' Theatre Quarterly* III (July–September 1973), 3–14. Finally, *Modern Drama* has published relevant article-reports from time to time: Walter Johnson, 'A Theatre that is National' [about Rigsteatret], *MD* I (December 1958), 192–5; P. M. Mitchell, 'Denmark and the Modern Drama,' *MD* II (May 1959), 51–6; Birgitta Steene, 'Critical Reception of American Drama in Sweden,' *MD* V (May 1962), 71–83; Glenn Loney, 'Bergman in the Theatre,' *MD* IX (September 1966), 170–78; and Horst Franz and Frederic Fleisher, 'Eugene O'Neill and the Royal Dramatic Theatre of Stockholm,' *MD* X (December 1967), 300–12.

Bibliography

Asterisked items contain useful bibliographies

SWEDEN

Arpe, Verner. *Das schwedische Theater.* Stockholm, 1969
Beijer, Agne. *Dramatik och teater.* Lund, 1966
——. 'Ett regihistoriskt dokument,' *Dikt och Studie* (Uppsala, 1922)
——. 'Le théâtre en Suède jusqu'à la mort de Gustave III,' *Revue de la société d'histoire du théâtre,* VIII (1956), 137–67, and 'Le théâtre de Charles XII et la mise en scène du théâtre parlé du XVIIe siècle,' *ibid.,* 197–214
——. *Slottsteatrarna på Drottningholm och Gripsholm.* Malmö, 1937
——. *Teaterrecensioner 1925–1949.* Stockholm, 1954
Bergman, Gösta M. *Den moderna teaterns genombrott.* Stockholm, 1966
——. *Pär Lagerkvists dramatik.* Stockholm, 1928
——. *Regihistoriska studier.* Stockholm, 1952
——. *Regi och spelstil under Gustaf Lagerbjelkes tid vid Kungl. teatern.* Stockholm, 1946
——. *Svensk teater. Strukturförändringar och organisation 1900–1970.* Stockholm, 1970
Bergman, Gösta M. and Brunius, Niklas, eds. *Dramaten 175 År.* Stockholm, 1963
Bergman, Hjalmar. *Samlade skrifter,* ed. Johannes Edfelt. 30 vols. Stockholm, 1949–58

Bjurström, Per. *Teaterdekoration i Sverige.* Stockholm, 1964
Brandell, Gunnar. *Svensk litteratur 1900–1950,* 2nd ed.
Stockholm, 1967
Børge, Vagn. *Strindbergs mystiske teater.* Copenhagen, 1942*
Cederblom, G. *Pehr Hillestrom som kulturskildare.* Stockholm,
1929
Collijn, Gustaf. *Intimen. Historien om en teater.* Stockholm,
1943
Dahlgren, F. A. *Förteckningen öfver svenska skådespel
uppförda på Stockholms theatrar 1737–1863.* Stockholm,
1866
Erdman, Nils. *Ur rokokoens liv.* Stockholm, 1925
Falck, August. *Fem år med Strindberg.* Stockholm, 1935
Flodmark, Johan. *Bollhusen och Lejonkulan i Stockholm.*
Stockholm, 1897
———. *Stenborgska skådebanorna.* Stockholm, 1893
Gran, Ulf and Lagerroth, U.-B., eds. *Perspektiv på teater.*
Stockholm, 1971
Gustaviansk teater skildrad af Pehr Hilleström, eds. A. Beijer
and G. Hilleström. Stockholm, 1947
Hallingberg, G. *Radioteater i 40 år.* Stockholm, 1965
Hedberg, Frans. *Svenska skådespelare.* Stockholm, 1882
Hedvall, Alfred. *Strindberg på Stockholmsscenen 1870–1922.*
Stockholm, 1923
Hillberg, Olof. *Teater i Sverige utanför huvudstaden.*
Stockholm, 1948
Hilleström, Gustaf. *Le théâtre et la danse en Suède.* Stockholm,
1951 (*Theatre and Drama in Sweden,* 1952)
———. *Swedish Theatre during Five Decades.* Stockholm, 1962
Hoogland, Claes and Kjellin, Gösta. *Bilder ur svensk
teaterhistoria.* Stockholm, 1970
Josephson, Ludvig. *Teater-Regie.* Stockholm, 1892
Klemming, G. E. *Sveriges dramatiska litteratur til och med
1875.* Stockholm, 1863–79
Lagerkvist, Pär. *Dramatik.* 3 vols. Stockholm, 1956
Lamm, Martin. *August Blanche som stockholmsskildare,* 2nd
ed. Stockholm, 1950
———. *August Strindberg.* Stockholm, 1948
Levertin, Oscar. *Gustaf III som dramatisk författare.*
Samlade skrifter XVIII, 2nd ed. Stockholm, 1911

——. *Teater och drama under Gustaf III*. Samlade skrifter XVII, 2nd ed. Stockholm, 1911

Lewenhaupt, E. *Bref rörande teatern under Gustaf III*. Uppsala, 1891

Lindberg, Per. *Bakom masker*. Stockholm, 1949

Linder, Erik H. *Fem decennier av 1900-tallet*. 2 vols. Stockholm, 1967*

Ljunggren, Gustaf. *Svenska dramat intill slutet af sjuttonde århundradet*. Lund and Copenhagen, 1864

The Modern Theatre in Sweden. Tulane Drama Review, VI, 1961

Molin, Nils. *Shakespeare och Sverige intill 1800-talets mitt*. Göteborg, 1931

Nordensvan, Georg. *I rampljus*. Stockholm, 1900

——. *Svensk teater och svenska skådespelare*. 2 vols. Stockholm, 1917–18

Nya teaterhistoriska studier (Föreningen Drottningholmsteaterns vanner XII). Stockholm, 1957

Ollén, Gunnar. *Strindbergs dramatik*. Stockholm, 1948

Personne, Nils. *Svenska teatern*. 8 vols. Stockholm, 1913–27

Petersson, August. *Studier i svenska skoldramat*. Göteborg, 1929

Rydell, Gerda. *Adertonhundratalets historiska skådespel i Sverige före Strindberg*, Stockholm, 1928

Silfverstolpe, Carl. *Käller til svenska teaterns historia*. Stockholm, 1877

——. *Svenska teaterns äldsta öden*. Stockholm, 1882

Sjögren, Henrik. *Ingmar Bergman på teatern*. Stockholm, 1968

——. *Regi: Ingmar Bergman*. Stockholm, 1969

Smitt, Isak Fredrik. *Teater förr och nu*. Stockholm, 1896

Stiernhielm, Georg and Columbus, Samuel. *Spel om Herculis Wägewal*, ed. A. Beijer. Stockholm, 1955

Strindberg, August. *Samlade skrifter*, ed. John Landquist. 55 vols. Stockholm, 1912–20

Strindbergfejden, ed. Harry Järv. Solna, 1968

Svanberg, Johannes. *Kungl. teatrarne under ett halvt sekel 1860–1910*. 2 vols. Stockholm, 1967

Teaterhistoriska studier (Föreningen Drottningholmsteaterns vanner II). Stockholm, 1940

Tigerstedt, E. N. *Ny illustrarad svensk litteraturhistoria,* 2nd ed. 4 vols. Stockholm, 1965–7*

Wettergren, Erik and Lignell, Ivar, eds. *Svensk scenkonst och film.* Stockholm, 1940

Widerström, C. H. *Minne af Kungl. dramatiska teatern.* Stockholm, 1825

Wieselgren, Oscar. *Bidrag til kännedomen om 1600-talsdramat i Sverige.* Uppsala, 1909

Wikland, Erik. *Elizabethan Players in Sweden 1591–92.* Stockholm, 1962

Wollin, Nils G. *Desprez i Sverige. Louis Jean Desprez' verksamhet 1784–1804.* Stockholm, 1936

DENMARK

Aschengreen, Erik. *Fra Trine Rar til Maria Stuart.* Copenhagen, 1961

Atlung, Knud. *Det kongelige Teater 1889–1939.* Copenhagen, 1942*

Aumont, A. and Collin, E. *Den danske Nationaltheater 1748–1889.* 3 vols. Copenhagen, 1896*

Billeskov Jansen, F. J. *Danmarks Digtekunst,* 2nd ed. 3 vols. Copenhagen, 1964

Birket Smith, S. *Studier på det gamle danske Skuespils Område.* 2 vols. Copenhagen, 1883–6

Bournonville, August. *Mit Theaterliv.* 3 vols. Copenhagen, 1848–77

Brandes, Edvard. *Dansk Skuespilkunst.* Copenhagen, 1880

Brix, Hans. *Analyser og Problemer.* 3 vols. Copenhagen, 1933–6

——. *Danmarks Digtere.* Copenhagen, 1951

Christensen, H. *Det kongelige Theater i Aarene 1852-9.* Copenhagen, 1890

Danmark i Fest og Glæde, eds. J. Clausen and T. Krogh. 6 vols. Copenhagen, 1935–6

Dreyer, P. *Odense Teater 1796–1946.* Odense, 1946

Engberg, Harald. *Pantomimeteatret.* Copenhagen, 1959

——. *Teatret 1945–1952.* Copenhagen, 1952

Fenger, Henning. *The Heibergs,* trans. and ed. with an introduction by F. J. Marker. New York, 1971

Friis, N. *Det kongelige Teater. Vor nationale scene i fortid og nutid.* Copenhagen, 1943

Friis, Oluf. *Den danske Litteraturs Historie.* I. Copenhagen, 1945

Gabrielsen, H., ed. *Teatret på Kongens Nytorv 1748–1948.* Copenhagen, 1948

Gade, Svend. *Mit Livs Drejescene.* Copenhagen, 1941

Hansen, P. *Den danske Skueplads, illustreret Theaterhistorie.* 3 vols. Copenhagen, n.d.

Heiberg, J. L. *Prosaiske Skrifter.* 11 vols. Copenhagen, 1861–2

——. *Vaudeviller.* 3 vols. Copenhagen, 1895

Heiberg, Johanne Luise. *Et Liv gjenoplevet i Erindringen,* 3rd ed. 2 vols. Copenhagen, 1913

Henriques, Alf. *Shakespeare og Danmark indtil 1840.* Copenhagen, 1941

Holberg, Ludvig. *Comoedierne,* ed. Carl Roos. 3 vols. Copenhagen and Christiania, 1922–4

——. *Epistler,* ed. F. J. Billeskov Jansen. 8 vols. Copenhagen, 1944–54

Holm-Hansen, H. *et al. Skuespil, opera og ballet i Danmark.* Copenhagen, 1970*

Jensen, Anne E. *Studier over europæisk drama i Danmark 1722–1770.* 2 vols. Copenhagen, 1968*

——. *Teatret i Lille Grønnegade 1722–1728.* Copenhagen, 1972

Kragh-Jacobsen, S. and Krogh, Torben. *Den kongelige danske Ballet.* Copenhagen, 1952

Krogh, Torben. *Bellman som musikalsk Digter.* Copenhagen, 1945

——. *Christian VII's franske Hofaktører.* Copenhagen, 1947

——. *Danske Teaterbilleder fra det 18de Aarhundrede.* Copenhagen, 1932

——. *Det kgl. Teaters ældste Regiejournal 1781–87.* Copenhagen, 1927

——. *Hofballetten under Christian IV og Frederik III.* Copenhagen, 1939

——. ed. *Komediehuset paa Kongens Nytorv 1748.* Copenhagen, 1948

——. *Musik og Teater.* Copenhagen, 1955

——. *Oehlenschlägers Indførelse på den danske Skueplads.* Copenhagen, 1954

——. *Skuespilleren i det 18de Aarhundrede, belyst gennem danske Kilder.* Copenhagen, 1948

——. *Studier over de sceniske Opførelser af Holbergs Komedier.* Copenhagen, 1929

——. *Studier over Harlekinaden paa den danske Skueplads.* Copenhagen, 1931

——. *Ældre dansk Teater.* Copenhagen, 1940

Mantzius, Karl. *Skuespilkunstens Historie: Klassicisme og Romantik.* Copenhagen, 1916

——. *Skuespilkunstens Historie i det 19de Aarhundrede.* Copenhagen, 1922

Marker, Frederick J. *Hans Christian Andersen and the Romantic Theatre.* Toronto, 1971*

Mitchell, P. M. *A History of Danish Literature.* Copenhagen, 1957

Nathansen, H. *William Bloch.* Copenhagen, 1928

Neiiendam, Robert. *Breve fra danske Skuespillere og Skuespillerinder 1748–1864.* 2 vols. Copenhagen, 1911–12

——. *Casinos Oprindelse og Historie i Omrids.* Copenhagen, 1948

——. *Det kgl. Hofteater.* Copenhagen, 1922

——. *Det kgl. Teaters Historie 1874–90.* 5 vols. Copenhagen, 1921–30

——. *Det kgl. Teaters Historie 1890–92,* ed. K. Neiiendam. Copenhagen, 1970

——. *Folketeatret 1845–1945.* Copenhagen, 1945

——. *Gennem mange Aar.* Copenhagen, 1950

——. *Mennesker bag Masker.* Copenhagen, 1931

——. *Scenen drager.* Copenhagen, 1915

Normann, J. C. *Holberg paa Teatret.* Copenhagen, 1919

——. *Teatret.* Copenhagen, 1939

Nyerup, R. *Efterretninger om Kong Frederik den Tredie.* Copenhagen, 1817

Nystrøm, Eiler. *Den danske Komedies Oprindelse.* Copenhagen, 1918

Overskou, Thomas. *Den danske Skueplads i dens Historie.* 7 vols. 1854–76

——. *Den danske Skueplads og Staten.* Copenhagen, 1867

——. *Oplysninger om Theaterforhold i 1849–1858.* Copenhagen, 1858

Poulsen, Knud, ed. *Mogens Wieth*. Copenhagen, 1962
Rahbek, K. L. *Breve fra en gammel Skuespiller til hans Søn*.
  Copenhagen, 1782
——. *Om Skuespilkunsten*. Copenhagen, 1809
Rosenstand-Goiske, P. *Den dramatiske Journal,* ed. C.
  Behrens. 2 vols. and Supplement. Copenhagen, 1915–19
Reumert, Poul. *Masker og Mennesker,* 3rd ed. Copenhagen,
  1963
Schyberg, F. *Dansk teater i tjugonde århundrade*. Stockholm,
  1942
——. *Dansk Teaterkritik indtil 1914*. Copenhagen, 1937
——. *Teatret i Krig (1939–1948)*. Copenhagen, 1949
——. *Ti Aars Teater*. Copenhagen, 1939
Swendsen, L. *De københavnske Privatteatres Repertoire
  1847–1906*. Supplement 1907–1919. Copenhagen, 1919
Teatervidenskabelige studier I, ed. Svend Christiansen.
  Copenhagen, 1969
Tode, C. *Dramatiske Tillæg til Museum og Hertha. Kritik og
  Antikritik*. Copenhagen, 1784
Wiingaard, J. *William Bloch og Holberg*. Copenhagen, 1966

NORWAY
Aarseth, Asbjørn. *Den Nationale Scene 1901–1931*. Bergen,
  1968
Anker, Øyvind. *Christiania Theaters repertoire 1827–99*.
  Oslo, 1956
——. *Den danske teatermaleren Troels Lund og Christiania
  Theater*. Oslo, 1962
——. *Det Dramatiske Selskab i Christiania. Repertoire 1799–
  1844*. Oslo, 1959
——. *Scenekunsten i Norge fra fortid til nutid*. Oslo, 1968*
Ansteinsson, Eli. *Teater i Norge. Dansk scenkunst 1813–1863*.
  Oslo, 1968
Bjørnson, Bjørn. *Det gamle teater. Kunsten og menneskene*.
  Oslo, 1937
Bjørnson, Bjørnstjerne. *Samlede Værker* VII-XI. Copenhagen,
  1901–2
Blanc, T. *Christiania Theaters historie 1827–77*.
  Christiania, 1899

——. *Henrik Ibsen og Christiania Theater 1850–99.* Christiania, 1906

——. *Norges første nationale Scene.* Christiania, 1884

Brandes, Georg. *Henrik Ibsen.* Copenhagen, 1898

Bødtker, Sigurd. *Kristiània-premierer gjennem 30 aar,* eds. E. Skavlan and A. Rønneberg. 3 vols. Christiania, 1923–9

Dale, J. A. *Nynorsk dramatikk i hundre år.* Oslo, 1964

Dalgard, Olav. *Det Norske Teatret 1913–1953.* Oslo, 1953

Due, Christopher. *Erindringer fra Henrik Ibsens Ungdomsaar.* Copenhagen, 1909

Elster, Kristian D. Y. *Skuespillerinden Johanne Dybwad.* Oslo, 1931

Fahlstrøm, Alma. *To norske skuespilleres liv.* Oslo, 1927

Gjesdahl, Paul. *Centralteatrets historie.* Oslo, 1964

Heiberg, Gunnar. *Ibsen og Bjørnson paa Scenen.* Kristiania, 1918

——. *Norsk teater.* Kristiania, 1920

Henrik Ibsen: A Critical Anthology, ed. James McFarlane. Hammondsworth, 1970*

Henrik Ibsens brevveksling med Christiania Theater 1878–1899. Oslo, 1965

Høst, Sigurd. *Henrik Ibsen.* Paris and Stockholm, 1924

Ibsen, Henrik. *Samlede Værker* (Hundreårsutgave), eds. F. Bull, H. Koht, and D. A. Seip. 21 vols. Oslo, 1928–57

Josephson, Ludvig. *Ett och annat om Henrik Ibsen och Christiania Teater.* Stockholm, 1898

Just, Carl. *Litteratur om norsk teater. Bibliografi.* Oslo, 1953*

——. *Schrøder og Christiania Theater.* Oslo, 1948

Koht, Halvdan. *Henrik Ibsen. Ett diktarliv.* 2 vols. Oslo, 1928–9

Linder, Sten. *Ibsen, Strindberg och andra.* Stockholm, 1936

Lorentzen, Bernt. *Det første norske teater.* Bergen, 1949

Lund, Audhild. *Henrik Ibsen og det norske teater.* Oslo, 1925

Meyer, Michael. *Henrik Ibsen.* 3 vols. London, 1967–71

Michelsen, J. A. *Det Dramatiske Selskab i Bergen 1794–1894.* Bergen, 1894

Midbøe, Hans. *Reinhardts Iscenesættelse av Ibsens Gespenster i Kammerspiele Des Deutschen Theaters Berlin 1906.* Trondheim, 1969

Nationaltheatret i Kristiania. Christiania, 1899

Normann, Axel Otto. *Johanne Dybwad: Liv og kunst.* 2nd ed. Oslo, 1950

Det Norske Teatret. Femti år 1913–1963, ed. Nils Sletbak. Oslo, 1963

Norsk Theaterliv. Utgit av Norsk Skuespillerforbund. Bergen, 1923

Paulsen, John. *Samliv med Ibsen*. Copenhagen and Christiania, 1906

Paulson, Andreas. *Komediebakken og Engen*. Oslo, 1932

Pettersen, Hjalmar. *Henrik Ibsen*. Oslo, 1928

Reimers, Sophie. *Teaterminder fra Kristiania Teater*. Kristiania, 1919

Rønneberg, Anton. *Nationaltheatret gjennem femti år*. Oslo, 1949

Skavlan, Einer. *Norsk teater: 1930–1953,* ed. P. Gjesdahl. Oslo, 1960

Sperati, Octavia. *Theatererindringer*. Kristiania, 1911

Svendsen, A. Strømme. *Den Nationale Scene. Det norske repertoire 1876–1964*. Bergen, 1964

Tennant, P. F. D. *Ibsen's Dramatic Technique*. Cambridge, 1948*

Waal, Carla Rae. *Johanne Dybwad, Norwegian Actress*. Oslo, 1967

Wiers-Jensen, H. *Billeder fra Bergens ældste teaterhistorie*. Bergen, 1921

——. *Nationaltheatret gjennem 25 aar 1899–1924*. Christiania, 1924

Wiers-Jensen, H. and Nordahl-Olsen, J. *Den Nationale Scene. De første 25 aar*. Bergen, 1926

Wiesener, A. M. *Henrik Ibsen og 'Det norske Teater' i Bergen 1851–1857*. Bergen, 1928

Index

Abel and Cain 22
Abell, Kjeld 239–40, 241, 255–9;
  Anna Sophie Hedvig, 241; *Den blå
  Pekingeser (The Blue Pekinese)*,
  258–9, Pl. 48; *Dage på en Sky
  (Days on a Cloud)*, 255–7, Pl. 46;
  Dronning går igen (Queen on Tour),
  241; *Ejendommen Matr. Nr. 267
  (Lot No. 267)*, 244; *Eva aftjener sin
  Barnepligt (Eve Serves Her Child-
  hood)*, 240; *Kameliadamen*, 259;
  *Melodien der blev væk (The
  Melody that Got Lost)*, 239–40;
  Silkeborg, 255; *Skriget (The
  Scream)*, 259; *Vetsera*, 258, Pl. 47
Abildgaard, N. A. 104, 107
Acis and Galatea 84
Adam og Eva 103
Addison, J. 75
Adélaide de Guesclin 86
Adelcrantz, Carl Fredrik 79, 92
Adlerbeth, G. J. 92
Adolf Fredrik 71, 77, 78, 83, 88
Aftenrøde (Evening Glow) 206
Albee, E. 247, 251, 268
Albrici, Vincenzo 46
Alceste 88, Pl. 15
Almqvist, C. J. L. 264

Alw, Gabriel 233
Ami de tout de monde, L' 83
Amorina 264
Andersen, H. C. 106, 115, 118, 119,
  124, 129, 141, 145, 180, 259
Anderson, Maxwell 247
André, Harald 218
Andria 26–7
Anouilh, J. 245, 247
Anseaume, L. 79
Antoine, A. 171, 173, 185, 186
Apollo 31
Appia, A. 204, 212, 218
Aquilo 36
Arnholdt, H. J. 59, 72
Aspenström, Werner 260
Asteropherus, Magnus Olai 25
Athalie 86
Auber, D. F. E. 100, 122
Auden, W. H. 268
Augier, E. 155
Aulularia 25

Badius, Jodocus 28
Baguette de Vulcain, La 75
Balders Død (Balder's Death) 103–4,
  105, 106
Ballet comique de la Reine 35

Ballet des plaizirs de la vie des enfans sans soucy 37
Ballet des 4 Elémens 41–2
Bang, Herman 162, 171
Baptiste, Marie Louise 88
Barba, Eugenio 206, 248f
Beaulieu, Antoine de 37, 38
Beaumarchais, P. A. C. de 80
Beckett, Samuel 247, 250, 251
Beijer, Agne 84, 236
Belasco, David 171
Belleval, Mariane 79, 80
Bellman, C. M. 94
Benavente, J. 227
Benktsson, Benkt-Åke 266
Bérain, Jean 51, Pl. 10–13
Berg, Christian 73, 74
Berg, Yngve 222, 261
Bergling, Birger 268
Bergman, Hjalmar 209, 225; Dødens Arlequin (Death's Harlequin), 209; Lodolezzi Sings, 213; Mr. Sleeman is Coming, 213, 250; Markurells of Wadköping, 225; Patrasket (Rabble), 225; Swedenhielms, 225, 252; En skugga (A Shadow), 209
Bergman, Ingmar 205, 232, 235, 237, 243, 247, 250, 261, 264, 265ff; Crisis, 265; Hetz (Torment or Frenzy), 247; The Seventh Seal, 267
Berlau, Ruth 253
Besekow, Sam 245, 255, 261
Béverlei 80
Beyer, A. P. 26
Beyer, Sille 125
Bibiena, Carlo 86, Pl. 14
Biederman, Jacob 63
Biehl, Charlotte Dorothea 76
Birch, Sixt 23
Birger Jarl 86, 92
Bjarme, Brynjulf see Henrik Ibsen
Björling, Manda 198
Bjørneboe, Jens 260
Bjørnson, Bjørn 159, 172, 174
Bjørnson, Bjørnstjerne 128, 134, 136, 137, 138, 144, 154, 155–8, 159, 173, 174, 178; En fallit (A Bankruptcy), 157, 158; Halte-

Hulda (Limping Hulda), 155, 156; En hanske (A Gauntlet), 158; Kong Sverre, 155; Leonarda, 158, 162; Maria Stuart i Skotland, 128, 156, 177; Mellem slagene (Between the Battles), 155; De Nygifte (The Newly Married), 128, 156, 157; Over Ævne I (Beyond Human Power), 175, 238; Redaktøren (The Editor), 157, 158; Sigurd Jorsalfer (Sigurd the Crusader), 174; Sigurd Slembe (Sigurd the Bastard), 156
Blanc, T. 134
Blanche, August 119
Bloch, William 159, 166ff, 172, 204
Blood Wedding 261
Boindin, N. 58
Boissy, L. de 78
Bonds of Interest, The 227
Borberg, Svend 217, 230
Bosse, Harriet 191–3, 227
Bournonville, August 106, 108, 113, 115, 127, 145, 163
Brandes, Edvard 120, 122, 127, 156, 161, 162, 163, 170, 182, 183
Brandes, Georg 106, 124, 130, 151, 156, 157, 158, 182, 183
Brandt, Enevold 81
Branner, H. C. 260
Brecht, B. 247, 253, 260, 264, 268; Leben des Galilei, 253; Mother Courage, 264; Puntila and his Servant Matti, 264; Schweik in the Second World War, 264
Brenøe, Anna see Anna Nielsen
Britannicus 250
Broen, Abraham de 99, 100
Brooke, Henry 95
Brun, Johannes 137, 153
Brunati, Antonio 46
Brunius, August 215
Brunswick, Duke Henry Julius of 45
Bruun, Thomas 106, Pl. 23
Bruun Olsen, Ernst 260
Brynilda 70, 72, 75
Bull, Ole 134, 137, 141
Burchard, P. H. 49
Börk, Isaac 31

Bøgh, Erik 162
Bøttger, Elizabeth 76, 77

Caesar and Cleopatra 252
Calderón de la Barca, P. 48, 115
Caligula 265
Calzabigi, R. de 86
Campbellerne (The Campbells) 136
Camus, A. 265
Capion, E. 54, 56, 57, 73
Castegren, V. 193
Cato 75
Cavling, Finn 260
Cavling, Viggo 231, 232
Cercle, Le 99
Certamen equestre 43, 90, 91
Charles XI 30, 42, 43, 47, 90, 91
Charles XII 49, 52, 78
Charles, Theodor of Schwetzingen
  79
Chekhov, Anton 186, 247, 250, 258
Chipart, M. 105
Christensen, C. F. 115, Pl. 25–6
Christian III 33
Christian IV 19, 27, 29, 32, 33, 34,
  35, 37, 45
Christian V 42, 43, 47, 48, 49
Christian VI 59, 69, 71
Christian VII 79, 80, 81, 82
Queen Christina 30, 32, 37, 38, 39,
  42, 43, 45, 46, 47
Christjern II 95, 106
Cicéri, P. L. C. 94, 114, 115, 136
Cinna 86
Clairon, H. 80, 81, 83, 86
Clementin, N. 76
Cleopatra 24
Cléricourt, Marie 80, 81
Cock-a-Doodle-Dandy 247
Collijn, Gustaf 205
Comedia de Mundo et Paupere 23–4
Concordia Regularis 1
Conquest of the Galtar Rock 89, 91,
  101, Pl. 18
Conscious Lovers, The 75
Copeau, Jacques 204
Cora and Alonzo 92

Corneille, Pierre 51, 52, 53, 58, 70,
  86, 103
Corneille, Thomas 49
Coward, Noël 240
Craig, Edward Gordon 150, 190,
  204, 205, 212, 218, 228ff
Cramer, P. 103, 104
Crébillon, P. J. de 86
Cromwell 112
Cyrano de Bergerac 252
Cysat, Renwart 9

Dagermann, Stig 260
Daguerre's Diorama 115
Dalin, Olof von 70, 72, 75, 77
Damm, Bertil 222, 261
Dancourt, F. C. 52
Daniel, Samuel 32
Darius 31
David and Goliath 22
Defresny, N. 75
Delavigne, C. 117
DePuy, Edouard 110, 111, 113
Descartes, René 38
Desprez, Louis Jean 94, 95, 96, 100,
  Pl. 20–2
Destouches, P. N. 75, 78
De uno peccatore qui promeruit
  gratiam 6
Deux Arlequins, Les 59
Diderot, D. 76, 103
Disa 24
Dissipateur, Le 75–6
Divine Words 266
Doctor Faustus 48
Doctor Simon 16–17
Don Giovanni 136
Dorotheæ Komedie 12–15
Drachmann, Holger 161
Dreyer, Carl 238
Drottning Christina 94–5, Pl. 20–1
Drottningens juvelsmycke (The Queen's
  Jewel) 264
Dürrenmatt, F. 252
Dumas, A. 112
Dumas, A. fils 155, 259
Duni, E. R. 79
Dybwad, Johanne 174, 175

Dyveke 106, 107, 110, 115, Pl. 23
Dødedansen (The Dance of Death) 23, 24
Dödsdömde, Den (The Condemned) 260

Eide, Egill 174
Eigtved, N. 73, 74, 79, 112
Ek, Anders 237, 265
Ekerot, Bengt 251
Eklund, E. 226, 228
Ekman, Gösta 224
Elmlund, Axel 178
Elves' Hill (H. C. Andersen) 145
Emilia Galotti 106
Enfant prodigue, L' 76
Engelbrecht, W. 179
Erixson, Sven 261, 263, Pl. 49
Essen, Siri von 179, 186, 187, 188
Ethelwold, Bishop of Winchester 1
Eugénie 80
Eunuch, The 26, 30
Eventyr paa Fodreisen (Adventures on Foot) 119
Everyman (v. Hofmannsthal) 208–9, 210
Eviga, Det (The Apes) 260
Ewald, Johannes 103–4, 105, 244

Fabris, Jacopo 74
Fahlström, Johan 174, 175
Falck, August 178, 184, 198, 199, 201, 202, 205
Fallesen, E. 169
Faust 267
Feast of Diana 89, 90–1
Festen i Albano (Festival in Albano) 115, Pl. 26
Fiskerne (The Fishermen) 104
Flies, The 262–3
Flotten (The Raft) 248, 249
Flygare, Anna 201
Flyttedagen (Moving Day) 118
Foech-Whirsker 80, 81
Foersom, P. 109–10
Forssell, Lars 260
Fouquet, Jean 15, 22
Fournenburgh, J. B. van 47

Français à Londres, Le 78
Frederick the Great 77
Frederik II 27, 29, 32, 33, 44
Frederik III 33, 39, 41, 46, 47, 48, 49
Frederik IV 49, 52, 54, 55, 59
Frederik V 60, 69, 71, 72, 77, 78
Frederik VII 120
Fredrik I 58, 71
Fridh, Gertrud 269
Friebach, C. 109
Frigga 94
Frischlin, N. 26
Fru Rangsuik (Lady Snob) 70
Fröken Snöhwits Tragedia (Tragedy of Snow White) 70
Fugleelskerne (The Bird Lovers) 260

Gabrielsen, Holger 204, 240, 241, 257, 261
Gade, Svend 210, 217, 241, 270, Pl. 37
Galeotti, V. 105, 108
Gallondier, Louis 84
Gamester, The 80
Garrick, David 83, 110
Genboerne (The Neighbours) 119, 252
George II 72
Gheradi, E. 59, 64
Gierow, Karl Ragnar 251
Giraudoux, J. 240
Gitrene (The Bars) 260
Glorieux, Le 78
Gluck, C. W. 72, 84, 86, 87, 88
Goethe, J. W. von 106, 107; *Rules for Actors*, 121, 202
Goldoni, Carlo 76
Gombrowicz, W. 264, 268
Gottsched, J. C. 72
Grabow, Carl 190, 193f, 197, Pl. 33–6
Granberg, P. A. 110
Grandison, Emil 188f, 190f, 193
Granville-Barker, H. 190
Grate, Eric 261
Green, John 45
Gregaard, Peer 245, 246
Grétry, A.-E.-M. 80, 87, 88, 111
Grevenius, Herbert 233, 235

Grieg, Edvard 152, 174, 244
Grieg, Nordahl 240–1; *Nederlaget (The Defeat)*, 240–1, 250; *Vår ære og vår makt (Our Power and Our Glory)*, 240
Grosch, H. 135
Grotowski, J. 206, 249
Grünewald, Isaac 218f, 220, 226, 227, 233, 238, 261, Pl. 41–3, 45
Gulmann, C. 230
Gundersen, Laura 137, 139, 146, 149, 171
Gustav II Adolf 22, 24, 45, 92
Gustav III 71, 78, 79, 81, 82–101
Gustav Adolf och Ebbe Brahe 94
Gustav Adolfs ädelmod (The Nobility of Gustav Adolf) 92
Gustav Vasa 6, 24, 27
Gustavius Vasa, Deliverer of His Country 95
Gustav Wasa (opera) 95–7, 101, Pl. 22
Gyldenløve, U. F. 43
Gyllenborg, Carl 58, 70
Gyllenborg, G. F. 86, 92, 94, 97, 99
Gyllich, Valdemar 129

Hallman, C. I. 94, 97
Hammarskjöld, Dag 251
Hamsun, Knut 206, 213
Hansen, Christiern 12
Hanson, Alfred 178
Hanson, Lars 206, 233, 235, 236, 251, 254, 263
Hans Wurst 19, 47
Happy Days 247
Harsdorff, C. F. 112
Haupt- und Staatsactionen 47, 64, 70, 72
Hedberg, Tor 195, 208f, 227
Hedeby, Kerstin 267
Hedqvist, Ivan 223
Hedvall, Y. 190
Hegel, F. W. 116
Hegelund, P. J. 23, 28
Hegermann-Lindencrone, C. 242
Heiberg, Gunnar 172, 173–4, 213
Heiberg, J. L. 106, 115–18, 119, 120, 124, 125, 127, 129, 134, 140, 141, 142, 145, 244; *Aprilsnarrene (The April Fools)*, 120; *Elverhøj (Elves' Hill)*, 120–1, 128, 130, Pl. 27; *Et Eventyr i Rosenborg Have (An Adventure in Rosenborg Gardens)*, 120; *Kong Salomon og Jørgen Hattemager*, 118; *Nei (No)*, 120; *On Human Freedom*, 116; *On the Vaudeville as a Dramatic Form*, 118; *De Uadskillige (The Inseperables)*, 120
Heiberg, Johanne Louise 103, 119ff, 142, 146, 150, 161, 162, Pl. 27–8
Heiberg, P. A. 115
Heimbach, W. 39, 41
Helmfelt 93–4, Pl. 19
Helmuth, Osvald 245
Hemmet (The Home) 248
Hennings, Betty 159, 162ff, 172
Henri III et sa cour 112
Hercules Furens 30
Herman von Unna 101, 108, 110
Hernani 112
Hertug Skule (Duke Skule) 150, Pl. 31
Hertz, Henrik 106, 118, 122, 124, 141, 147, 244
Hettner, H., *Das Moderne Drama* 142
Hiärne, Urban 30
Hillberg, Emil 154, 179, 197
Hilleström, Pehr 86, 87, 90, 94, Pl. 13, 15–19
Hippolytus 31
Hjelm, C. J. 113
Hjortsberg, Lars 91, 100, 110
Hjulström, Lennart 248
Hofmannsthal, Hugo v. 208
Hogarth, W. 268
Holberg, Ludvig 54, 55–68, 70, 72, 73, 74, 75, 76, 78, 115, 118, 119, 121, 133, 141, 174, 244; *Barselstuen (The Lying-In Room)*, 66; *Den danske Komedies Ligbegængelse*, 67–8; *Don Ranudo de Colibrados*, 61; *Ellevte Juni (Eleventh of June)*, 57, 250; *Erasmus Montanus*, 61, 62, 73;

Henrik og Pernille, 64; Jacob von Tyboe, 61, 63; Jean de France, 60, 61–2; Jeppe paa Bjerget (Jeppe on the Hill), 60, 63, 133, 206; Julestuen (The Christmas Party), 66; 'Just Justesen's Reflections', 56, 63, 64; Kildereisen (The Healing Spring), 66–7; Maskarade, 57, 66; Mester Gert Westphaler, 60, 63; Melampe, 64; Den pantsatte Bondedreng (The Pawned Peasant Boy), 58; Peder Paars, 60; Pernilles korte Frøkenstand (Pernille's Brief Ladyship), 64; Plutus, 67; Den politiske Kandestøber (The Political Tinker), 56, 60, 61, 64, 73, 133, 245; Den Stundesløse (The Fussy Man), 58, 61, 62; Ulysses von Ithacia, 64, 74; De Usynlige (The Invisible Lovers), 64, 73; Den Vægelsindede (The Weathercock), 60, 62, 137

Holofernis och Judiths Commoedia 22, 28
Holst, H. P. 164
Honnête criminel, L' 80
Horace 65
Hostrup, J. C. 119, 244, 252
Hr. Burchardt og hans Familie (Burchardt and His Family) 118
Hugo, Victor 112
Hunderup, H. R. 182, 183, 187
Hwasser, Elise 146
Händel, G. F. 72, 84
Høedt, F. L. 125, 127, 142, 164

Ibsen, Henrik 106, 121, 128, 129, 130, 132, 134, 136, 137, 138–54, 155, 158, 159–75, 178, 180, 183, 237, 239, 266; Brand, 151, 154, 175; Bygmester Solness (The Master Builder), 166, 171, 174, 252; Catiline, 137, 138–9; Et dukkehjem (A Doll's House), 106, 159ff, 179, Pl. 32; En folkefjende (An Enemy of the People), 159, 166ff, 172, 174; Fruen fra Havet (Lady from the Sea), 166, 174;

Fru Inger til Østeraad (Lady Inger of Østeraad), 146; Gengangere (Ghosts), 162, 166, 172, 186, 250, 252; Gildet paa Solhaug (The Feast at Solhaug), 124, 147, 156; Hedda Gabler, 166, 268–9; Hærmændene paa Helgeland (The Vikings of Helgeland), 142, 149–50; John Gabriel Borkman, 161; Kejser og Galilæer (Emperor and Galilean), 154; Kjæmpehøjen (The Warrior's Barrow), 139, 145; Kongs-Emnerne (The Pretenders), 128, 129–30, 150, 151, 156, 161, 179, 228–32, Pl. 30; Kærlighedens Komedie (Love's Comedy), 128, 146; Naar vi døde vaagner (When We Dead Awaken), 175; Olaf Liljekrans, 147–9, Pl. 29; Peer Gynt, 151–4, 180, 213, 244, 250, 252, 254; Rhymed Letter to Fru Heiberg, 130, 142–3; Rosmersholm, 171, 173, 175, 250; Samfundets støtter (Pillars of Society), 161, 162, 165; Sancthansnatten (Midsummer Eve), 145; De Unges Forbund (The League of Youth), 128, 154, 252; Vildanden (The Wild Duck), 166, 172, 173, 174, 175, 244, 254, 269
Iffland, A. W. 109
Iliad 64
Inconnu, L' 49
Indenfor Murene (Inside the Walls) 204
Intruder, The 202
Investigation, The 268
Ionesco, E. 247, 250, 251
Iphigénie 86
Ipsen, Bodil 205, 236, 240, 252, 254

Jacobi, Hans 2
James I 27, 35
Jardin, N. H. 80
Jerndorff, Peter 169
Jessner, L. 231
Johanne von Montfauçon 108, 111
Johan Ulvestjerna 227
Jon-And, John 227, 228, 261, Pl. 44

Jones, Inigo 35
Jonson, Ben 35
Josephson, Ludvig 127, 138, 146,
    149, 151f, 154, 159, 167, 178, 193,
    205
Joueur, Le 52, 73
Judas Redivivus 25
Juel, Jens 104
Juel, Peder 39
Julestuen og Maskarade 66
Jungfrau von Orleans, Die 107
Jørgensen, Olaf 153

Karrig Niding (Niding the Niggard)
    25–6
Karsten, Christofer 88, 95
Kayser, Johan 54
Kellgren, Johan 94, 95
Kemp, Will 44
Kexél, Olof 97
Kierkegaard, Søren 106, 115, 239;
    Crisis in the Life of an Actress 125
Kingo, Thomas 43
Kjer, Bodil 245, 259
*Kjærlighed paa Nicolai Taarn (Love on
    St. Nicholas Tower)* 118
*Kjærlighed uden Stromper (Love
    Without Stockings)* 104
Klausen, Henrik 153
Klemming, G. E. 6
Klingenberg, Gyda 137
Knutzon, Per 239, 261
Koht, Halvdan 159
*Kongen Drømmer (Dreams of the
    King)* 129
Kong Midas 213
*Kong Renés Datter (King René's
    Daughter)* 122, 126, 130, 141
*Kong Salomons Hyldning (Allegiance
    to Solomon)* 22–3, 29, 30
*Kong Sverres Ungdom (King Sverre's
    Youth)* 135
Konung Gustaf Then Första 24
Kotzebue, A. von 101, 108, 109, 111
Kreuzfahrer, Die 108
Krogh, Torben 41, 48
Krogh, Wilhelm 137, 153
Krum, Johanne 183

Kückelson, A. von 35
Kuhlau, F. 120
Kulle, Jarl 251
Kyd, Thomas 48
König Phineus 37

Laading, Herman 143
Lagerbjelke, G. 112–13
Lagerkvist, Pär 202, 203, 209, 219–
    26, 242, 270, 273; *Bödeln (The
    Hangman)*, 224, 241; *Han som fick
    leva om sitt liv (The Man Who
    Lived His Life Over)*, 223; *Himlens
    hemlighet (The Secret of Heaven)*,
    220–2, 226; *Mannen utan själ (Man
    without a Soul)*, 225; *Midsommar-
    dröm i fattighuset (Midsummer
    Dream in the Poorhouse)*, 225–6;
    Modern Theatre, 202, 204, 210,
    217, 219, 226; *Den osynlige (The
    Invisible One)*, 222; *Seger i mörker
    (Victory in the Dark)*, 225; *Sista
    mänskan (The Last Man)*, 209;
    *Den svåra stunden (The Difficult
    Hour)*, 220; *The Tunnel*, 220, 222–3
Lagertha 105, 106
Lalin, Lars 84
Lamm, Martin 234
Landé, J. B. 58, 59
Lange, H. W. 127
Lange, Sven 166, 208
Langlois, Charles 70, 71
Larsen, Thorvald 244–5
Larson, Yngve 264
Laube, Heinrich 143
Launai, Pierre de 77, 78
Lauremberg, J. 30, 36, 37, 41, 42, 45
Le Boeuf, Sr. 83
Le Clerc, Mlle. E.-M. 80
Leclercq, T. 117
Legrand, M. A. 83
Lehmann, Julius 230
Lekain, Henri Louis 80, 81, 86
Leopold, Carl G. 94, 97
Le Sage, A.-R. 74
Lessing, G. E. 103, 106
Lewis, M. G. 101
Lindahl, P. 71

Lindberg, August 159, 167, 172, 173, 174, 178, 183, 186, 189
Lindberg, Per 205, 207, 209ff, 217, 218, 222ff, 226ff, 232, 238, 261
Lindeberg, Anders 119
Linschöld, Erik 43
Livet i Vold (In the Throes of Life) 213
Livets Spil (Game of Life) 206
Londemann, Gert 76
Londel, Jeanne du 77, 78
Lorca, F. Garcia 261
Louis XIV 37, 46, 48, 78, 83
Queen Louise (Denmark) 69
Lovisa Ulrika 69, 71, 77, 78, 79, 80, 84, 88
Ludus de Sancto Canute duce 7–11
Lugné Poë, A. 171, 189
Lund, Troels 113, 115, 135, 136, 137, Pl. 24
Luther, Martin 21
Lying Lover, The 58
Läkaren (The Doctor) 119
Löf, Fredrika 99, 100
Løgneren 58

Maeterlinck, M. 202
Magdalene Sibylle of Saxony 19, 35, 45
Magnon, Jean 49
Malmquist, Sandro 217, 223, 261
Mantzius, Karl 120, 204
Mariane 76
Maria Stuart (Schiller) 107, 121–2
Marivaux, P. de 78
Marlowe, Christopher 48
Marmontel, J.-F. 88, 92
Marriage, The 264–5
Mars, Mlle. A. F. 91
Masreliez, Adrian 79
Mazarin, Cardinal 83
Melanchton 21
Mendelssohn, F. 157
Ménechmes, Les 83
Menteur, Le see *Løgneren*
Mérimée, Prosper 117
Mérope 80, 86
Merry Widow, The 266

Messel, Oliver 245
Messenius, J. 24, 27, 92, 196
Meyerhold, V. 211
Miller, Arthur 247
Mingotti, Pietro 72
Moberg, Vilhelm 260
Modée, R. G. 70
Moissi, Alexander 207
Molander, Harald 188, 197, 205, 232
Molander, Olof 195, 205, 208, 218, 222, 228, 232ff, 238, 251, 261, 270, 272
Molière, Jean Baptiste Poquelin de 49, 52, 53, 56, 57, 58, 60, 61, 65, 66, 70, 74, 75, 78, 156, 266, 267; *Amphitryon*, 58, 74; *L'Avare*, 56; *Le Bourgeois gentilhomme*, 56, 66; *Don Juan*, 76, 267; *L'École des femmes*, 252; *Le Malade imaginaire*, 58, 252; *Le Mariage forcé*, 56; *Le Misanthrope*, 267; *Les Précieuses ridicules*, 252; *Tartuffe*, 57, 236, 244, 252
Monde rejovi, Le 37, 42
Monde renversé, Le 74–5
Monsigny, P. 80, 86
Montaigu, Marie Magdalene 56, 62, 68
Montaigu, René Magnon de 49, 52, 53, 54, 55ff, 70, 71, 72
Monteverdi 35
Monvel (Jacques-Marie Boutet) 91, 94, 98
Moore, E. 80
Mort de César, La 71
Mozart, W. A. 135
Mrozek, S. 251
Muette de Portici, La 122, 124, Pl. 28
Mulatten (The Mulatto) 124
Munch, Andreas 135, 150
Munk, Kaj 238–9, 241, 242, 244; *Cant*, 238; *En Idealist (Herod the King)*, 238–9, 252; *Ordet (The Word)*, 238; *De Udvalgte (The Elect)*, 238
Musset, Alfred de 155, 156
Mystère de Saint Apolline 22
Mörk, Lennart 261, 264, 272, Pl. 50

Mörner, Stellan 261, 262

Naissance de la Paix 38
Nanine 76
Nansen, Betty 238
Nathansen, H. 204, 205, 244
Naumann, J. G. 92, 95
Neiiendam, Sigrid 204
Neuber, Caroline 72
Nielsen, Anna (Wexschall) 102, 109, 119, 121, 125, 142
Nielsen, Carl 218
Nielsen, Christoffer 105
Nielsen, N. P. 102, 109, 119, 121, 126, 142
Nilsen, Hans Jacob 244, 261
Ninon 124
Nordgreen, Erik 259, 261, Pl. 48
Nürenbach, Martin 82, 132–3

O'Casey, Sean 247
Odyssey 64
Oedipus Rex 207, 227
Oehlenschläger, Adam 103, 106–9, 115, 124, 134, 139, 157, 178, 238, 244; Aladdin, 106–7, 180, 217–18; Axel og Valborg, 109; Correggio, 108; Dina, 124, 130; Guldhornene (The Horns of Gold), 106; Hagbarth og Signe, 109; Hakon Jarl, 107, 130, 141, 252; Hugo von Rheinberg, 108; A Midsummer Night's Dream (trans.), 157; Palnatoke, 108; Poems 1803, 106
Olin, Elisabet 84, 86
Olivet, Jean St-Hillaire d' 51, Pl. 10–12
Olivier, Lawrence 251
Olof Skottkonung 24
O'Neill, Eugene 247, 251; Hughie, 251; The Iceman Cometh, 254; Long Day's Journey into Night, 251–2; More Stately Mansions, 251; A Touch of the Poet, 251
Oracle, L' 78, 94
Orondaat en Statira 47
Orphelin de la Chine, L' 80, 86
Orpheus and Eurydice 84–6, Pl. 13

Oscar II 172
Othello (Vigny) 112
Our Town 247, 249
Overskou, Thomas 118, 141

Palmberg, Petter 71
Palme, August 191
Palme, Ulf 251
Pamela 76
Paris' Dom (The Judgment of Paris) 16
Parnassus triumphans 38
Pasch, Johann 78
Passow, Anna Materna v. 76
Paulli, J. R. 66
Paulsen, Carl Andreas 47
Peintre amoureux de son modèle, Le 79
Perfall, Karl v. 189, 190, 199
Petersen, Carlo M. 248
Petersen, Clemens 121, 126, 156
Petri, Olaus 6
Phèdre 228, Pl. 44
Philidor, F.-A. 80
Philomela 30
Philosophe marié, Le 78
Phister, Ludvig 103, 119, 142
Piccini, Nicolo 88
Pickelhering 47, 72
Pilloy, Frederik de 56, 72
Pinter, Harold 247, 250, 251
Pirandello, Luigi 264, 266
Plautus 22, 25, 27, 64
Poel, W. 190
Poinsinet, A.-A.-H. 99
Pontoppidan, Clara 204, 239, 241
Pope, Thomas 44
Port de Mer, Le see Toldboden
Positiv-hataren (The Hurdy-Gurdy Hater) 119
Pot of Gold, The 25, 27
Poulsen, Adam 229
Poulsen, Emil 161f, 166, 168
Poulsen, Johannes 204, 217, 218, 229, 230, 231, 238, 261
Pram, Christen 105
Preciosa 113
Preisz und Ruhm 41

Price, John 259, 261
Prytz, Andreas 24
Pätges, Hanne *see* Johanne Luise Heiberg

Quem queritis 1
Quingey, Falbaire de 80
Qvoten, Julius Heinrich von 72, 73, 75
Qvoten, Samuel Poulsen von 54, 73

Racine, Jean 51, 52, 53, 77, 103, 228, 250
Radcliffe, A. 101
Rahbek, K. L. 103, 106
Raimund, Ferdinand 119, 142, 145
Rake's Progress, The 268
Ranch, H. J. 25, 29, 30
Ranft, Albert 193, 197, 205
Rebecka 22, 26
Rebolledo, Bernardino de 39, 40, 41
Refn, Helge 225, 240, 257, 261, Pl. 46–7
Regnard, J.-L. 52, 58, 60, 73, 74, 75, 78, 83
Reimers, Sophie 171
Reinhardt, Max 199, 207ff, 211, 220, 226, 231, 232, 262, 267, 270
Resande teatersällskap, Ett (A Travelling Troupe) 119
Reumert, Poul 204, 205, 235–6, 238, 252–4, 255
Rhadamiste et Zénobie 86
Richard Coeur-de-Lion 111
Richardson, S. 76
Rifbjerg, Klaus 247
Ristell, A. F. 55, 98, 99
Rivière, Henri 189
Robbers, The 177
Roi et le Fermier, Le 80
Roland 88, Pl. 16
Rolf Blaaskæg 108
Rolf Krage 103
Rolland, Romain 227
Roller, Alfred 208
Romdahl, Axel 214
Rondeletius, J. 25
Roose, Thorkild 205

Rosenkilde, C. N. 103, 119, 121, 142
Rosenstand-Goiske, P. 112
Rosidor, Claude 49, 52, 73
Rosidor, Jean Guillemoys du Chesnay 48
Rosimunda 30
Rostand, E. 252
Rovsing, Michael 104, 108
Rudbekius, J. 26
Ryge, J. C. 102, 108, 109, 110, 119, 121

Sackville, Thomas 45
Saint-Foix, G.-F. P. de 78, 94
Saint-Saens, C. 218
Samson and Delilah 218–19, 220, 226, Pl. 41–3
Samsons Fængsel (Samson's Prison) 29
Samsøe, O. J. 106
Sandlåden (The Sand Box) 248
Sanquirico, A. 114, 136
Saroyan, William 247
Sartre, Jean-Paul 247, 257, 262
Saurin, B.-J. 80
Saxo Grammaticus 103, 105
Schall, Claus 105
Schanche, Ingolf 206, 227–8
Schiewe, Viggo 187, 188
Schiller, F. von 106, 107, 110, 121, 146, 177
Schinkel, K. F. 114
School for Scandal, The 99, 245
Schowburg 46, 47
Schrøder, Hans 167
Schröderheim, E. 97
Schultz, Heinrich 35
Schwab, Per 261
Schyberg, Frederik 233
Scott, Walter 91, 101, 112, 136, 197
Scribe, Eugene 94, 100, 116, 117, 118, 122, 128, 136, 140, 141, 142, 155, 156
Seendes Blinde, Den (The Blind Man's Vision) 66
Selander, S. 251
Sémiramis 80
Seneca 30

Seuerling, C. G. 109

Shakespeare, William 45, 47, 48, 103, 106, 109ff, 124, 125, 146, 157, 189, 197, 226, 237, 238, 262f; *Antony and Cleopatra*, 227; *All's Well*, 125; *As You Like It*, 125, 141, 252; *Hamlet*, 109, 110–11, 112, 125, 130, 141, 142, 146, 212–13, 227, 241, 250, 252; *Julius Caesar*, 252; *King John*, 264; *King Lear*, 48, 110, 121, 141, 213; *Love's Labour's Lost*, 125; *Macbeth*, 110, 125–6, 146, 162, 252, 265; *The Merchant of Venice*, 218, 254; *A Midsummer Night's Dream*, 145, 157, 191, 207, 228; *Othello*, 213, 254; *Richard III*, 95, 263, Pl. 49; *Romeo and Juliet*, 109, 125, 141, 213, 263, Pl. 39; *Troilus and Cressida*, 264; *Twelfth Night*, 125, 207, 262

Shaw, G. B. 160, 206, 252

Sheridan, R. B. 99, 245

Signill 27

Simonson, Lee 260

Siri Brahe 99

Sjöberg, Alf 205, 225, 237, 250, 261ff, 265, 268

Skawonius, Sven Erik 233, 235, 261

Skjöldebrand, A. P. 101, 108

Sonnambula, La 113

Sophie Amalie 39, 41, Pl. 9

Sophocles 227

Soya, Carl Erik 244, 260

Spanish Tragedy, The 48

Sparekassen (The Savings Bank) 119

Spindlarna (The Spiders) 260

Stanislavski, C. 166, 171, 173, 246, 253

Steele, R. 58, 75

Steffens, Henrik 107

Stege, H. T. 24

Stenborg, Carl 83, 84, 86, 87, 88, 95

Stenborg, Petter 71, 83

Stiernhielm, G. 37, 38, 43

Stoora Genius, Den (The Mighty Genius) 43

Stopani, Donato 79

Stravinsky, I. 268

Strindberg, August 6, 24, 92, 100, 154, 155, 157, 175, 176–203, 204, 205, 206, 213ff, 218, 219, 226, 227, 232ff, 237, 242, 251, 252, 266, 270f; *Bandet (The Bond)*, 181; *Bjälbo-Jarlen (Earl Birger of Bjälbo)*, 196; *Brott och brott (Crimes and Crimes)*, 189, 270; *Brända tomten (The Burnt House)*, 199; *Ett drömspel (A Dream Play)*, 179, 193–5, 202, 208, 210, 220, 232–4, 236–7, 270–2, Pl. 34–7, 45, 50; *Dödsdansen I–II (The Dance of Death)*, 181, 201, 235–6, 252; *Engelbrekt*, 196; *Erik XIV*, 196, 270; *Fadren (The Father)*, 177, 181–4, 200, 201, 202, 252; *Folkungasagan (Saga of the Folkungs)*, 196, 215–16, 235, Pl. 38; *Fordringsägare (Creditors)*, 177, 187, 213; *Den fredløse (The Outlaw)*, 178; *Fröken Julie (Miss Julie)*, 177, 184–8, 200, 202, 252, Preface to, 185–6, 200; *Första varningen (The First Warning)*, 270; *Gildets hemlighet (The Secret of the Guild)*, 179; *Gustav Adolf*, 196; *Gustav III*, 196; *Gustav Vasa*, 196-7, 213, 252; *Hemsöborna (The People of Hemsö)*, 189; *Herr Bengts hustru (Sir Bengt's Wife)*, 179; *Himmelrikets nycklar (The Keys of Heaven)*, 179; *Holländarn (The Dutchman)*, 270; *I Rom (In Rome)*, 178; *Karl XII*, 189, 196; *Kristina (Queen Christina)*, 196, 198–9, 200, 202; *Kronbruden (The Bridal Crown)*, 266, 270; *Leka med elden (Playing with Fire)*, 250, 270; *Lycko-Pers resa (Lucky Per's Journey)*, 179, 180, 188; *Mäster Olof*, 6, 178–9, 213–15; *Occult Diary*, 191; *On Modern Drama and Modern Theatre*, 181; *Open Letters to the Intimate Theatre*, 189, 201f; *Oväder (Storm Weather)*, 199, 200, 270; *Paria (Pariah)*, 187;

301

Pelikanen (The Pelican), 199, 200, 208, 270; *Påsk (Easter)*, 189, 200–1; *Spöksonaten (The Ghost Sonata)*, 199, 207–8, 266–7, 270; *Den starkare (The Stronger)*, 187; *Stora landsvägen (The Great Highway)*, 180; *Svanevit (Swanwhite)*, 201; *Svarta Handsken (The Black Glove)*, 202; *Till Damaskus* I-III *(To Damascus* I-III*)*, 177, 179, 227; Part I, 175, 177, 188, 189–93, 199, 202, 235, Pl. 33; Part III, 216–17, 227, Pl. 40

Struensee, J. F. 81
Ström, Carl 227
Ström, Carl Johan 265
Ström, Knut 200, 211ff, 217, 218, 220, 222, 226, 261, Pl. 38–40
Strömberg, J. P. 134, 135
Strömstedt, B. 272
Sundström, L. 84
Sune Jarl 94, 99
Susanna 23, 28
Svartsjuke neapolitanaren, Den (The Jealous Neapolitan) 100
Svend Dyrings Hus (Svend Dyring's House) 123, 130, 147
Svendsen, Laura *see* Laura Gundersen
Svennberg, Tore 197
Svenska Sprätthöken (The Swedish Fop) 70
Swedenborg, Emanuel 196
Sydow, Max von 267
Sæverud, Harald 244
Søskende (The Judge) 260

Taine, H. 77
Tairov, A. 228
Teahouse of the August Moon 266
Teenagerlove 260
Teje, Tora 228, 233, 235, 236, 253
Terence 22, 25, 26, 28, 30
Tessin, Carl Gustav 77
Tessin, Nicodemus the younger 49, 51
Thaulow, Fritz 153
Théâtre de la Foire 75

Théâtre Italien 59, 60, 64, 75
Then fångne Cupido (Cupid Captured) 38
Thermopylæ 260
Thetis and Pélée 83–4, 86
Thielo, C. A. 72, 73
Thielo, Caroline 76
Thisbe 25
Thorvaldsen, B. 115, 178
Thum, C. 45
Thøgersen, P. 24
Tidblad, Inga 251
Tieck, L. 157
Tiemroth, Edwin 245, 261
Tilfälle gör tjufven (Chance Makes the Thief) 94
Tobie Comedia (Sweden) 6, 22
Tobiæ Comedie (Denmark) 23, 28–9
Tode, Clemens 80
Toldboden 58
Topsøe, V. 161, 163
Torelli, G. 42
de la Tour, Henry 80, 81
Tragoedia von den Tungenden und Lastern 18–20, 36, 45, Pl. 7
Treu (Drey), Michael Daniel 46, 47, 48

Udsen, Bodil 247
Udviklinger (Developments) 247
Uncle Vanya 250
Unterschiedliche Oracula 39, 40–1, Pl. 9
Utopia 63
Utro Hustru, Den (The Unfaithful Wife) 16, 17
Uttini, Francesco 78, 83

Valle-Inclan, R. M. del 266
Valse de toréadors, La 245
Vedel, V. 231
Ved Rikets Port (At the Kingdom's Gate) 206
Vega, Lope de 47, 48
Velten, Johan 46, 47
Verdi, G. 100
Vereinigte Götter-Streit, Der 49
Vergnügung und Unvergnügung 41

Vigny, A. de 112
Visé, J. D. de 49
Visit, The 252
Voltaire, F.-M. A. 70, 76, 77, 78, 81, 86, 87

Wahl, Anders de 197, 209
Wallenstein 107
Wallentin, Arne 261
Wallich, Aron 113, 114
Walpole, R. 95
Wegener, Henrich 64
Wegener, Paul 207
Weiss, Peter 268
Welhaven, J. S. 137
Wellander, J. 83, 84
Wergeland, H. 136, 137
Wergmann, P. F. C. 137, 150, Pl. 30–1
Werner, A. F. 39, 41
Wessel, J. H. 76, 104, 244
Who's Afraid of Virginia Woolf? 268
Widerberg, Andreas 100
Wied, Gustav 187, 244
Wiehe, Michael 103, 122, 127, 142

Wiehe, Vilhelm 141
Wieth, Mogens 241, 245, 254–5, 259
Wilder, Thornton 247
Wilhelm Tell 108
Williams, Tennessee 247
Wolf, Andreas J. 46, 47
Wolff, Lucie 144
Wolff, P. A. 113
Wolves, The 227
Woyzeck 267
Wrangel, Erik 70

Yeats, W. B. 202, 204
Yvonne, Princess of Burgundy 264–5

Zaïre 80, 86
Zemire et Azor 88, 90, Pl. 17
Zirkelgesellshaft 15–16
Zola, E. 182, 184, 185

Østergade og Vestergade (East Side, West Side) 118

Åbergsson, Gustaf 110